Health

Health and Medical Public Relations takes a fresh look at media relations and news values. It examines how information about medical research from the academic, pharmaceutical and charitable sectors is disseminated to target audiences through a variety of PR techniques. Scrutinising a wide range of health-related public relations activities, the book combines a critical, analytical and cultural overview of these methods with helpful guidance on their practical application.

Key features include:

- Advice on how to write and place effective press releases, plan and budget for campaigns, and anticipate responses from different sectors and the wider public
- Coverage of different types of communication and consultancy, including the controversial areas of lobbying and access to influential policy makers
- Case studies on the way in which experienced journalists and public relations practitioners gain coverage for their work, with plentiful examples drawn from both recent media scares and long-running issues
- A survey of the way challenging public relations issues have been perceived in the past, analysing the attitudes of both legislators and the public
- A user-friendly format designed to reinforce learning, including handy tips, definition boxes explaining key words and concepts, and exercises and reflection points to stimulate group discussion and reflection on specific examples of science and medical PR practice

Wide-ranging and highly accessible, this book will be an essential resource for undergraduates, postgraduates and professionals learning to specialise in health public relations.

Myc Riggulsford is a science journalist and broadcaster with extensive experience in PR, media training and issue management. He is also a visiting lecturer at the Universities of Manchester, Sheffield and St Andrews.

Health and Medical
Public Relations

Myc Riggulsford

Routledge
Taylor & Francis Group

LONDON AND NEW YORK

First published 2013
by Routledge
2 Park Square, Milton Park, Abingdon, Oxon OX14 4RN

Simultaneously published in the USA and Canada
by Routledge
711 Third Avenue, New York, NY 10017

Routledge is an imprint of the Taylor & Francis Group, an informa business

British Library Cataloguing in Publication Data
A catalogue record for this book is available from the British Library

Library of Congress Cataloging in Publication Data
Riggulsford, Myc, 1956-
Health and medical public relations / Myc Riggulsford.
p.; cm.
Summary: "*Health and Medical Public Relations* takes a fresh look at media
relations and news values. It examines how information about medical
research from the academic, pharmaceutical and charitable sectors is
disseminated to target audiences through a variety of PR techniques.
Scrutinising a wide range of health-related public relations activities, the
book combines a critical, analytical and cultural overview of these methods
with helpful guidance on their practical application"–Provided by publisher.
I. Title.
[DNLM: 1. Health Communication. 2. Public Relations.
3. Communications Media. WA 590]
362.1–dc23
2012044006

ISBN: 978-0-415-61330-9 (hbk)
ISBN: 978-0-415-61331-6 (pbk)
ISBN: 978-0-203-14369-8 (ebk)

Typeset in Galliard
by Taylor and Francis Books

MIX
Paper from
responsible sources
FSC
www.fsc.org   FSC® C013056

Printed and bound in Great Britain by
TJ International Ltd, Padstow, Cornwall

Contents

Figures

Author's note and acknowledgements

For those expecting a conventional academic tome with all the usual references, I did indeed debate writing a book for you that would be stuffed full of source notes, ideas taken from standard texts, and a classic bibliography, until I realised that the references would take up half the allotted word space, and take so long to track down the arcane sources that the thing would never get finished. And as a haphazard collector of unconsidered trifles, many of my original sources are simply lost in the mists.

The advice and thoughts contained in this volume are shamelessly crowd-sourced from the thousands of postgraduate students, postdocs, senior executives, scientists, doctors, engineers, midwives, press officers, and academic lecturers among others, whom I have had the enormous pleasure of meeting, debating with and teaching on media training workshops over the last 30 years. So this tries to be a book of content, not historical reference, and in many cases I simply have no idea where I first heard the idea, meme or telling phrase.

Many other tips will have come as invaluable nuggets from Tim Radford, formerly Science Editor of the *Guardian*, Nigel Hawkes, formerly of *The Times*, Steve Connor of the *Independent*, and David Derbyshire, formerly of the *Daily Mail*, and the other dozen or so medical and science journalist friends and colleagues I have worked with over the years, and who do a tremendously difficult job every day under enormous pressure. They still manage, on the whole, to get a reasonable first draft of history out into the public domain in a way that their publics and audiences actually wish to hear about this stuff.

If I have inadvertently plagiarised someone or failed to credit an idea, meme, or method to some long-forgotten source, then I am truly sorry, but 30 years of practice at speaking without notes is a long time. And anyway, these days, you can always check my assertions on Wikipedia, where many of my scientist friends and colleagues, who are the anecdotal and original sources of much of my small store of acclumulated knowledge, gallantly spend unsung hours correcting public misconceptions for the benefit of us all.

Without Jon Cope who proposed the original book, but sadly and understandably had to drop out due to a new job and new baby, Dylan Evans who accidentally talked me into it on our Café Sci trip to Monterrey some years ago, my friend and former director Prof Ben Bradley who gave me my first chance at public relations management, and above all without my friend, work colleague and wife Jenny, this would never have happened.

Part I
Health PR in context

1 What is PR?

An introduction to public relations

When I first became aware of the existence of public relations as a distinct activity that grown adults could actually be paid for performing it was still in its early youth as a management discipline. In those dark days it was roughly described as 'managing internal and external communications', which really meant 'sending out press releases to the media, and maybe in-house produced newsletters to customers, and possibly letting the staff know stuff too'. Or, in radical, bleeding-edge thinking, for campaigning organisations or ones dealing with any sensitive issues, as 'managing our interests and protecting the organisation's reputation'.

By 2013, definitions of public relations have become more widely accepted, and the industry has matured somewhat. So, according to the UK public relations industry's professional trade body, the Chartered Institute of Public Relations (at which point I have to declare an interest, as I have been a member for more than 15 years and once gave a breakfast seminar on pressure groups and issue management at their annual conference), public relations is

> about reputation – the result of what you do, what you say and what others say about you.
>
> Public relations is the discipline which looks after reputation, with the aim of earning understanding and support and influencing opinion and behaviour. It is the planned and sustained effort to establish and maintain goodwill and mutual understanding between an organisation and its publics.[1]

Just in case this statement is too difficult for its own practitioners to understand, the CIPR then goes on to define what it means by each of the trickiest jargon terms in this definition:

> 'Organisation' can be a government body, a business, a profession, a public service or a body concerned with health, culture, education – indeed any corporate or voluntary body large or small.
>
> 'Publics' are audiences that are important to the organisation. They include customers – existing and potential; employees and management; investors; media; government; suppliers; opinion-formers.

'Understanding' is a two-way process. To be effective, an organisation needs to listen to the opinions of those with whom it deals and not solely provide information. Issuing a barrage of propaganda is not enough in today's open society.

My first proper public relations boss, an ex-sports reporter called Tony Court, defined it to me way back in 1980 as: 'If you pay for the space and claim in a newspaper that you are brilliant, that's advertising. But if you can get someone else to say that you are brilliant, in an editorial, that's public relations.'

Tony's attitude recognised the pragmatic if unpalatable truth that it doesn't really matter what people *should* think, it matters what they *do* think, even if that opinion is based on false or erroneous information. Thus public relations activity is at the mercy of the wisdom of crowds – if people think that something is wrong, even if it isn't, then you are going to have to do something about it.

Of course, by 2013, most students of public relations no longer go to the CIPR or the other industry bodies' own websites, or even to cynical former sports hacks, as the first port of call for their information. Rather, they go to that crowdsourced favourite fount of all knowledge, Wikipedia.

As a minor digression, it is telling that one of the first major contributions to theoretical thinking on the subject of public relations from the new chief executive of the CIPR, Jane Wilson, who was, among other posts, the former director of communications for Capital Radio in London, has been on the subject of Wikipedia. And her thoughts were placed elegantly in that mainstream media outlet, the *Huffington Post*, on 6 February 2012.

Wilson wrote: 'Wikipedia is the world's fifth most-read website. It is an online encyclopaedia with over 20 million articles and often the first port of call for millions of people researching a topic, individual or company.'[2] Jane's contribution pointed out that Wikipedia therefore has enormous influence on an organisation's reputation and therefore it is also understandable that public relations people are interested in it as a way of taking the temperature of public opinion. And for precisely that reason it is basically unethical for public relations executives to be editing Wikipedia entries that refer to their clients as part of their PR activity. As Jane says:

> [It] is questionable whether it is ever right for a retained advocate to edit a Wikipedia page that relates to their employer or client ... the neutral point of view rule is clear. It amounts, in my mind, to a 'thou shalt not edit' for public relations professionals. An encyclopaedia should not be leveraged for competitive advantage, whatever your perspective, or point of view. Those wishing to interact with the Wikipedia community must first understand it.
>
> Public relations professionals must be clear about its aims and ambitions, and before engaging they need to adopt its etiquette. You do not have to accept mistakes or misunderstandings on Wikipedia, but you do not have the right to edit the content so that it reflects what you want it to say. Wikipedia is not going to provide a public relations professional with a quick win for a

client or employer. Accepting that and explaining it should now become part of our professional etiquette.

I entirely agree with Jane Wilson, and also with her savvy choice of the *Huffington Post* as a showcase for these essentially new media sentiments. The world is changing, and changing again, and the government diktat school of press freedom has no place in today's society. And neither has the deficit model of communication (if they just knew more they would like us better), as practised for so long in science, and medical, and health communications.

As I was finishing this book the debate moved forward and the CIPR now has draft guidelines for editing and using Wikipedia.[3]

So to return to the main point, a working definition of what public relations actually is, or should be. Wikipedia itself defines public relations as:

> **Public relations** (PR) is the practice of managing the flow of information between an organization and its publics. Public relations provides an organization or individual exposure to their audiences using topics of public interest and news items that do not require direct payment. Their aim is often to persuade the public, investors, partners, employees and other stakeholders to maintain a certain point of view about the company, its leadership, products or of political decisions. Common activities include speaking at conferences, winning industry awards, working with the press, and employee communication.[4]

Actually on the day I checked, some lovesick wag had inserted the word 'aileen' instead of 'practice' in the first line. And it will have changed by now anyway. Which neatly encapsulates the twin-edged sword of encouraging interaction as a way of building brand awareness and loyalty by getting crowds to participate. This opening definition is mainly culled from the highly respected industry textbook by James Grunig and Todd Hunt called *Managing Public Relations*, first published in 1984 and still in print today.[5] This book remains an eminent source of underpinning theory for the practice of public relations.

And in my view, the aim of managing information is a fairly honest and workaday description of much of public relations' aim. In passing, I particularly liked the Wikipedia contributor's cynical 'speaking at conferences, winning industry awards' as the key examples of common public relations activity, doubtless also destined to be deleted by industry worthies.

Modern definition of public relations

The Public Relations Society of America announced 'a modern definition of public relations' on 1 March 2012 in an article by Stuart Elliott in the *New York Times*,[6] followed by a press release from the PRSA itself dated three days later, with links on its website suggesting that the *New York Times* article was published on 2 March, which seems an altogether odd practice for a communications industry body.

The new definition, chosen from 927 definitions submitted during the four-month industry and community consultation exercise, which drew 1,447 votes (46 per cent of which eventually chose this new definition from among the top three), called Public Relations Defined,[7] says:

> **Public relations** is a strategic communication process that builds mutually beneficial relationships between organisations and their publics.

The response to this redefinition has been predictably critical among bloggers and those on the industry chat forums, who seem to feel that the new definition is simply 'more of the same' rather than a radical redefinition suitable for the internet and social media age. Several commentators have been critical of the 'corporate speak' language used, rather than plain English.

The PRSA itself also seemed surprised that the consultees rejected the word 'ethics' as part of the definition. However, ethics is a concern that might be expected to feature more highly in discussions of medical and health communications, than in PR activities for other areas of business.

Communications skills

So public relations is about communicating in some planned way, and about trying to manage how others see us. But how should this apply to health and medical activities? And why should doctors, nurses, scientific researchers, or the entire pharmaceutical industry, wish to involve themselves in so grubby an activity? Surely all proper medical news is published in peer-reviewed journals and undertaken as part of a noble and self-sacrificing higher calling, rather than as a tawdry, commercial, money-chasing transaction?

Unfortunately, the interested publics have become rather more interested in health and medical practices than many members of the noble Hippocratic professions feel that they should be. The ability to communicate with ordinary members of the public such as government representatives and patients has almost entirely withered in some of the members of our associated medical professions. As some wit said back in the late 1980s when I was still working in the NHS: 'Consultants are now having to give communication skills training to their junior doctors. Being taught communication skills by the average NHS consultant is a bit like being taught to fly by a pastry chef.'

We need to communicate our science, our research, our ethics and our intentions better, and we may well have to do this using both conventional media such as television, radio, newspapers, and public debates, and the newly enabled internet and telecommunications platform-based social media.

This book is therefore an attempt to demystify some of the everyday practices of public relations practitioners, and among other things, offer a self-help guide to publicising stuff in a practical manner through various media. It is decidedly not another highly technical, theoretical, and esoterically academic textbook, replete with arcane references and endnotes.

Readers who were hoping for another explanation of the history and theoretical underpinnings of the practice of public relations as such are referred to my old friend Prof Anne Gregory, former President of the Chartered Institute of Public Relations, for almost any of her excellent publications over the last 25 years. Her sound and solid work is underpinned by a thorough knowledge of the subject, and she more than almost anyone else has helped public relations to develop into a highly respectable academic discipline. Do read her excellent textbooks. This volume is instead about the craft, practice, and practical side of public relations activity, an area that often seems to get missed.

Profession or trade?

One of the first questions that I usually get asked by dewy-eyed public relations students when I am speaking as a visiting lecturer to eager classes is 'Do you believe that public relations is a profession, or is it a trade?' This reflects the point in their degree teaching at which I am asked to come and give a seminar, and is also the pressing essay question that they have to answer this week.

My old-fashioned view is that the professions are properly a small and distinct group of businesses in which the practitioner is putting her own professional reputation, her credibility and either her own money or her own life on the line. So a professional soldier, a partner in a law or accountancy firm, do count as such, since the principals stand to lose their own money, lives, or livelihood.

If you are risking other people's money, with limits on that risk (such that your clients, creditors and suppliers are the ones most likely to suffer any lasting financial loss as a result of your mistakes), and if you are accepting a salary or regular wage, pension and all the usual employment protections, then you should do the best possible job that you can, but you should probably not think that you are in a profession. You are a journeyman, a businesswoman, a competent tradesman, or hopefully an artisan practising your craft. Or possibly, in 2013, bankers, who have lately earned a whole taxonomic class of their own, outside the realms of normal society.

The title 'profession' or 'professional' should perhaps be reserved as an honorific awarded by your grateful clients or possibly your working partners in the media, not a self-designated title to make you feel better about pursuing an ordinary commercial calling, or as a spin doctor. Our own consultancy is structured as an unlimited liability partnership.

As a journeyman, an artisan, what craft skills should you hone and what activities will you be expected to undertake? One of the most compelling arguments for public relations activity as an ethical practice takes its justification from the concept of advocacy in the law courts – which suggests that everyone has the right to a fair trial.

Western society says that everyone should be allowed legal representation to put the mitigating factors of their case, no matter how heinous a crime they have committed, or are accused of. There may be extenuating circumstances that have contributed to the criminal's actions and that may be taken into consideration when passing sentence, such as dire need, coercion, or simply ignorance.

So, for instance, stealing is wrong. But stealing a loaf of bread to feed your starving children, when the theft is from a very rich person's house where unwanted bread is thrown away every day, may not be viewed by most people as being as serious a crime as some other forms of stealing; such as persistently and knowingly manipulating the money markets to cream off invested money intended to provide hard-working people's pensions in their old age, for instance. I'm sure that you can think of better examples.

In the same way, a central tenet of public relations is that everyone deserves the right to fair advocacy. So no matter how apparently transgressive an organisation has been in its dealings, which have since led to a public furore, it still has the right to put its point of view forward and to have a fair public hearing. And, today, that point of view will often be put out, or prepared for a senior representative, by the public relations staff. Although they may well call it something else, such as corporate communications, lobbying, public engagement, stakeholder dialogue, publicity, press relations, or public affairs.

Stockholm Accords

The World Public Relations forum met in Stockholm, Sweden, on 15 June 2010 and produced a set of agreed guidelines or principles on the role of public relations and its value to an organisation, summed up as a set of accords between public relations and communication management industry leaders from every continent.

The final agreement is known as the Stockholm Accords[8] and is titled 'A Call to Action for Public Relations and Communication in a Global Society', published by the Global Alliance for Public Relations and Communication Management by their editorial board, comprising Ylva Skoogh from Sweden, Gary McCormick from the USA and Toni Muzi Falconi from Italy.

According to the UK's Chartered Institute of Public Relations, the Stockholm Accords is designed to change the perception of public relations from a tactical discipline to one that sits at the heart of what organisations do and plays a significant part in their success. It is also designed to help professionals have conversations with their organisations about the way PR can be used strategically, to support and defend investment in public relations, and to provide a platform from which public relations professionals can outline their value to different stakeholders.

The UK Chartered Institute of Public Relations was represented by Prof Anne Gregory, Director of the Centre for Public Relations Studies at Leeds Metropolitan University, at the forum. For a full text and the exact wording go to www.stockholmaccords.org, but these short extracts and summaries should give you an idea of their scope:

Stockholm Accords: The organisational value of public relations and communication management:

- **Sustainability:** The organisation's *sustainability* depends on balancing today's demands with the ability to meet future needs based on economic, social and environmental dimensions. The public relations role in this is to involve and engage stakeholders and ensure transparent and authentic reporting to them.

- **Governance:** All organisations operating under the *stakeholder governance model* empower their leaders – board members and elected officials – to be directly responsible for deciding and implementing *stakeholder relationship policies*. This will let them identify and deal with opportunities and risks. The public relations role is to help define organisational values, apply appropriate communication skills, sustain the organisation's licence to operate and create an internal listening culture, allowing the organisation to anticipate, adapt and respond.
- **Management:** In today's accelerating, globally competitive *network society*, the quality and effectiveness of an organisation's decisions are increasingly determined by the speed and context within which it implements those decisions. The public relations role is to shape the two-way communication process, act as a conduit for intelligence and trends, identify and solve issues, and communicate the organisation's values to stakeholders, so creating its reputational capital.

Stockholm Accords: The operational value of public relations and communication management:

- **Internal Communication:** Internal communication is vital to the organisation, fostering trust, commitment, purpose and shared goals. Public relations professionals seek constant feedback for a mutual understanding of how the internal community accepts and communicates its strategy and how the organisation's reputation depends on the actions taken by internal stakeholders.
- **External Communications:** Organisations must review and adjust their policies, actions and communicative behaviour to improve their relationships with their stakeholders and society at large, including customers, investors, communities, governments, active citizen groups, industry alliances, mainstream and digital media and other stakeholders. Public relations professionals craft and deliver effective messages, advocate for stakeholder groups and sustain an appropriate dialogue.
- **Coordination of Internal and External Communications:** Organisational communication today is a complex, multidimensional, multi-stakeholder enterprise involving concurrent engagement across diverse *value networks* and legal frameworks. It must balance transparency, finite resources and time sensitive demands against rapid change and conflicts of interest. All organisational communication must be coherent and coordinated. The public relations role is to oversee internal and external communications to assure consistency and accuracy, to research, develop, monitor and adjust the organisation's communicative behaviour and to manage, measure and evaluate programmes for improvement.

What is health and medical PR?

This section might easily be entitled 'So how does health public relations differ from other types of PR?' Just as science and medical journalism have increasingly been recognised as print and broadcast media specialisms that do not just require a talent for reportage but also an in-depth specialist knowledge of the subject area, so too science communication and health and medical public relations are increasingly becoming specialist areas within the broader public relations trade. Health and medical public relations arguably has developed distinct rules and conventions that may require a specialist knowledge of the subject area and the recipient audiences.

It is no longer good enough to tell a general reporter that she is now medical editor of a magazine, newspaper, or television channel. Or indeed any other media outlet. The subject requires a good contacts book (for 'comment and reaction' in newspaper jargon) to provide on-tap expertise to analyse, discuss, and verify new discoveries, a long memory for previous relevant incidents, and a thorough knowledge of the arcane terminology used by the academic and pharmaceutical research industries to translate their stories into news of interest to wider publics.

Science and medical journalists are unusually long and stable holders of their posts (by which I mean they successfully fight off the competition, not that they aren't given to personal misgivings, bouts of depression, or weird flights of fancy), especially compared with the high turnover in other specialist positions. This deliberate churn within the media is supposed to bring a fresh eye and new ideas to otherwise jaded topic areas. But the health and medical reporters consistently resist it, even to the extent of turning down promotions.

By the early 1990s there were probably still only a dozen or so full-time science journalists working in UK national newspapers or in the media (outside the BBC), and another dozen full-time medical journalists (again, outside the BBC, which has long recognised the need for specialists), plus twice as many freelances.

There were also surprisingly few full-time medical or science press officers working for universities, research councils, professional academic societies and institutes. Or even within the pharmaceutical industry, although within PR consultancies, some people and indeed whole agencies were already specialising, recognising the financial advantages of a thorough knowledge of the pharmaceutical marketplace and its peculiar regulations.

Public relations was, if anything, seen mainly as a discipline allied to marketing, and therefore most suited to selling more packets of cornflakes rather than as one of the normal functions of a serious academic organisation or research funding body. Even today some research-focused universities in the UK and Europe, and even some academic societies, still do not have specialist medical and health press officers. Which means that they have no one to proactively act as advocates for the subject or their institution.

Others, however, including UK examples such as Manchester University and Imperial College, London, or the Society for General Microbiology, do, and consequently they get more and better coverage for roughly the same volume and quality of research output, peer-reviewed publications, or academic conference papers than their rivals. I'd love to see some research findings on this, if such findings exist. But anecdotally, my science journalist colleagues, usually on a tight time schedule, tend to go to the press officers that they know will understand the question.

By the 1990s (and obviously earlier in some cases) many UK-based academic societies were appointing press officers to manage their media and public relations functions, though in all too many cases these incumbents were recently graduated (and therefore cheap) postgraduates, who had an up-to-date knowledge of their subject but remarkably little idea of how to successfully promote their science activities. This book is a result of more than 25 years of working with many of those struggling, well-intentioned press officers.

Some universities and academic organisations, for example Manchester University, have now started planned programmes aimed at engaging with their local communities through outreach programmes. These include science weeks and festivals, local museum talks and events, Café Sci, and a whole raft of other activities designed to both enthuse the public about their work and to teach their postgraduate students and researchers interpersonal communication skills.

Meanwhile the university academics gain valuable feedback about the wishes, concerns, and misconceptions about medical science currently held by the public, media, and business community. Other universities have appointed professorial chairs in Public Understanding of Science or Public Engagement.

The airport and railway bookshops are stuffed full of management self-improvement manuals which often take a relatively simple idea – such as de-clutter your desk, or take regular breaks – and then parley it into an entire homespun philosophy for turning your life around and becoming a success in business. Public relations, and especially health and medical public relations, has no such magic wand to wave. Getting good at this is hard graft. I turned down several early potential clients for our consultancy simply because they had the notion that advertising costs money, but gaining free editorial coverage through public relations is itself free. This is nonsense.

Media editorial coverage and social recognition gained through public relations activities costs exactly as much, if not more, than a similar amount of coverage gained through advertising. So if you want a quarter page article about your latest work in the *Financial Times* or equivalent quality newspaper somewhere across Europe, then as a rule of thumb, find out how much that would cost to buy as advertising today, and that's roughly what your budget will need to be once you have costed everything in, to achieve the same volume of coverage by public relations routes.

Public relations today is about much more than just getting media coverage, but in the rush to turn it into an all-encompassing discipline, partly driven by public relations academics trying to park their tanks on other departments' lawns, media coverage gets all too easily forgotten. If no one finds out about what you are doing, then much of your effort has been wasted. Unless of course you are a banker, and if everyone did know what you were actually doing with their money, they might feel driven to tar and feather you instead, rather than pay you a bonus.

No one can give you the secret of public relations in a nutshell, all we can offer is a broad overview of the field, some useful guidance notes, and an eclectic selection of the hints, tips, tricks, and techniques that we all learn through experience.

The social psychology writer Oliver Burkeman, in an article for the *Guardian* newspaper, recently brought to my attention the musings of Glen Whitman, professor of economics at California State University. Glen has become a fan of the Two Things game. Apparently, 'for every subject there are only Two Things you need to know. Everything else is just the application of those two things, or just not important.' Whitman has blogged about it and received in turn a flood of suggestions for his website.[9] As the Two Things for economics he suggests: 1) Incentives matter; 2) There's no such thing as a free lunch.

I got interested because he also listed the Two Things for medicine: 1) Do no harm; 2) To do any good, you must risk doing harm; the Two Things about journalism: 1) There's no such thing as objectivity; 2) The end of the story is based on your deadline; and the Two Things about public relations: 1) Perception is reality; 2) Perception is rarely reality.

References

1. 'What is PR?' at www.cipr.co.uk/content/careers-cpd/careers-pr/what-pr.
2. Wikipedia comments at www.huffingtonpost.co.uk/jane-wilson/wikipedia-the-real-public_b_1252257.html.
3. Wikipedia guidelines at http://uk.wikimedia.org/wiki/Draft_best_practice_guidelines_for_PR.
4. http://en.wikipedia.org/wiki/Public_relations.
5. James Grunig & Todd Hunt, *Managing Public Relations*, New York: Holt, Rinehart & Winston, 1984.
6. *New York Times*, 1 March 2012.
7. More definitions of PR at http://prdefinition.prsa.org.
8. www.stockholmaccords.org.
9. 'The Two Things' game at www.csun.edu/~dgw61315/thetwothings.html.

2 Health and medical PR sectors

So far we have identified public relations as a discipline concerned with reputation, aiming to gain support and understanding and trying to influence an audience's behaviour and opinions. But what does this actually mean in practical terms? For some clients from mainstream commercial companies, this may simply mean 'gaining favourable media coverage' for a product or service.

But in medical and health public relations, changing behaviour such as stopping smoking, or changing public or parliamentary opinion about groups of disabled or sick patients, or lobbying to change business economics, may be higher priorities for many of the key players in the sector. And for the big companies involved, the commercial equivalent of selling more packets of cornflakes, which might be thought to be selling more medicines, is strictly regulated in most UK, European, American and, to a lesser extent, in world markets.

You are simply not allowed to try to actively create a public demand for more and stronger branded pharmaceuticals in most developed countries. And if you did, most of the Western world publics would consider that you were behaving unethically, anathema in the medical and health environment.

So who can you work for, and what can you expect to do in a health and medical public relations agency, pharmaceutical industry in-house position, public sector, or charity, campaigning and the not-for-profit organisations?

It might help to think first of the different types of players in the field of health and medical activities. There is an enormous crossover of aims, activities and sponsorship money from each of these sectors to the others, and several organisations may be pursuing a specialist interest in one sector while funding the activities of other, sometimes apparently opposed, interests. You will be able to think of many more organisations that can be fitted into this matrix, I am just suggesting a few which may be considered to be indicative types of major players with similar aims, activities and opinions.

Incidentally, the words you choose to describe the different organisations will provide an insight into your perception of them, and may even alter the way you view them. So as an industry sector would you just list drug companies or medicines manufacturers as a description?

Or do you refer to them as pharmaceutical companies, or big pharma for the handful of major international companies, and then think vaguely of all the others as simply medicines manufacturers? If you subdivide further you can consider a whole range of organisations involved in manufacturing, producing and marketing drugs and treatments that could be thought of as health and medical companies.

As well as by the major international companies, other drug products are developed by small-scale specialist producers targeting niche markets or neglected diseases. These include laboratory and university spin-outs and users of new techniques such as genomics, looking at the interactions of different genes as well as studying the function of single genes, and bioinformatics, the use of computers and information technology to mine data and analyse it.

These smaller companies may have a specialist expertise that enables them to develop a new method of targeting a particular disease, or identify new drug targets by accurately identifying and imaging a particular protein (such as those used by viruses to gain access to our cells) and then intelligently designing a drug to block its action.

Smaller-scale companies may manage to develop a treatment, but once they have proved a treatment in principle, they will often need to enter into a licence agreement with a major pharmaceutical company to gain assistance and investment for clinical trials, international marketing and distribution.

Some of these specialist and smaller companies are now starting to target lesser-known or rare diseases, and the neglected tropical diseases, which are economically unviable to develop treatments for by the pharmaceutical majors. Particularly rare diseases simply do not have enough people suffering from them to make modern medical research by commercial companies an economic proposition.

Similarly until now it has not been economically viable to develop and patent treatments for the neglected tropical diseases, a group of 13 diseases formally recognised by the World Health Organization,[1] which includes for example Chagas disease, a Central and South American parasitic disease transmitted by biting insects, similar to African Sleeping Sickness.

The people who suffer from these diseases typically cannot personally afford the new drugs once developed, and neither can their own countries' hospitals or health systems. Existing treatments for neglected diseases are typically brutal, having been first developed around 100 years ago, and are often based on arsenic and other poisons, which work by hopefully killing the parasite before they kill the patient.

Today a combination of modern air travel for business, exotic holidays, and growing wealth in the developing countries, mean that these diseases are now appearing in the UK, Europe and the US, and demand for new effective treatments is growing, creating an opening for specialist medical companies.

Generic medicines producers specialise in producing cheaper versions of drugs whose patent protection has expired, and so they do not have the massive overheads and development costs of research, efficacy and safety testing faced by the major pharmaceutical companies. They simply need to show that their version of the drug is functionally and chemically the same as the patent expired version. US patent protection gives 20 years to the original manufacturer, but since patents are usually sought before clinical trials begin, market protection for a drug is often only from seven to 12 years before generics can market a cheaper non-branded version.

Me-too medicines companies take a slightly different approach. Their technique is to chemically analyse a newly developed drug and then make a very similar formulation that has practically the same properties, targeted at exactly the same disease and market, but with sufficient technical differences to allow it too to be patentable. This may seem a morally reprehensible course of action, but sometimes these me-too variants can be used to treat patients unlucky enough to react badly to the original drug, or for whom it does not work effectively. The slight chemical differences can make a huge difference in the drug's side effects, and the competition from me-too producers helps to keep drug prices down.

In addition there are medicines, treatments and therapies designed for mental illnesses and disorders. Mental illnesses are heavily stigmatised in our society, so many sufferers do not wish to admit to having them and may not seek proper treatment, relying instead on self-diagnosis and self-medication, sometimes using illegally obtained medicines. These illnesses may be caused or contributed to by chemical or hormonal imbalances in the brain, and may not even be recognised as genuine sickness by many people in society, for instance in depression, anorexia, or obesity.

In other cases, disease diagnoses themselves are questionable, with growing concern about increasing medicalisation of such experiences as feelings of sadness or loss after bereavement, mild anxiety, or dissatisfaction with personal appearance. It may be a normal part of the cycles of everyday experience that many people are not happy all of the time.

However, to obtain medicines paid for by insurance companies, patients in the US must be diagnosed with a formally recognised syndrome. So there is a financial incentive for pharmaceutical companies to lobby to get mild, cyclical or seasonal disorders defined as mental illnesses, or to identify brand new conditions for which they can then develop and market a drug treatment.

A further section of the medicines and drugs market is occupied by the illegal producers of drugs used by recreational users, ravers and clubbers. Any discussion of the drugs industry as a whole should take some account of the phenomenal economic value of the illegal and criminal market, with its network of users, suppliers, pushers, dealers, importers and producers.

The Executive Director of the United Nations Office on Drugs and Crime, Yury Fedotov, announced in June 2012 that 230 million people, or 5 per cent of the world's population, used an illicit drug at least once in 2010, according to their *World Drugs Report 2012*, and 27 million people are problem users, mainly heroin and cocaine dependent.[2]

Another section of the medicinal market covers the producers of traditional remedies, herbal medicines and Chinese medicines. These remedies all contain active ingredients that may or may not actually exhibit the properties claimed for them, but many are certainly likely to cross-react when taken along with conventional medicines.

Herbal medicines, made directly from plants and other natural ingredients, are likely to have widely varying amounts of the chemically active substance in each dose, depending upon how it was harvested, from where and at what time of year the ingredients were collected and who prepares it as a medicine.

Chinese medicines often contain strongly active ingredients, including some substances that would normally be regarded as poisons, and may sometimes be extremely effective, although others – such as bear bile or tiger penis – owe more to the power of myth than rational prescribing.

Vitamin pills and supplements, which are regulated in the UK and Europe, restricting the health benefit claims that can be made about them, are not currently regulated in the UK's Crown Dependencies since the UK Department of Health, and therefore its subsidiary the UK Medicines and Healthcare Products Regulatory Agency, has no jurisdiction over them. This has led to a lucrative internet-based mail-order industry in Guernsey, part of the Channel Islands, worth up to £100 million a year according to a *Guardian* newspaper investigation in 2012.[3] Some Channel Islands companies have used catalogues sent to the UK to make unsupported claims about products to treat cancer, dementia, diabetes and other diseases, claims that have been criticised by the Advertising Standards Authority. The supplements are not manufactured on Guernsey, just sold on from there.

Cosmetics, grooming and beauty products such as shampoos and creams can be considered as a further, if peripheral, section of the market, and are often a triumph of marketing over substance. Many make optimistic-sounding claims to treat problems that you didn't know you had. The marketers think up the new problems to make consumers feel insecure, and then offer the new product as a solution to this recently identified problem. The original product to use this marketing technique was Lifebuoy Soap, a carbolic soap produced by Lever Brothers in Port Sunlight, which famously dealt with BO or body odour, a previously non-existent condition (although of course many people did smell badly). By 1969, Lifebuoy wrappers claimed that it knocked out BO. This was a problem that, according to the advertising, even your closest friends would not tell you about. Today similar quasi-health products and advertising target body image, insecurities and other neuroses, and are marketed as treating such problems as the seven signs of ageing, or uneven skin tone (for women), dry and lifeless hair (hair is actually a dead structure), or signs of tiredness and fatigue (for men).

However, if the marketers make any genuine medical or health claims (in the US, UK and Europe) the product manufacturers must now produce evidence of this, and the products would come under strict medicines and advertising legislation, so the claimants are careful to target the appearance of wrinkles, rather than wrinkles themselves.

Patent diet products, which typically replace fats with sugar (otherwise the foods would taste like cardboard), and neutraceuticals (and even some weird diets and massage therapies) may be similarly marketed and make optimistic-sounding but unverifiable claims for the health benefits of everything from probiotic yoghurts to enemas.

A further sector of the medicines market could be categorised as magic, or faith treatments, or at least as cures and treatments that defy all the known laws of physics. This sector includes homeopathy (for which there is still no convincing empirical evidence), and supernatural interventions such as prayer. These treatments are harmless, unless used instead of genuine treatments, but generate millions of pounds a year for their practitioners.

To be fair, homeopathy and other alternative therapies, which usually involve long personal consultations so that the supposed medication can be individually assigned, may have genuine psychological benefits by giving the patient the undivided attention of a sympathetic expert listener, time that an overworked GP is unlikely to be able to spare. Wealthy but lonely attention-seekers may derive real comfort and benefit from this. And have no risk of developing side effects, drug dependency, or alcoholism.

In addition to the wide variety of alternative treatments offered by the less empirically testable ends of the market, the genuine or conventional medicines and health sector could be further subdivided by rules governing the distribution of the products:

- Medicines or products which can be bought over-the-counter in ordinary shops and pharmacies (such as hay fever pills, antiseptics, cough medicines, anti-diarrhoea and headache pills).
- Those which can be bought on the high street but can only be supplied by qualified pharmacists (in the UK) as they contain stronger formulations, have some side effects, are not advised with some other existing conditions, or may react with other common medicines.
- Medicines that can only be prescribed by GPs or family doctors in surgeries.
- Those which must be taken under expert supervision and that can therefore only be prescribed by hospital doctors (usually consultants). This last group of medicines would include some of the few remaining new antibiotics for instance, in an attempt to prevent antibiotic-resistant bacteria becoming tolerant of them too.

Your particular choice of name, and the way you view the medicines sector, will depend upon your own experience of health interventions, loyalties, politics, employment history, and – just possibly – the PR activities of both supporters and critics of the particular group you are naming.

So as another example, are 'animal rights groups' distinct in your opinion from animal welfare charities, pressure groups, special interest groups, antivivisectionists, protestors, campaigners, or animal extremists?

The five overlapping sectors within society

However you decide to name them, and in whatever sector you work in, we have always found it very helpful to think about the needs of the many different but overlapping sectors by dividing them into five key ones: industry and business; government and public bodies; campaigners; academic and research institutes; and, of course, media, all of which operate within our wider society.

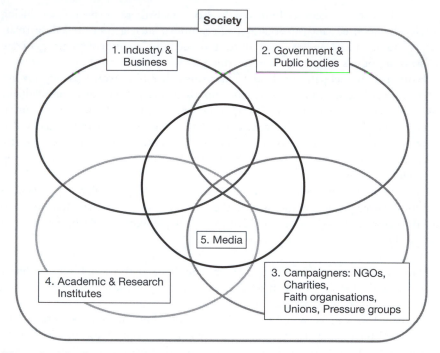

Figure 2.1 The five overlapping sectors within society: industry and business; government and public bodies; campaigners; academic and research institutes; media.

Most areas of public relations, such as in consumer goods or fashion brands, do not usually need to consider government, academics or even pressure groups as quite such a significant influence on public opinion as the activities of the commercial sector. But in the health and medical field I suspect that all four of these distinct but overlapping sectors, or five if you include widespread media effects as well, may have fairly equal weight in shaping public trust.

The European Commission's annual autumn and spring Eurobarometer surveys[4] do not show how public opinion is actually shaped, but they do give an indication of concerns across Europe. In the latest published results, from 2011, healthcare ranked as the fourth most pressing national concern, ahead of crime but behind unemployment, the economic situation and rising prices.

According to Eurobarometer, trust in national institutions is not very high across Europe at the moment, with only 28 per cent of Europeans trusting their government and 31 per cent trusting their parliaments, although as with all these measures, this varies from country to country, and the political parties fare particularly badly with only 15 per cent trusting them.

Big companies are trusted by 30 per cent of Europeans compared with 59 per cent who distrust them, although this distrust rose to 79 per cent in Greece, compared with 67 per cent in Germany and 66 per cent in the United Kingdom.

I. Business and Industry	II. Government and Public Bodies
Pharmaceutical companies	Government ministers
Generic drug manufacturers	Civil servants
Alternative medicine suppliers	Members of Parliament
Laboratory equipment makers	Members of European Parliament
Chemists and Pharmacies	European Commissioners and officials
Health food stores	Local government elected members
Royal Colleges (Anaesthetists, GPs, Surgeons, Physicians, Nursing, Veterinary Surgeons and so on)	Local government staff
NHS Hospitals	Publicly funded research bodies (such as National Institute of Health Research), UK Research Councils (such as Medical Research Council, BBSRC, NERC, STFC, EPSRC, ESRC)
Private Hospitals	
Insurance companies	UK National Health Service
Trade groups such as Confederation of British Industry, Association of the British Pharmaceutical Industry	

III. Campaigners, Charities, Unions, Faith Groups and NGOs	IV. Academic and Research Sector
British Medical Association	Universities
Wellcome Trust	In-service research groups (such as at Nursing and Midwifery colleges, Hospitals, Veterinary colleges)
Medical welfare charities	
Medical research charities	Regulatory bodies, professional practice registries
Umbrella bodies (such as Association of Medical Research Charities, Genetic Interest Group)	Benchmarking organisations (such as Medicines and Healthcare products Regulatory Agency, General Medical Council, National Institute for Health and Clinical Excellence)
Patients' associations (such as National Federation of Kidney Patients Associations, Transplant Sports Association of Great Britain, Genetic Alliance)	
Trades Unions (such as Unite)	Academic societies (such as Society for General Microbiology, British Transplantation Society, Federation of European Neuroscience Societies)
Animal rights groups (such as BUAV)	
Animal welfare charities (such as RSPCA)	
Industry and patient funded pro-science campaign groups (such as Pro-Test, Understanding Animal Research)	Peer-reviewed academic journals (such as *The Lancet*, *New England Journal of Medicine*, *British Medical Journal*, *Cell* and *Nature*)
Science-sceptical campaigning groups (such as Genewatch, What Doctors Don't Tell You)	
Alternative medicine, homeopathy and alternative therapy practitioners, their trade bodies and registries	
Church leaders and faith based campaigning bodies (opposed to contraception, stem cell research, abortion, sex education, euthanasia and assisted dying)	
Pro-choice patient campaigners (such as Dignity in Dying, Action on Addiction, Marie Stopes clinics)	
Social groups (such as Women's Institutes, Mumsnet, Rotary Clubs)	
Guilds and trade bodies (such as Institute of Laboratory Animal Technicians)	

Figure 2.2 A working map for different sectors.

Similarly only a minority trust trade unions (38 per cent, compared with 49 per cent who distrust them), although this trust rose to 67 per cent in Finland, 66 per cent in Denmark and 59 per cent in the Netherlands. Religious institutions are only trusted by 40 per cent of people in Europe, a drop of 10 per cent in the last four years.

Scientific research is generally seen as an area in which decisions should be taken at the joint European level (73 per cent), whereas health is seen as an area for national decision-making by 60 per cent, compared with 38 per cent favouring European-level decisions.

When you are preparing any public relations actions or campaigns, you may therefore need to consider how your activities will be perceived by representatives from each of these sectors, and what kinds of criticism or responses you can predict.

A working map for different sectors

You may find it useful to jot down the names of organisations that you come into contact with regularly, or who publicly express opinions about your work, even if you do not do this in any particular order of importance or systematically. You can classify the list more logically later, such as when identifying specific groups to target, consult, or respond to in formal campaigns. Examples listed in Figure 2.2 apply to the UK, but similar organisations will exist in most other countries.

We will consider my remaining fifth sector, the press, media, or more grandly, the fourth estate, throughout this book. The way you decide to think about the different players in the media and communications sectors will affect your own perception of any problems you are facing, and will, if you are working in public relations as a management discipline, ultimately affect the way your organisation relates to organisations from other sectors and responds to their activities. Communication is a competitive (and sometimes collaborative) activity, and everyone is pushing their own agenda through competing public relations channels.

The way you choose to classify the competing sectors and the names you assign to different groups may limit your expectations of their activities and their capabilities, leading to some serious miscalculations or oversights. So as well as considering the health and public relations and media landscape from your own perspective, you should also step back sometimes, and carry out the equivalent exercises from the perspective of the other sectors that you have identified. We hate surprises in public relations.

References

1. For more on neglected tropical diseases see www.who.int/neglected_diseases/en.
2. United Nations Office on Drugs and Crime, *World Drugs Report 2012*, published 26 June 2012.
3. *Guardian*, 29 June 2012.
4. Eurobarometer surveys, European Commission, http://ec.europa.eu/public_opinion/index_en.htm.

3 Roles within health and medical PR

Having identified some of the different players in the field of health and medical public relations in the previous chapter, we also need to identify some of the distinct roles that individual practitioners may be expected to carry out. The following chapters will then look at some of the core skills, expertise and techniques that you will need.

Part of the great attraction of working in public relations is the variety, the need to learn new skills almost every day and the opportunities to speak enthusiastically to people who actually wish to hear from you. In no particular order, some of the tasks or roles you may be expected to master include:

Spokesman, advocate, public speaker

Some PR people think that their role is simply to find the correct person to represent their organisation for this particular event, brief the speaker and then let him loose on the public, media, or gathering of experts. Be afraid. Eventually the system will break down. One day you will not be able to find just the right expert to explain something to a journalist, or to do your promised interview for BBC local radio.

One day the keynote speaker from your organisation will fall ill, or miss an aeroplane, and you will have to step up to the microphone instead, even if the audience was expecting your chief executive, or the office cleaner. You are the last fallback option for every single possible communication activity for your organisation. If you feel that you simply could not do this, it is time to find another job. Do not go into public relations.

Expert, tactician

You will be expected to know how to achieve the impossible at various times in your public relations career. How do you contact difficult to reach audiences? What will appeal to the key people? How can you avert a crisis or create a buzz? Everyone gets nervous eventually, and seeks a second opinion, even chief executives. You need to be an expert on every conceivable communications activity and every possible crisis that could strike. Part of your role is to know how to find things out, and then know what tactics are likely to work to convince the public and media that you are in control.

You will get asked by your senior managers whether they should walk out of the front door as usual and face some protestors down, or should they sneak out the back way to avoid conflict. You need to have thought this through in advance. If you are going to make suggestions to your senior staff about the way they should phrase a statement or press release, you must be able to back up your assertion with a convincing argument, or they will just change the text back to the form of words they are most used to using, which will sound stuffy and boring.

Ethicist, conscience

The Public Relations Society of America's shiny new, 2012 crowdsourced, 'modern definition of public relations' does not include the word 'ethics', which surprised the society's senior officers. And me. But that was for a general definition, suitable for all possible public relations sectors. We are working in health and medical PR: you definitely do need to consider the moral and ethical aspects of almost every activity that your organisation undertakes. Do not ever, ever, let the lawyers have the last word.

Sometimes you and your organisation have to do stuff just because it is right, no matter what the cost. I do not care if you are primarily a deontologist with a fixation on duties and keeping your promises; or a utilitarian who judges that the greatest good is the best path; or even a follower of rights theories; or a casuist fixated by precedents; or a fan of Aristotelian virtue. You may at times face problems that just cannot be reconciled, in which case you must simply try to do the least harm, and welcome to the world of postmodern ethics.

You are not a Machiavellian veiled figure in the shadows, subtly manipulating your colleagues, the media and public opinion. Sometimes you will need to speak up as the conscience of your organisation. Just figure out when to do the right thing. You have a spine for a reason. In a crisis almost everyone else in your organisation will probably be protecting their backs, or their jobs, or their face.

Press officer, press relations manager

Knowing what the media and journalists want and how to deal with them is the vital, everyday core of public relations. Traditional newspapers are moving from being print media that also run a website, to being website content providers that also currently produce a print version of some of their output.

Remember, you are acting as a liaison officer between two warring tribes, the two cultures, so try not to allow your good judgement on what the media actually needs to be overruled by your senior managers from other disciplines. The fourth estate is there to perform an important function in our society, which is to cast light into murky corners and assemble a hasty first draft of history. Support them, but do not go native.

Publicist, promotions, photo opportunities

We are a visual species. Humans hunt by sight. Get good pictures and learn how to recognise a good photo opportunity. If you want to get your event onto television or featured in magazines, where are the pictures? Don't waste money on expensive fripperies, only use celebrities with a real connection to your cause and giveaways with a genuine purpose. To do otherwise would be like expensively bidding to hold the world's biggest sporting event in the UK to promote this country and then inviting a US fast-food company to be the major sponsor. The public can and will spot the disconnection.

Online and social media manager, blogger

The Web 2.0 has changed our audiences from being passive consumers of any particular content that we care to post online, to actively interacting with other members of virtual communities who network, share information and expect user-friendly and user-focused design. You need to work out how to convert your target audiences from being viewers and readers into being a supportive, involved and interactive community who understand and share your values. You need to monitor your organisation's formal and departmental, and in some cases employees' web logs, or blogs, to check what messages and tone are being given out; and similarly check what others in the blogosphere are saying about you.

Events, exhibition and conference organiser

In the world of medicine and health many of the most active or involved organisations are not principally commercial entities whose public face is closely controlled by their marketing department, or medical charities whose principal PR aim is to support fundraising efforts. Your organisation's public perception may be public relations led, which means that your department will also need to take responsibility and project its image at conferences, exhibitions and public events such as ethical debates, café scientifque, science and art crossover exhibitions, schools liaison, or by providing speakers and sessions at science festivals.

Community liaison, social events, sponsorship and fundraising

You may need to get out and speak to real people in the community if you are trying to build grassroots support or recruit volunteers for an activity. Cause-related marketing activities, when an organisation hopes that some of the stardust attaching to a sport, good cause or other community activity will rub off in exchange for sponsorship, is a worthwhile but dangerous course to steer. Why should your organisation, or for instance all general taxpayers who happen to own nearly all of a failed bank, be spending millions of pounds and euros subsidising one particular sport such as rugby? Bankers are not, on the whole, bruisers. On the other hand a fun physical activity, such as the iconic London to Brighton Bike

Ride, which has been organised by the medical charity the British Heart Foundation for more than 25 years now, fits well with their mission to promote activities that increase fitness and reduce heart disease, and also gives them a huge fundraising boost. It raises the charity's profile among participants, their families and friends, and thousands of spectators who turn out to see it, gaining favourable PR and media coverage every year.

Crisis and issues management

Most organisations will face unexpected and suddenly media-sensitive issues, environmental and ethical concerns, threats, pressure groups, public criticism, financial problems, or staff difficulties at some time or another. You will need to become an expert in crisis management and public consultation, find ways to promote dialogue, consensus-building and mediation. You need a plan. And make sure that it is clearly labelled as an emergency or contingency plan, not mistaken for a projection of what is likely to happen, in case it leaks out. In medical and health public relations you are also going to have to do some long-term planning in issue management, for the slow-burning issues that simply are not going to go away. For instance as a medical charity, using animals in research or assisting women with pregnancy terminations; as a pharmaceutical company, patenting medicines or cherry-picking data; as a government body, trying to privatise the National Health Service or appointing all-male committees; as an academic body, not crediting the indigenous people you were studying or not allowing public access to research they have funded.

Internal relations and communications

One of your most engaged and important audiences is your organisation's own staff. In most companies the public relations function reports through separate channels to the directorate, as it is seen as a management function, even though, in organisations still struggling with the dark ages, it may not yet qualify for a dedicated management board seat. So when a strike threatens, or during payroll disputes, you are still going to have to put out press statements and internal newsletters telling everyone what is going on. European Union legislation means that workers have a right to be informed and consulted. As a Department of Health mandarin told me many years ago, when talking about NGOs, you can divide them into those we inform; those we consult; and those we cooperate with. For internal audiences the same philosophy is true when you are communicating some of the trickier management decisions. There are policies that you tell as simple top-down decisions; those you sell (when you're expecting some resistance); those you consult about (already decided, but hoping for some input to modify the impacts); and those you involve the staff in, where the whole process of change is collaborative. The larger your organisation, the bigger the audience, especially when you factor in their families and friends, your board or trustees, and some random subcontractors, suppliers and a few friendly customers as well. In many cases internal audiences are so large, or so dispersed on multiple sites, that it is worthwhile to produce dedicated newsletters, websites, podcasts and video messages to keep them up to date on new developments, research findings, or simply communicate with them.

Lobbyist, parliamentary liaison, public affairs

Legislation, regulation and regime change can all affect the financial and political environment in which your organisation is operating. As public relations people, you need to keep abreast of proposed or likely changes that could adversely affect your employer or area of work. And as a lobbyist, try to encourage legislators to make beneficial changes. Changes in the financial situation of your target audiences, or major cultural shifts, such as privatising the National Health Service, can also radically affect the business and communication environment that you are working in. For instance the international pharmaceutical industry is constrained by UK and European, US and other national laws, which regulate how prescription medicines may be marketed, and in many countries forbids their direct sale to the public. In the same way, within the UK especially, registered charities, which receive substantial tax benefits, are constrained by Charity Commission regulations that govern the lobbying activities they can legitimately undertake, and their ability to call for a change in the law. Until relatively recently this was interpreted as forbidden in the UK, and charities had a duty to operate within the law as it is. Pressure groups that wanted to change the law, such as animal activist organisations and others with similar political ambitions, were banned from holding charitable status or attempting to pass themselves off as charities. This has now relaxed a little, so that charities can lobby for legislative changes that fall within their core remit, such as welfare charities which may call for tighter laws to protect disadvantaged or disabled people, or prevent discrimination. And some radical animal rights groups have gained charitable status by claiming educational or animal welfare purposes.

Financial public relations, business-to-business communications

Financial public relations is another area that comes with its own special rules. Registered companies and other financial entities such as charities have specific duties to file properly audited accounts at set times of the year. For commercial companies, any information that is deemed to be price-sensitive, affecting the share value of the company, such as takeovers, mergers and major acquisitions, must be delivered to all shareholders and other interested parties simultaneously and by following specific rules to avoid market manipulation and insider dealing. Do not attempt to muddle through – you could end up with a substantial fine, or in jail. Get proper advice on what is required and the specific format it needs to be delivered in from your finance department or accountants. Do not accidentally leak price-sensitive information to journalists. As with most misdemeanours, affecting the pockets of the city grandees and bankers is considered far more serious, and will be dealt with far more harshly, than simply behaving unethically or insensitively.

Similar to financial public relations, but without the legal constraints, business-to-business communication or B2B aims to impart industry-relevant information to companies and trade bodies, usually through specialist trade publications, exhibitions and conferences, rather than via the wider mainstream media. The B2B communication channels tend to be more direct, shorter and simpler, but at the same time B2B tends to be more price-sensitive. You are not trying to create consumer demand, you are working within an area where consumer demand has in turn created a business need for a new product, more of something, or a different formulation. The problem here is often that because a lot of the people working within a major industry all speak using the same shorthand terms and discipline-specific jargon, you may get institutionalised into doing the same. Do not ever draft a story aimed at a trade body or produce a trade press release that contains language and terms which your chief executive or the government minister responsible for this sector would not understand. Using jargon may make you look as though you are a cool insider, but you are storing up problems for the future and adding to obfuscation, not clearing the fog.

Speechwriter

Speechwriter. Says it all really. Try not to make them sound like robots. Remember, speeches are meant for saying out loud, not reading, so actually try it out yourself. If you manage to asphyxiate or lose the will to live while you are still speaking it, the sentence is too long. Repetition, repetition, repetition, and the rule of three is handy for making things memorable. Find out what a soundbite is. Last time I was working in BBC local radio, the lunchtime news clips had come down from 22 seconds to 17 seconds so that they could get an extra item in. That's enough time to say 51 words. Use it.

Brand champion, viral marketing

Brands, reputation and people make up the intellectual capital of an organisation. Originally confined to commercial organisations, and a concept borrowed from marketing, brand championing is, as its name suggests, the practice of looking at a particular product, service, or defined aspect of an organisation, and working out how to enhance it and incorporate it into our lives. Brand championing often tries to bundle together different aspects or traits and combine them with lifestyle markers rather than focusing on a single attribute. Public relations brand champions may use viral and stealth marketing techniques, trying to create word-of-mouth interest through social networks and discussions on internet chat forums, through attractive images and video clips that can be shared and circulated, and by developing online competitions and games.

Dark arts and dirty tricks

The dark arts of public relations are the negative and ethically questionable techniques that members of the public might disapprove of, but can help an organisation to win, or at least steal, the media coverage, at the expense of competitors or critics, however unfairly. Negative public relations can also be used to try to discredit competitors or critics.

Tricks include ambush marketing, hijacking, flash mobs or other PR stunts, when an event arranged and paid for by another organisation, usually a high-profile event where television cameras and reporters are expected, is used as a platform for a PR stunt by someone else. Everyday examples include streaking at sporting meetings such as horse races or football matches. Radical pressure groups have thrown red paint over catwalk models at fashion shows in protest over the use of fur, or dressed protestors as animals and invaded pharmaceutical and healthcare companies' annual shareholder meetings to protest over animal use in research and testing. Ambush marketing is less confrontational and usually involves an organisation using an event sponsored by another company to distribute their own competing product samples without permission or paying for sponsorship themselves. They may dress some telegenic supporters in brightly branded or message T-shirts, but originally disguised by normal outerwear, and then simultaneously reveal them at the appropriate time when cameras are present. A flash mob is created when groups of people who may not know each other are invited to a particular venue, typically through social media or cascade text messaging, to perform a particular action at a particular time, often pointlessly, such as lying on the floor or whistling a particular tune. You could imagine 1,000 individual morris dancers suddenly unveiling themselves and starting to dance among the spectators at the opening ceremony of the Olympic Games. As a public relations officer, you need to consider how your events, public meetings, press conferences, photocalls and open days could be hijacked.

Propaganda, spin-doctoring and cover-ups all involve deliberately misrepresenting the truth, adopting overly emotive language, and seeking to mislead the public or regulators in order to gain an unfair advantage, garner media coverage and sway public opinion. The point of propaganda is to influence or form opinions, not to impart unbiased information, and so it relies on deception and confusion rather than genuine education, persuasion and understanding. Examples include animal rights leaflets suggesting that medicines that were safety tested on animals cause side effects (they are also tested on tissue cultures, computer models and in clinical trials, but some people will still inevitably have adverse reactions).

White propaganda comes from an easily identifiable source, such as in a government anti-smoking campaign; black propaganda pretends to be from one source but actually comes from another; grey propaganda has no identifiable source and may be used to start rumours or cast slurs that later turn out to be untrue, leading audiences to believe that a second party is being maligned, and therefore gaining sympathy or belief for this second position, even though it is itself erroneous. This is similar to disinformation, which is the positive planting of untrue information, which through widespread repetition, especially by authority figures such as religious leaders, and especially during school-age years, becomes generally accepted as true. Selective cherry-picking of facts or entire research papers can give the impression that some medicines or alternative therapies are effective, or conversely ineffective. Linking two unrelated observed effects can suggest a causal relationship which does not actually exist, such as examples of people recovering from cancer after taking homeopathic remedies.

Spin-doctoring is the art of choosing which selected facts to highlight, and is often used to put a positive spin or slant on an otherwise negative outcome. In an astonishing display of this, I was once present when the Prime Minister of the time berated my boss via his speakerphone because I had told a journalist that one in four patients waiting for heart transplants died while on the waiting list due to the shortage of organs, and that the number of heart transplants in the last six months had fallen. The Prime Minister insisted that my boss find a six-month period within the last year, which when compared with the same six-month period from the previous year, showed a rise instead. We declined, she was furious. Spin-doctoring can also suggest a pleasant, ethical, or attractive connotation, such as calling attempts to bully women into accepting the outcome of rape or abuse as being 'pro-life' rather than 'anti-choice'. Similarly removing the right to be treated in a local hospital but instead forcing people to shop around for hundreds of miles for one with an empty bed and reasonably competent staff might be termed 'giving patients a choice'.

The flip side of building genuine grassroots support for a campaign, where ordinary people are outraged and object to some proposals or current practices, is astroturfing, named after the fake or artificial grass product. In astroturfing, a fake grassroots campaign is organised by vested interests, usually political or commercial ones, to counter the changes being suggested, or to challenge existing systems. For example a political pressure group, such as animal rights activists, might set up a supporters' group for patients harmed by drug side effects, and get them to call for a ban on animal testing as one of a suite of changes needed; or faith-based extremists might set up a supporters' group calling for, among other measures, a ban on stem cell research because of an imagined danger of cross-contamination or cancer. Other examples were the smokers' alliances that sprung up when smoking bans were first suggested, but which were actually pressure groups created by public relations companies on behalf of their tobacco giant clients. A recent form of astroturfing has seen public relations agencies placing supportive online comments on behalf of their clients in blog discussions and chat forums, which pretend to be from ordinary members of the public. Note that this may be illegal in some countries.

Critical friend, fool, court jester

Finally, as a last task, and one that can frequently make you unpopular, or get you shot as the messenger, is the role of critical friend, traditional court jester, or fool (in its medieval sense, when kings kept court fools to remind them not to get too grand or above themselves). When your chief executive has appeared on television last night, being interviewed or sounding off, everyone else in your office who gets into the lift with her the next morning will say: 'Saw you on the news last night, you were great.' It is your job to go into her office first thing and run through all the good points she made, and the areas where she made serious mistakes in fact, style, messages, or tone. No one else, not even her family, is going to do this for her. But those simple mistakes are going to rebound on you, your organisation, and possibly your chief executive, all day. And may, if you sell particularly cheap jewellery, continue until your company collapses. So get in first, tell it fast, tell it all, and above all, tell the truth. I have become lifelong friends with a couple of former chief executives who really appreciated this service. I have also lost major public sector clients who simply could not take the suggestion that anything was amiss, as their organisation still operated in a blame culture. You win some, you lose some, but you personally have to be able to look at yourself in the mirror every morning.

Part II
Media relations

4   Getting your voice heard
Basic health public relations activities

Press and information releases

Press or information releases sent to the media are still the main way that findings from science and medical research reach a wider public audience. They are also one of the ways these advances become much more widely known within the medical and health community, especially in other countries. Key decision-makers and funding bodies only tend to discover about, adopt and fund new techniques based upon scientific advances after they reach the wider press, radio, television and internet discussions.

A press or information release is a standard way of conveniently packaging information that you want to publicise. Press releases should be written in a news format and simple language so that they could go directly into a newspaper, magazine, or internet newsletter, or be quoted directly by broadcasters. If you write them in any other way you risk that the information will be misinterpreted or accidentally changed during the editing processes.

A press release is an official document from your university, research institute, or funding organisation, so it should usually only be sent out through your official press office as it may become part of the permanent record.

Some funding bodies have strict rules about agreeing press releases for work they have funded. Most peer-reviewed journals also have rules preventing information about work which has been accepted for their journal being released until the official publication date. Breaching these rules may mean that the journal article is withdrawn before publication, which can affect the researcher's career or the institute's future grants. Some research work done for commercial and industrial partners may also have confidentiality restrictions placed on it.

Press coverage vs. media management services

PR agencies, which are principally in the business of making money, not predominantly philanthropists dedicated to increasing the sum total of human knowledge, know just how difficult it is to write, distribute and place good stories on behalf of their clients. And to keep doing it. Consequently many PR agencies prefer to sell their clients other services – such as reputation management, brand awareness activities or management advice – and add on their percentage mark-up, rather than to try to promote their clients and their clients' products and services through editorials and press releases.

However, many clients and in-house managers want more than anything else, good, apparently unbiased editorial, and apparently free media coverage. So it is essential for anyone working in public relations, public affairs or a press office to learn the discipline of writing good press releases that will be picked up and used by the media.

It is worth noting, as a counter to this argument, that the increasingly common practice by some news outlets and some science journalists of simply reprinting word-for-word the contents of commercially produced press releases is coming under heavy criticism and categorised as 'churnalism' rather than journalism.

A website set up by the Media Standards Trust spots and exposes these unresearched and unchecked articles as they appear in mainstream news channels.[1] It has been welcomed by media commentators and pundits, including members of the Association of British Science Writers. For more background on churnalism see Nick Davies' book *Flat Earth News*,[2] which brought it to public consciousness, based on a University of Cardiff study, and in Wikipedia under Churnalism, although I gather that Davies denied inventing the term.

To be fair to science and medical journalists, the first they hear about proper academic research should be when they receive a well-prepared press release highlighting the fact that this particularly interesting or newsworthy piece of research is about to appear in a respected peer-reviewed journal.

Journalists cannot and should not be the first people to hear about new medical or scientific findings – their academic colleagues and competitors should be the people to give these new claims a proper scrutiny at a conference or in print in peer-reviewed journals. And under current academic rating systems, a scientist's career will be made or broken by their publication record.

These official releases of information are a long way removed from churnalism, where a commercial company or PR agency gives an unwarranted puff to a piece of poorly supported work, some dodgy survey results or simply a blatant advertising message about pseudoscience or a new 'health' product or service, and manages to get their release reported as scientific fact in mainstream news media.

We have all seen these type of reports: 'young mums are most likely to be depressed after abortion' or 'new skin cream with (insert any meaningless algebraic symbol and chemical) stops ageing say users'. When you investigate the scientific provenance of these stories you quickly discover that the abortion story was placed by a committed faith group and based upon their expectations rather than any sort of independent academic research. And the skin cream story is based upon interviews with three unspecified users, two of whom were convinced that their wrinkles looked smoother afterwards.

The Science Technology Engineering & Medical Public Relations Association is so concerned about rogue press officers, who issue sloppy or inaccurate press releases that get the industry a bad name, that it issued a helpful booklet in 2009, the STEMPRA guide to being a press officer, subtitled Promoting Research Responsibly.[3]

BBC News science and medical correspondent Pallab Ghosh, who was President of the World Federation of Science Journalists, says:

> Press officers play a vital role in helping connect scientists and journalists. It is vital that they do not over-hype or exaggerate findings as this can lead to misunderstanding and unrealistic expectations and could ultimately damage public trust in science. I welcome these guidelines and hope they have a beneficial effect on the communication of important science-related issues.

The misuse of statistics by public relations agencies, pharmaceutical companies, pressure groups, the media and government bodies has frequently been criticised by both the academic community and science and medical journalists.

In 2008 a pressure group called Straight Statistics[4] was formed to 'detect and expose the distortion and misuse of statistical information, and identify those responsible'. It comprises a group of statisticians, senior politicians and journalists, funded by a grant from the Nuffield Foundation. Its director is the well-respected journalist Nigel Hawkes, former health editor of *The Times*, and other contributors include Dr Ben Goldacre, the campaigning GP and author of the Bad Science columns in the *Guardian* newspaper.

Churnalism 2

In 2010, comedy science activist Tom Scott got so incensed by churnalism that he designed and printed journalism warning labels that he anarchically fixes to random newspapers on newsstands. They include, among others:

- **Warning:** Statistics, survey results and/or equations in this article were sponsored by a PR company.
- **Warning:** This article is basically just a press release copied and pasted.
- **Warning:** Medical claims in this article have not been confirmed by peer-reviewed research.
- **Warning:** This article contains unsourced, unverified information from Wikipedia.

You can download the template free from his website.[5]

Press release format

Press releases should normally be written in a news format (for feature writing see later). The style should be chatty, spoken-style language, not formal, stuffy and ponderous like so many written reports. But correct punctuation and spelling please – former microbiologist and Amsterdam-based head of media relations for the Global Reporting Initiative Lucy Goodchild reminded me recently of the importance of good grammar with her example: 'Let's eat grandpa' – no, that should be 'Let's eat, grandpa'. So remember, commas save lives.

News

The news format was developed in the days when newspapers were printed using hot lead typesetting, when the type was physically cast in metal and laid out on a flat plate called a stone. To edit or cut a story short, the compositor simply took a hammer and chisel and bashed off the last few lines of metal type to make a story shorter.

We still set newspaper stories the same way because it helps the readers, who can stop reading at any line and not miss any of the main points. So the most important bit in any story has to come first and so on, getting less important as you go. Do not start with background, like traditional academic reports, abstracts and formal science writing.

As the great medical communicator Sir Peter Medawar probably said, don't begin with a resounding platitude or background fact such as 'malaria is a source of great morbidity around the world' – we already knew that. Tell us something new.

The first paragraph of your press release should only be about four lines long. It has to grab your readers' attention and contain all the essential information that makes the item news. You can think of this as 'who, what, why, when, where and how'. In other words it says what key thing you have done or discovered. Almost every science or medical story written could thus start with the words 'Researchers announce today that … '. If you are having trouble writing your story, you could try putting it like this for your first draft.

But 'news in brief' items in newspapers are often only 25 words long. They are essentially a normal story cut down to just the first paragraph. So your first sentence should always try to sum up the most interesting aspect of your discovery within the first 25 words. If you want people to read on, put the next most interesting thing next.

You should also try to put the most interesting words at the start of the sentences. So the first sentence should not start with the words 'Researchers announce today that … ' followed by your killer 25 words. Instead you need to re-order your sentence so that it now reads 'Killer 25 words, announce researchers today'.

This hook makes people want to read more while making it obvious what the story is about. An example might be 'You risk a heart attack if you don't brush your teeth, say scientists'.

You may also want to give the provenance or authority of the story fairly early on, in the first few paragraphs, so that journalists know whether they can trust your press release as a source. Put it on your headed notepaper so they know who you are.

If the research is being published in a respected peer-reviewed journal such as the *Lancet*, or being announced at a major conference where presentations have been chosen by an academic committee such as at a meeting of the Society of General Microbiology, then you should say so.

In this example the first paragraph might now become: 'You risk a heart attack if you don't brush your teeth, according to scientists speaking today at the Society of General Microbiology's annual conference in Dublin'.

The final version of the story that appears in a newspaper may have the provenance moved to very much lower down by the sub-editors, after all the other main points have been covered, although it will usually still get into the text somewhere. This is one of the few differences between a newspaper story format and a press release format.

Science is often difficult to understand and the significance or relevance of some research findings may not be obvious to many readers. The second paragraph of a press release should still follow the news format by answering the question 'So what?' Why is this new finding relevant or important and how does it affect ordinary people? If the story's importance is already obvious, then your second paragraph (or second sentence) should include your second best fact.

To continue with the same example, your second paragraph might be: 'New research has discovered that poor dental hygiene leads to bleeding gums which can allow bacteria into the bloodstream. Bacteria in the blood can make platelets clot and form a blockage, causing a stroke or heart attack.'

The third paragraph of a medical press release often contains the names of people involved and what they said, or a direct quote from one of the researchers to provide some human interest. This is because new medical science is often very technical and complicated, so having a real person speaking about it humanises the subject and makes it more accessible for readers.

The human interest in a news story will often be how the new work, treatment or research affects people, rather than the technical details of the finding itself, or how the research was done (which is often the part of greatest interest to other scientists).

Other researchers will also often want to know how to repeat an experiment, to check the findings for themselves. This is usually of little interest to general readers – we expect the peer-review process used for science publications to check that the experiment was done properly and that the results can be trusted.

The body text or following paragraphs expand and repeat the information given in the first two or three paragraphs in more detail and explain the significance of the issue. This body text often provides further names and quotations from key people such as doctors who work on the disease or some patients and their families, or patient-support groups who may be affected. This is what journalists call reaction.

For controversial issues, the journalists will probably get reaction responses from pressure groups and people opposed or concerned about the news, but you may prefer to simply give the viewpoint of other stakeholders in your press release. The body text should include all the rest of the key points and follow in order of importance while developing the story logically.

The body text should also include some fascinating facts such as statistics and numbers of people who could benefit, the type of benefit they can expect, costs, or brief technical information about new medicines or equipment and the timescales for when it will be introduced. These precise details help us to judge whether we trust a story or not.

So if a story says that many people in major cities will benefit from a new procedure, which is quite a vague statement, this is less believable than a story which says that 250 people every year in Brussels, Manchester and Berlin will benefit from a new type of abdominal drain using plastic made from corn starch. The only question left unanswered is what the unspecified benefit is. So we also need to know that this new plastic causes fewer allergic reactions, or naturally dissolves over two months, removing the need for further surgery to take it out. Every story needs enough fascinating facts to make it credible, without having so many facts and figures that it becomes confusing.

The news format of the press release should make it clear from the start why the story is news. This is often because the announcement is being made today, if it is at an academic conference, or as a briefing statement to the press, or because an academic article is appearing in a peer-reviewed journal which is published today, even if the work itself was done two years ago. In this sense 'new' really means 'new to our readers and listeners', because it concerns something important that they have not heard about until now.

In our earlier example, where bad teeth can cause heart attacks say scientists today, 'today' needs to be defined, because press releases are sent out about a week early to give journalists a chance to interview the researchers and prepare and check their story properly. So our press release might now read: 'You risk a heart attack if you don't brush your teeth, according to scientists speaking today (Monday 3 January 2011) at the Society of General Microbiology's annual conference in Dublin.'

The words in brackets disrupt the normal flow of the sentence, which is bad, but they fix for the newspaper journalists and sub-editors when 'today' is, which is very important. As a rule of thumb, if you put words into brackets (or, to give them their proper name, parentheses), you are inviting journalists and sub-editors to cut them out of the final copy.

Headlines

The title or headline of your press release is almost as important as the content of the release itself. How you craft your headline depends upon what you want your press release to achieve, where you want the story to appear and who your target audience is. If you are thinking of tweeting about your story, you may also want it to be fewer than 140 characters.

There are two major mistakes made by many scientists when trying to write a press release about their work, or when invited to contribute an article for publication in the non-academic or popular press. First, they try to write a witty, funny headline, similar to those they have seen in newspapers. Second, they imagine that people will read both the headline and the story, so they do not need to repeat things in the body text that they have already said in the title. Both of these misconceptions are wrong, mainly because of the technical way that newspapers are put together.

Crucially this applies to the physical paper-and-print versions of newspapers. Journalists write the stories. But then a group of technicians known as sub-editors trim the articles to length, check facts and make sure that the stories contain all the elements that they need such as quotes, visual language and human interest.

Once the length and shape of the story has been decided, the sub-editors finally write a headline that somehow sums up the story's content and grabs the interest of readers. This headline has to fit the column width and shape chosen for the piece and be the appropriate font size for the story – not the other way round. Inevitably this means that newspaper staff view the headlines and the text of stories as two completely separate items, not as a connected whole.

If a story is moved to a different position on a page in the paper in later editions, because more important news has come up in the meantime, then the headline in large bold type changes because it will no longer fit the new shape of the story.

So the first thing that happens when you as a scientist or your press office sends in a beautifully crafted health article or press release is that your headline is separated from the story. And it is usually discarded, because it won't be the right shape for the eventual printed version of the piece. It is also a point of honour among sub-editors to think of a better, wittier headline than the one you sent in. So if you think of a great line, which brilliantly sums up your story, put it into the main text as well.

A third reason why headlines sometimes misfire is because of the way science, health and medical journalists view the hundreds of new press releases released every day online these days. Typically journalists will have notifications sent to their computers according to keyword searches from the big international science media websites, such as AlphaGalileo[6] in the UK and Europe or EurekAlert! in the US, used by hundreds of academic, publicly funded and research organisations.

Alternatively, many journalists just view a list of newly posted online press releases by headline on the science media websites and on the dedicated press websites of their favourite medical and science organisations such as CERN and relevant government departments. This means that your headline has to stand out. But it mustn't be too clever or too much of a tease. It has to quickly and concisely convey the main news content of your press release, preferably while including a few of the sexiest keywords that you can.

So use active language and short punchy words. And somehow you need to convey the authority or provenance of the story without sounding pompous or self-important. A headline like 'Brushing your teeth could prevent heart attacks, says Manchester scientist' should grab attention without promising more than your research finding justifies.

You also need to decide who your audience is and where you want your story to appear. That way you can target your press release and its keywords at specific journalists, or specific regions and areas of the country.

Notes to news editors

After the main body text of your press release you should put the word 'Ends' and then 'Notes to news editors' or 'For further information'. This section should contain any technical information that journalists may need, such as the full name and title, job title, institute address, email and telephone number for anyone mentioned in the text. Preferably this will include their work, home and mobile telephone numbers, as international news outlets in different time zones and 24-hour rolling news channels may be interested in your story and will need to contact people outside normal office hours for comments.

If your press office is going to be the first point of contact or screen calls from journalists then you may just want to give a duty press officer's name and contact telephone numbers. But you will then need a foolproof system for contacting your researchers who carried out the work, as journalists will often still want to talk to them directly to get exclusive quotes, or radio and television broadcast interviews with them.

Personal details

Bloggers and website owners now scour the internet for relevant content to paste into their sites to attract traffic. Increasingly, we are finding that complete press releases with all their 'notes to news editors', including home telephone numbers, which journalists would automatically keep in confidence, are sometimes being published for anyone to see. So you may wish to screen all contact details through your press office first. If you do not you may find that your experts and senior spokespeople become the target of internet trolls, stalkers and understandably worried patients.

You may also want to put brief biographies and paragraphs about the research team, listing all the members and their institutions, the research funding bodies and other details into your notes to news editors. You can also include any technical information, including the proper scientific names of animals, plants or bacteria, and graphs, tables and other technical data into this section as it would break up the story you are telling if they were all included in the main text.

You can include a web link to the original research paper and further background information such as the researcher's departmental website or any pictures you have available. The journalists will find this very useful, especially if they are asked to write a longer article or feature about the story.

Contents of press releases

Medical researchers often want to know how much technical language or jargon they can put into a press release for different audiences. Ideally the answer is none, and your story should not require any specialised knowledge to understand it. If you even wonder whether a word is jargon, it probably is, so try not to use it if a simpler word could be used instead. So refer to cancer rather than oncology, call it a heart attack not a cardiac arrest. Talk about breathing, chest, throat and lung problems, not respiratory disorders.

You should use short sentences of no more than 25 words and simple language. The longer the sentence, the more difficult it is to understand. Ideally everything you write in a press release should be easily understood by an average nine-year-old child, and this is the reading age aimed at by most popular newspapers. People do not want to have to work hard to understand news stories, they just want to know what has happened. Often they are reading their news in a short break over a cup of coffee, or on public transport.

Longer words are usually more difficult to understand, and medical stories often contain a lot of technical language and difficult concepts, so stick to short and simple words if you possibly can for the rest of your sentences. So you should use words like 'get' instead of 'achieve' and 'find' instead of 'acquire'.

We humans rely on sight for gathering most of our information about the world. Visual language that triggers pictures in our minds is much easier to understand than a theoretical concept, abstract ideas or words that refer to general classes of things.

A word such as 'organs' is harder to grasp than examples of organs, such as kidney, heart or liver. Often the more precise a word is, so long as it is a familiar, everyday one, the more likely it is to trigger a picture, which is the easiest sort of all to understand. The effect of an illness or a description of the outcome may convey the importance of a disease and will help to get your press release some coverage. So having painful headaches, falling over or needing a wheelchair are all descriptions of effects that can be caused by neurological disorders.

We want people to quickly understand our story and to care about it, which means we need to use emotive language that people identify with. So home is a more emotional word than house; brothers and sisters more emotive than siblings or relatives. Try to think of people as 'people' not as persons, members of the public, humans, hominids or as one of the many species of great apes, even if these other terms may be more technically correct at times.

Science is traditionally written about in an impersonal way and in the passive case – so 'an experiment was designed' as though it was never touched by human hands. Exactly the same information sounds more interesting and more exciting if you write about it actively and in a personal way – so 'we set up an experiment' or 'we did this'. Active language will engage your readers.

Timing your press release, embargoes and exclusives

The date on a press release should be the date the press release is allowed to be used, not the date you sent it or wrote it, otherwise journalists may think that it is an old news story and throw it away without reading it first.

Journalists, like everyone else, need time to plan, so you should send out your press release to journalists and publish it under embargo on science news websites such as AlphaGalileo about a week in advance. This gives everyone a chance to prepare their story properly, and interview the researchers who have done the work, in time for the story to appear by the embargo date.

Embargoes are not legally binding, but there is a general agreement among journalists that they help both the media and the authors of the work, so they are usually respected (for a slight exception see Sunday stories below, p.43).

The embargo date on a press release is the formal date and time that the press release can be used by anyone. This system makes sure that everyone gets the same fair chance to cover a story, especially if the research was done using public funds. If there is no reason that it cannot be used immediately then mark it 'For immediate release'.

A normal format for a news embargo is to allow the press release to be used at one minute past midnight Greenwich Mean Time on the day the event happens. For example, 'Embargo: 00.01 hrs GMT Monday 3 January 2011' means that all the daily newspapers, radio and television stations can cover the story that day.

If you set your embargo for the time that the announcement is being made, for example at 10.00 hrs, then that day's newspapers would not be able to cover the story as they are already on sale before the embargo time. But by tomorrow the story will have become old news because it will have already been covered by the rest of the broadcast and web media and evening newspapers. So setting the wrong embargo time may mean that your story is unlikely to be covered by daily newspapers at all.

Even if a medical conference paper is being delivered by the author at 10 o'clock in the morning, the embargo should usually be set for one minute past midnight that day. If the story is sufficiently important that it is likely to become international, then you may also wish to state the US Eastern Standard Time, or other equivalents, in addition to the GMT under the embargo time given.

If you have set an embargo, do not break it yourself (for instance by going on television to talk about the story the night before) or you will find that journalists will not respect your embargoes in future.

Do not give exclusive access or information about your news story to just one newspaper, radio or television programme if it is publicly funded research. Although the favoured newspaper may give you much more space in exchange for having an exclusive story, it is unfair on the other media channels.

If your story is quite interesting, but not so important that you are likely to get wide media coverage, then you should still issue (or post on the science media websites) a general press release, but you can also tip off a particular newspaper journalist or broadcaster in advance so that they can prepare a major story in time for the embargo deadline. This often works well by publishing the story as a Sunday story, which increases your chances of getting a longer news or feature piece published, although fewer publications will cover it.

Sunday papers are always at a disadvantage because so many of the top English language science and medical journals around the world are published on Thursdays, Fridays and Saturdays. This means that Sunday papers are very rarely able to cover a new medical advance as breaking news. It also explains why they are more likely to break embargoes if they hear about a story in advance. So it is a good idea to build up good relationships with the Sunday papers by giving them some stories embargoed for Sundays.

If you have good relations with them, the Sunday papers are more likely to offer you the chance to comment in response to exclusive or investigative stories they are about to publish themselves, giving you advance warning and a chance to respond to any criticisms or concerns if the story is a critical one.

Alternatively you could talk in advance to a Monday daily newspaper or broadcaster and choose to publish your research story as a Sunday-for-Monday story, which will usually be prepared and written on the previous Friday. This will be welcomed by the journalists as Monday is traditionally a quiet news day. You should still issue a general press release embargoed for the Monday.

The same principle which means that science stories are more likely to get used and published on a Sunday or Monday, which are quiet news days, also applies to quiet times of the year such as the Christmas holiday period, Easter and summer breaks. These periods when the national and European parliaments are in recess or away on holiday mean that politicians are not making new laws, formal announcements or causing other excitement, so there is much more space available in the media for other types of stories.

The long summer break is called the silly season because we see trivial or lighter news items, including science stories, published then which would not normally be considered important enough to beat other news. If you have a major medical announcement to make you may want to time it for the summer to take advantage of this effect. However, newspapers sell fewer copies during the holiday period and news broadcast viewer and listening figures also drop – because many people are away on holiday themselves.

Financial announcements, basically anything that can affect the share price of a company, have their own special rules, and have to be disclosed to all potential investors and shareholders simultaneously. I am not an expert in financial or investor relations, you should take specialist advice on this, but your company accountant will know about the particular rules for the industry sector that your company operates in, and for the jurisdiction in which its shares are listed. Breaches of the rules for stock exchange price sensitive information, even inadvertent ones, are extremely serious and can attract massive fines or jail terms for people and companies suspected of trying to manipulate the international money markets.

The sort of information that is price-sensitive in the pharmaceutical industry can include adverse clinical trial results, or Federal Drug Agency approval for a new medicine or treatment, and announcements about this type of news will need to be coordinated across different time zones for global release.

Different countries also have different rules for what can and cannot be advertised directly to patients (see the Association of the British Pharmaceutical Industry guidelines[7]).

Distributing your press release

If your press release is about publicly funded research then you should give all news outlets an equally fair opportunity to publish the information and not give it to just one newspaper, magazine, radio, television or web-based news outlet as an exclusive story. However, if a journalist comes to you for comment, background information or a quote on a story idea that they are planning to run, then you should respect their exclusive and not tip off other media that the story is about to break.

You will quickly build up your own additional list of key contacts, including freelancers, as your own press list, and you will usually want to tip these individuals off personally (normally by email or telephone) in addition to publishing your press release generally when you have a strong news story.

You can also obtain targeted media lists, often as website downloads or on disk, from commercial suppliers. These will give you the name, address, telephone number, email and other contact details of key journalists and publications for different areas of interest such as medicine and health or even specific types of disease such as cancer or heart problems. There are thousands of trade magazines and specialist publications that appear every month in the English language alone and internet newsletters are increasingly popping up on websites which may also cover your story.

A general press release should be published for any news outlet to use, preferably by listing it for a small fee on one or both of the two major international science media websites, which can be accessed free by all journalists. AlphaGalileo specialises in European, UK and world stories, and EurekAlert! in United States based stories, although they will both carry stories from anywhere if asked.

AlphaGalileo is an independent foundation, originally set up by UK and European publicly and government-funded research bodies, now paid for by subscriptions from academic organisations, universities and some industries and businesses that publish their research on it. EurekAlert! is a commercial website owned by the American Association for the Advancement of Science, which also publishes the journal *Science*, and charges fees for carrying press releases.

In addition you may want to release your news story simultaneously through the major international and national news agencies such as Reuters, the Press Association and Agence France-Presse, who will all prepare their own version of the story if they are told about it in confidence, in advance, and if they judge it to be newsworthy enough.

This inevitably means that some major news outlets may receive as many as five different versions of a news story, packaged as press releases and highlighting different aspects, organisations or individuals involved in the research.

These could include press releases from:

- the institute or university where the researcher is based;
- associate organisations who collaborated on the work such as a university in another country which carried out some of the tests;
- the government funding body, industry partner or charity that originally paid for the research;
- the peer-reviewed journal or academic conference organiser where the work is first being published or is now being announced;
- a short version of the story distributed by a regional, national or international news agency.

Do not worry, it increases your chances of getting recognition for the work, but it does mean that the best written of the press releases with the best quotes is the version most likely to be used. So make sure that it's yours.

Press conferences

Journalists do not come to press conferences as readily as they used to in the days before the internet age. In some countries such as Spain, France and Italy, with many large and distinct regional centres, the rivalry between cities and regions, or simply the lack of resources, may make national media reporters reluctant to leave their desks for a time-consuming trip out to a distant press conference. In the UK, the national media is fixated on the capital city, London. But the main daily newspapers are no longer physically clustered in offices in Fleet Street near the city centre, so it is logistically harder for the reporters to reach a central venue to attend a press conference.

Most of a reporter's job can now be done by searching the web and by using telephones, so pressure of work deadlines and the drive to cut costs mean that journalists (and their editors) are now reluctant to leave their offices. On the other hand, this does mean that if reporters can be enticed to attend a major national or international conference such as the European Society of Cardiology, National Science Festival or Federation of European Neuroscience Societies meeting, they will give the event good coverage. They will expect a selection of rapid press conferences arranged for them every morning highlighting key presentations. This also gives them a chance to question the scientists in person, make personal contacts and catch up on general advances in the particular field.

Journalists are much less likely to report on any presentations which are not featured in the press conferences, or in press releases available from the official conference press office. Even when away from their office distractions, they simply do not have time to go and sit through the speaker's talk on the off-chance that it will be interesting. And the timing of the key talks themselves within conference schedules rarely fit with key publishing and broadcasting deadlines.

Specialist press conference venues: the Science Media Centre, London

In the UK, in an attempt to prevent a repeat of the GM foods debacle and the pressure group rout of rational science, an ancient and respected science body, the Royal Institution, tried to redress the reluctance to attend press conferences by opening the Science Media Centre in the year 2000, to host press conferences on behalf of academic organisations, universities and science-funding bodies. The centre is now housed in the offices of the Wellcome Trust, one of the world's largest medical research charities.

Originally the Science Media Centre allowed organisations such as regionally based patients groups, non-London-based universities and smaller and less wealthy research organisations to showcase their top-class science research to a wider national and international audience. It also originally provided a much-needed point of contact and a reliable source of access to nationally recognised expert scientists for regional newspapers, radio and television stations, and web-based news portals. In addition for the first time Scottish, Welsh and Irish media were given the same access to UK news as the London-based English media.

However, according to some critics among regional media and public relations consultancies, as the Science Media Centre became better known and more successful over the next ten years at hosting and showcasing the top science stories, it served to restrict access to the top scientists by anyone other than the already well-resourced London-based media such as the BBC, ITV and English national daily newspapers – on the apparently reasonable grounds that they have to prioritise the invitations due to demand.

The Science Media Centre also restricted access to these top journalists for less-well-resourced and regional science research organisations – on the grounds that due to demand it has to prioritise the organisations which it allows to use its facilities, to make sure that the most important stories get properly covered.

This inevitably means that the already well-resourced main funding bodies such as UK Research Councils, which previously held their own press conferences, are now monopolising the Science Media Centre. This has created an elite and cosy club of those journalists who are lucky or famous enough to be considered worthy of an invitation to Science Media Centre events, and also those few well-favoured science research organisations who are lucky, famous or powerful enough to be granted press conferences by the Science Media Centre.

This development, although hugely successful in time and resource saving for the elite members of the inner club, has diminished the chances of other media outlets and other regional research organisations, such as all the other UK and European universities, from getting their equally excellent medical and scientific research findings publicised to a wider national and international audience. By 2011, the Science Media Centre's Advisory Panel of 16 experts reflected this bias, with 15 of them in Oxbridge or London.

The undoubted success of the Science Media Centre in London makes a strong case for any country, or even any city, which is also a major media base to develop its own science, technology, medical and engineering media centre to showcase research by the not-for-profit sector. Science Media Centres have already been set up in Australia, New Zealand and Canada.

So in the UK these could include strong regional centres such as Manchester, Sheffield, Newcastle, Bristol and Birmingham, and the national capitals of Cardiff, Belfast and Edinburgh (or Glasgow). And across Europe, at least one media centre in each country, major city and centre of regional government which is also a medical research hub, such as Brussels, Paris, Barcelona, Madrid, Milan and Rome.

How these regional science media centres would get staffed and funded is a major sponsorship or subscription problem, so for now the majority of regional medical and science research organisations are relying on the internet press websites such as AlphaGalileo for virtual launches, and rarely hold their own physical press conferences, unless attending a major science or medical congress.

Press conferences: what is the reason for your event?

If you do decide to arrange and host a press conference, you need to start by clearly identifying the reasons why journalists and photographers would wish to attend, what they will realistically get out of it compared with the effort of attending and what you hope to realistically achieve. So what is your event about?

- **Visual**: is your event primarily visual, offering an unusual, one-off or exciting video or photo opportunity that cannot be achieved elsewhere? Examples might include the final chance to film inside the Large Hadron Collider in Geneva after all the building and installation work was completed but before it was sealed, turned into a vacuum and fired up for the first time.
- **News**: is your event simply genuine news, caused by a new scientific advance, a world first, a health problem solved or an outbreak of disease? If so, what do you imagine the front-page headlines will say? What will you do if the news leaks out early or if your embargo is broken, such as when Dolly the first cloned sheep was announced? Will you still hold the press conference?
- **Human interest**: is your story about people we are interested in or care about, such as an attempt to separate conjoined twins, the world's oldest mother or youngest father, or the first successful two-way communication using brainwave-reading computers by a locked-in patient?

- **Celebrity**: are you trying to build news values by association, by having royalty, politicians, sports personalities, pop stars, actors or other celebrities attend or open your event? Do the celebrities have a genuine link to the health problem, such as having a disabled child themselves? Why don't you think your issue is sufficiently newsworthy on its own, and how will you get your event mentioned rather than all the focus being on the celebrity?
- **Finance**: is the story really just about money? If so, is it money raised, money saved, massive grants or investments? It may be obvious to you why this change in finance is important to you or your organisation, but why do you think anyone else will be interested in this?
- **Policy**: are you announcing a major change in health policy, delivery of services or priorities? Policy changes usually make news stories for the politicians making the announcements, not the hospitals, doctors and nurses who have to cope with the proposed changes and who are invited to comment or respond to the announcement. Why are you in particular holding the press conference to launch a policy change?
- **Politics**: is the story really about politics and the triumph of one ideology over another? If so how will you prevent politicians taking all the credit and stop them using your health or medical event to make party political speeches? Will your association with this political stance cause you or your organisation problems in the future when the regime, economy or fashion changes?

Press conferences: timetable

You will need to start the preparations for your press launch well in advance of the planned press conference. Once you have decided what kind of event you are going to hold, and what the main thrust of the story is, you will need to prepare your press list of key contacts you want to invite. Be realistic here, and only invite journalists that you genuinely think will be interested in this particular announcement or type of event. The shorter your list, the more individual effort you can put into contacting each person on it and convincing them that attending your press conference will be worthwhile.

You need to give away enough information so that the journalists are convinced that the event is newsworthy, but not so much that they realise they don't need to attend. But then you need to give enough information to the media who genuinely can't be there so that they can report on the launch as though they had attended. It's a fine line.

In an ideal world you will know about your event well in advance, so you should be able to send out an initial diary notice to your press contacts several months beforehand, notifying them that the event is happening. In the case of an awareness campaign such as National Transplant Week or the World Transplant Games, you want the news organisations to put the launch date in their forward-planning diary. This lets them build it into their longer-term schedules and arrange to have news crews, freelances or photographers available to cover the main events when they happen.

This will also give features editors and long-lead time publications such as monthly magazines the opportunity to commission supporting features and build the launch date into their schedules. You will also want to contact any key personalities such as government ministers, sports stars or other celebrities who could speak at the launch, or lend their support to your campaign, to make sure that they keep your key dates free as well.

Closer to the event, and to help with fundraising efforts, you may also want to hold a press launch and send out a formal advance notice of your story about a month in advance of the main event. In the example of the World Transplant Games, famous sports personalities who have agreed to endorse the awareness campaign and some previous gold medal winners of Transplant Games events can be invited to a press launch or photocall to announce that the main event will be happening in a month's time.

This is your first real opportunity to get the key messages of your campaign across, so your celebrities and stars should be properly briefed beforehand. Ask them to try to make opportunities to talk about the health problem being addressed – such as the lack of organ donors and the reluctance of doctors and nurses to offer relatives the chance to save lives with hearts, livers and kidneys.

When you launch your event with a press conference and main photocall you will usually want to hold it the day before the main events start, so that it can be reported by the newspapers, television and radio as 'National Transplant Week starts today' rather than 'National Transplant Week started yesterday', which sounds less newsworthy. Remember that photographers and television crews will need something active to take pictures of, or an interesting background that adds something to the story, so do not just concentrate on the speeches and announcements, plan your press conference schedule backwards from the photo opportunity.

You will need to choose the day and date of your launch carefully. If you are having a national awareness event, you may naturally think of Monday to Sunday as a logical length for a week. But your supporters, and especially patients, may find it easier to be available at weekends, so you may want to schedule your 'week' to be formally launched on a Saturday and go right through to the following Sunday, nine days later, which also allows you to announce how successful the initiative was on the following Monday, another quiet news day.

So your press conference and photocall will need to be held on the Friday before the 'week' starts (giving government ministers a chance to announce their support). Friday may still be the best day to hold the press conference, even if you have decided to technically start your week on the following Monday, taking advantage of Saturday as a quiet news day to trail the coming events.

Your press conference speakers will usually be a maximum of three people, plus yourself to orchestrate the question-and-answer session after the main presentations. A former medical correspondent of the *Guardian* newspaper once told me that nothing makes your heart sink quite like turning up at a press conference to see 12 chairs behind the top table, as there cannot possibly be 12 different opinions on anything which could be written up in a normal news story.

Your three key speakers (maximum) should be:

- The press conference chair, who will be your chairman, chief executive, government minister or other top dignitary who introduces the event, demonstrating how important your organisation thinks it is, and saying why something needs to be done about the problem.
- The person responsible for the event itself, who may be a researcher, medical doctor, scientist or administrator who can say what is going to happen or what will be happening, outline the medical problem being addressed, or stressing the human interest angle.
- A technical expert, who may be a medical doctor, researcher, scientist or engineer who can answer technical and detailed information about any new kit which is being used, new types of treatments or scientific problems being addressed.

If, instead of an event, you are announcing the start of a major academic conference, your supporting speakers may be two of the key session chairpersons who can outline some of the most interesting issues that will be covered. If your press conference is announcing a major medical advance, then one of your supporting speakers may be a representative from a patient support group or a charity which has funded the work, or even a person who suffers from the disease and who has now benefited from the advance or new treatment.

Once each person has spoken, for a maximum of five minutes each, either you or the press conference chair should then orchestrate the question-and-answer session, inviting journalists to identify themselves and their media outlet, and ask their questions. This means that you need to be able to recognise who each journalist is. Which means that you probably should have been hanging around or actually manning the registration desk when they arrived, to greet them, get them to sign in and give them a name badge. These name badges will also be useful afterwards if you are offering refreshments and an informal opportunity for journalists to mingle with your speakers, patient representatives and other relevant interviewees.

When journalists ask a question from the floor during the press conference, especially if they do not speak up or have an accent that is difficult to understand, you should repeat any key points clearly so that everyone in the room can hear both the question and the subsequent answer (this can also give your panel a few moments of vital thinking time).

If a journalist asks a question of the form 'So, are you saying that … ?' listen very, very carefully, as you are probably hearing the quote that will be used in their story being tested on the speaker, but in a new, clearly expressed form that has not so far been stated explicitly. Make sure that the speaker understands that this quote needs to be absolutely right and accurate, and be prepared to intervene if the form of the journalist's question has substantially altered what was actually intended by your speaker.

Preferably, knowing in advance that quotes will be needed, you will have helped each speaker prepare a distinct soundbite that sums up their own key aspect of the announcement being made. The speaker may wish to point this up during their part of the press conference presentation by using speech acts such as 'The most important thing we discovered is … ' or 'Perhaps the key point to make is … ' so that the journalists realise that these are the key messages.

After the press conference, your main event should then go ahead as planned, as a one-off announcement of a major scientific advance, an awareness week, academic conference or other news. Your press releases and press conferences should signal the main event or events, giving enough detail, key times, dates and places, interview opportunities and quotes from your representatives.

If you have several events happening around the country (or the world) then list all the key places in your notes to news editors, and provide a web link where journalists can get further details and full information. Events with a local connection to audiences are always more newsworthy, so if you are trying to gain grassroots support, you may also want to send your press releases to local newspapers, local radio and television stations, and even parish magazines and patient-support groups, which usually publish their own newsletter or magazine.

After your press conference you should schedule a follow-up press release or contact with key journalists, letting people know what was achieved and what difference the event made.

Finally you should build into your timetable a review of the whole event, including your press conference and timetable, so that you can identify afterwards what went right and what could have been improved. If you don't build this in from the start, then reviews are only held when things go disastrously wrong and people are looking for a scapegoat. If you always hold reviews, especially when things go right, it cements the post-mortem as part of the normal routine, allowing you to address the real reason why things may have gone wrong, and make the case for a proper budget next time.

Press conferences: information packs

Your press conference information pack for journalists who attend should include your latest press release giving all the main information about the event or news story. It could also include copies of recent previous press releases if these are still relevant and include key information not included elsewhere.

You should include the text of speeches for all of the speakers at your press conference, with a footnote saying that the draft text should be checked against actual delivery. The discipline needed to get this text in on time should give you a chance to check that your speakers are intending to include their key messages, speak in simple jargon-free language, and not repeat each other. When you review their draft texts, try reading them out loud yourself – if the language is convoluted, formal and dry then suggest rewrites.

Your information pack can also include sample literature if you have any helpful patient's leaflets, or quick reference guides which give useful background information. You can include a fact sheet summarising the aims and history of your organisation, and some data sheets showing the key statistics and any relevant costs or numbers such as how many bricks were used to build a hospital, how many local jobs were created or how much money will be invested over the next ten years. These are all examples of the quirky details that are known as fascinating facts and help journalists to personalise their stories.

You will also want to include a brief relevant biography of each of your press conference speakers – please note that this does not mean following the academic convention of listing every single post the person has ever held and every single academic paper that they have ever managed to get published.

If you have relevant pictures such as photographs of the speakers or research site, medical images, graphs and scientific diagrams, then samples of these can also be included in the information packs. Pictures and graphics give visual help to the journalists who are trying to understand the issue your press conference is addressing. They will also suggest to their graphics departments ways that newspapers, magazines and television can make the subject understandable to the public, even if they do not use your pictures themselves.

If you have a large stock of copyright-free images that you are prepared to release for general use, wish to make the original scientific abstracts and papers available as background, or simply have a lot of supporting data which some of the more technical or industry publications may need to include in their stories, then you can publish these on a relevant website and give the link address in the press packs.

However, remember that many journalists are under-resourced compared with scientists and medical researchers, so do not rely on the media to access your web links for all their information – they may be writing the story up on their laptops on a train, in a café or hotel, so make sure that the key facts and figures are included in the printed press information packs and given out at your press conference.

Many larger budget organisations now give out a CD, DVD or USB data stick or flash drive containing huge amounts of background information, promotional videos and other publicity material as part of their press packs. These rarely get used, or indeed even looked at, so make sure that you are not being persuaded by a support organisation, marketing agency or other content provider to supply these in a vain attempt to make your organisation look slick and modern. Or so that the agency can justify their fees and mark-ups, when all the journalists really want is a good story.

Press conferences: checklist and preparation

You will need a checklist of equipment and resources for your press conference, starting with the venue itself. The venue will be dictated by the type of event you are running – if it is a one-off press conference to make a major medical announcement then you may want to hold it at your organisation's headquarters, or the funding body's premises if public or charity grants were involved. It could be at the hospital where the clinical trials were carried out, or the university or research laboratory where the key advance was made.

If none of these is suitable or appropriate, hold your press conference at an exhibition centre, media centre or similar dedicated venue, or in a suitable central hotel, but remember that journalists attending may then wonder why money is being spent on glitzy promotion rather than patient care or medical research.

If your press conference is promoting an academic congress or longer-running public event, such as a science festival, then you are probably going to have several press conferences spread over a few days, and finding a suitable room close to the main action will be the most important consideration.

Your press conference room should ideally be set up in lecture theatre style, with a top table for the speakers, a bank of seats for the journalists and, if it's a very large room, microphones to make sure that the speakers can be heard, with at least one roving one, so that questions can be taken from the journalists afterwards. Microphones can also allow you to keep a record of exactly what was said in controversial situations.

In an ideal situation you will have another small side room with a separate entrance for the speakers, where they can make their last minute preparations – so it will preferably have wireless broadband access and an A4-sized photocopier – and to which they can retreat afterwards, especially if they are making an unpopular announcement. It is handy if this side room has a telephone, or you have your mobile available, so that missing speakers can be located or last-minute instructions given.

You will need standard conference room equipment for the press conferences such as a data projector, laptop computer, screen or suitable wall for projection, a flipchart or whiteboard (which help during questions). Make yourself a standard press conference toolbox that includes black, red, blue and dark green thick felt tips and dry-wipe whiteboard marker pens and an eraser. Alternatively some better equipped conference venues now have a rostrum camera type of overhead projector, which will project a plain paper image through a standard data projector.

You should try to get responses from your press list invitees confirming that they will attend, so that you can prepare an invitation list for them to sign in on when they arrive, and provide name badges with the name of their media organisation, and country if it's an international press conference. Don't overlook local freelances, who may appreciate the chance to make personal contact with some of your top executives. You should hand out your press pack to the journalists when they sign in, giving you a complete record of who attends, which will help you to track press cuttings.

If you want your speakers to have a chance to mingle informally with journalists and staff afterwards then you can provide refreshments, but preferably in the same room, at a side table. Remember that you are trying to provide something for busy journalists, not an expensive treat for your own staff, so all the food should be capable of being picked up in one hand and eaten easily without any mess, or stuffed into a pocket, while the journalist is still taking notes. You may need to cater for some vegetarians. Don't provide exotic, hot food that needs a plate, or knife and fork. And don't be surprised if none of the journalists stay to eat, they may have deadlines to meet or other events to attend.

To prepare your speakers properly you should brief them beforehand, reminding them what they are trying to achieve, and prepare a list of key questions and answers, especially any tricky ones, which could come up at the press conference. Just in case the media do not respond as enthusiastically as you would like, you should also have your own photographer at the press conference, which will also give you some pictures of the eager press hordes asking questions.

You will need to make arrangements for individual radio and television interviews by reporters, so make sure that you build in time for these before your key speakers are scheduled to leave. You may want to use the small side room reserved for your speakers for the radio interviews, but the television crews will often want to choose their own backdrop, which may be in a lobby or laboratory, or even outside, against the main building.

Your choice of venue will also offer you the opportunity to allow a site visit for any dignitaries and the reporters, which also gives television crews and press photographers the chance to update their stock shots if you are based at a major scientific facility. Make sure that you have a technical expert on hand who can talk the visitors through the most interesting parts of the site. Remember that the journalists are not visiting because they want entertaining, they are looking for stories, so have some fascinating facts, interesting science and engaging anecdotes ready for key points during the visit. Keep it short.

Finally you need contingency plans, in case some other news event clashes with or overshadows yours, or you get much less interest than you were hoping from your press invitations. If appropriate, are you ready to take out an advertising campaign to make sure that your key messages get into the press? If you need local awareness of an issue, can you achieve it instead through leaflet drops to homes and posters in community centres?

Once your main plans are fixed hold a brainstorming session to predict what could go wrong. You need to know whether any statements could be taken out of context, or if there is any likelihood of demonstrations, hijacking of your press conference by special interests and pressure groups, or other types of misrepresentation. Reporters do not usually have a hostile agenda, but as individuals they are likely to share the same prejudices as the public, especially if you are using controversial technologies such as animal experiments, genetic modification, stem cells or nanotechnology.

References

1. To check for churnalism go to http://churnalism.com, the Media Standards Trust website.
2. The prevalence of churnalism: Nick Davies, *Flat Earth News*, London: Chatto & Windus, 2008.
3. STEMPRA guide to being a press officer, Promoting Research Responsibly, see www.stempra.org.uk.
4. For examples of misused statistical evidence see Straight Statistics at www.straight statistics.org.

5. Tom Scott's churnalism warning labels template is at www.tomscott.com/warnings.
6. New and archived science press releases can be found at www.alphagalileo.org.
7. Association of British Pharmaceutical Industry guidelines on drug promotion can be found at www.abpi.org.uk/our-work/library/guidelines/Pages/code-2012.aspx.

5 Why health is big news

What makes health news

We are a social species, choosing to live in villages, towns and cities. Above all other news, we are most interested in other members of our species, as a glance through the pictures in any newspaper, any day, anywhere in the world will confirm. So the most important aspect of any health and medical news story is explaining how it affects people, especially if you can tell some real human interest stories.

Within the broad category of people, we can identify with particular sub-groups. Or we may be interested in them or sympathetic towards them, especially if they are vulnerable. So babies, children, elderly people, patients, the injured, ill, disabled, blind, deaf, mute, allergic, asthmatic, overweight, underweight and those with mental impairments or social and health deprivations, all gain special attention as we can visualise and empathise with their situations, and any difficulties they face. Any of us could get sick.

It is always wisest to check with a patients' group representing the interests of people with these vulnerabilities to find out how they prefer to be described. Don't simply categorise them as Parkinson's disease victims or sufferers, which may accidentally offend, if the patients themselves prefer the phrase 'people with', for instance. Labels shape our attitudes.

However, being too careful can smack of political correctness gone mad, so don't use complicated circumlocutions either. Don't confirm stereotypes and prejudices such as the unfounded fear that all people with mental illnesses are violent or crazy, stigmas that charities and health experts are working hard to overturn.

Readers and viewers are usually less interested in the cleverness of the new scientific advance, or how it was achieved, and more interested in how it may affect them and people they care about, such as their family, friends and neighbours. Within that broader area of human interest, news is made up of a mixture of elements, some of which vary from day to day, and all of which become more or less important depending upon the other elements that are making up the news agenda on that particular day.

Science and medicine can often supply a lighter or more uplifting note compared with the standard news diet of murder, sudden deaths, train and car crashes, robberies, violence, rapes, frauds, bankers' bonuses, politicians' expenses, volcanoes, tsunamis, earthquakes and disasters that fill the main news pages and broadcast bulletins every day.

News values

News value is a strange and indefinable quality that old hacks feel in their bones, the shiver generated by a good story. Science and medical journalists still argue about the key elements that make a news story, and I am grateful to my colleagues for their collective wisdom in arriving at the following incomplete and unsatisfactory list.

The most obvious thing that makes something news is if it is new. If this is the first time that something has been discovered, said or done, or at least the first time that readers can remember hearing about it, then it usually has news value. We are also fascinated by extremes or superlatives, so we like the best, the biggest, the fastest, the slowest or the smallest things, or anything else that breaks records. A research institute starting the biggest study ever into cancer or heart disease may make the news, but winning the biggest grant you have ever received is unlikely to generate more than local interest unless it is a truly phenomenal sum of money, such as a banker's bonus.

But be cautious and do your research thoroughly. As the legendary medical and science writer Tim Radford said in his 25 commandments for journalists:[1]

> Beware of all definitives. The last horse trough in Surrey will turn out not even to be the last horse trough in Godalming. There will almost always be someone who turns out to be bigger, faster, older, earlier, richer or more nauseating than the candidate to whom you have just awarded a superlative. Save yourself the bother: 'One of the first' will usually save the moment. If not, then at least qualify it: 'According to the Guinness Book of Records.'

Unexpected or surprising things also make us stop briefly to reconsider our worldview, so for instance the news that chocolate is poisonous to dogs comes as a shock to many pet owners. But stories that are predictable and unsurprising are rarely front-page news, unless the surprise is that anyone bothered to do or fund the research, which is probably a type of publicity that you don't want. So bears do defecate in forests, and psychologists have discovered that people do play more sport in summer – possibly because the weather is usually better and evenings are lighter. Both stories hardly come as a surprise. Malaria is a great source of morbidity.

Something that overturns our previously held beliefs is also intrinsically interesting, so counterintuitive stories grab our attention. The most famous example is 'man bites dog', but Darwin disproved, the world is cooling, the earth is actually flat, or homeopathy works would do equally well.

Because newspapers, radio and television want to appeal to as wide an audience as possible they need to include stories from all over their coverage areas, so from time to time they have to include stories from their regions as well as their central base city. This makes geography one of the elements that can sometimes promote a story higher up the news agenda – it may simply be some time since that area was covered. For a medical or health story this can be a cluster of disease outbreaks, the region where the research was carried out, or even simply the location of the institute or hospital leading the study.

Medical and science editor Tim Radford, in another of his 25 commandments for journalists, says:

> Remember that people will always respond to something close to them. Concerned citizens of south London should care more about economic reform in Surinam than about [football team] Millwall's fate on Saturday, but mostly they don't. Accept it. On 24 November 1963, the *Hull Daily Mail* sent me in search of a Hull angle on the assassination of President Kennedy. Once I had found a line that began 'Hull citizens were in mourning today as … ' we could get on with reporting what happened in Dallas.

This effect is also known by old newspaper hacks as the Times Square Law, where public interest in a news story is reckoned to be inversely proportional to its distance from Times Square itself. So one pedestrian killed outside the offices of the *New York Times* will receive equal coverage or column inches of newsprint as the deaths of a million people thousands of miles away across the world during a famine in Africa, an earthquake disaster in China or floods in India. We should care a million times more about a million individual deaths. But we don't. Medical charity fundraisers know this and exploit the impact of a named individual's personal story of suffering, disease or hardship.

So news is often simply what is relevant to the readers and their current interests or concerns. This could include consumer stories about the latest applications for mobile phones, such as a heart monitor app for doctors, which will get coverage even though most people will never load or use it. In tough economic times, relevance to readers could be rising costs or news that is significant to the world, such as descriptions of mining companies saying that they are running out of the rare raw materials needed to produce medicines or major pieces of hospital equipment. These stories may affect anyone and everyone.

When I was first working in newspapers and broadcasting on the radio the famous maxim was 'sex, death and royalty, that's what sells newspapers'. Today, royalty being slightly out of fashion in a more republican world, the equivalent would be 'sex, death and celebrities'. And possibly chocolate. Members of the British and other European royal families are now a small subset of the wider group of celebrities such as pop stars, footballers and television personalities who form our popular news fodder. So a disease with a celebrity angle will gain extra coverage. Even a disease that Gregor Mendel suffered from.

But so will a well-known or celebrity disease such as cancer, compared with a relatively unknown disease such as Friedreich's ataxia. One particular tabloid newspaper in the UK, the *Daily Mail*, is famously testing every single known substance in the universe to see whether it either cures cancer, or causes it. They publish a new story about the cancer-causing properties of a new substance almost every week, and people are still buying the paper. So one test of newsworthiness is whether the subject of the story is popular, if disease notoriety can ever be properly described as popular.

From an editor's point of view, an exclusive increases the news value of a story, making it more valuable to the one media outlet that has the sole coverage rights. However, this means that other media outlets will in turn be less likely to cover the story, as they did not have it at the same time as the original publication or broadcast. If you are discussing a serious piece of academic research or discovery achieved through publicly funded work, then you should offer the story to all media outlets simultaneously to gain the most widespread coverage.

A story that is less important, or of limited interest to a select audience, may be offered as an exclusive to just one media outlet, but do not then be surprised if no one else covers it. Try to spread your exclusives around fairly among several different media outlets, or you may find that after a while other good stories of yours are not getting the coverage they deserve.

The other elements that make a good health or medical story are harder to define. Some stories simply tickle the public's fancy, have a bizarre or unusual element or are just weirdly compelling. Journalists sometimes call these 'fancy that' stories or, to put it more technically, 'other stuff'. They include the strange and unexpected, such as finding a fish with legs, or a child who has swallowed 50 spoons. They help to make up some of the lighter side of news reporting, which balances the otherwise unremitting diet of gloom, doom and disasters.

Bad news or threats and danger are usually more newsworthy than good news. *The Times* newspaper famously once held a staff competition to find the most boring headline, which was won by 'Nobody hurt in small earthquake'. So a hospital that completes 20 operations without having any mishaps, or losing any instruments or other equipment inside patients, is unremarkable. But a hospital that makes three such mistakes in quick succession may easily find itself the target of unwanted media attention.

Exotic viruses reaching new countries or mutated antibiotic-resistant bacteria spreading through hospitals will grab our attention. We are hardwired as humans as part of our survival strategy to pay attention to threats and dangers. But when everything is going well and as planned, we don't really need to give our everyday surroundings much thought.

Health news, like any other type of news, moves up the agenda on slow news days or when people are taking a special interest in a particular issue. So one element of a medical or health story may simply be its topicality. Once one newspaper or broadcaster has run a particularly harrowing story of a flesh-eating superbug that destroys human tissue in hours, which few people had ever been particularly aware of before, other news outlets will try to find other victims. The story can go from an unusual curiosity to an apparent epidemic sweeping through hospitals across the country within days.

The imitative element of news – newspapers, radio and television all tend to report on things like the things that already made it into the news – means that one of the main sources of inspiration for news stories is other stories already in the media. But don't leave it too late if you have another, better, example of something which has hit the headlines recently. The news moves on.

However, there are some times of year and some days of the week when it is much easier to get a medical or health story into the media. For more information on this see Chapter 4, 'Timing your press release', but briefly just remember that it is easier to get items into the news when there is less competition from politicians. That means on Sundays, at Easter, Christmas and during the long summer holiday break. If you are prepared to spend Christmas Day morning on the telephone, personally contacting news desks with a reasonably good story, you can almost guarantee good coverage.

Quiet news days: cloned humans

Few news desks actually believed the story, but the Raelians, a religious cult who believe that all life on Earth was created by an alien species from outer space, managed to get worldwide coverage by releasing a startling story one Boxing Day. The Raelians claimed that the world's first cloned human was born to one of their members, an American woman, after using a cell fusion machine. Her daughter Eve was born on 26 December 2002. As no one could realistically check with the usual scientific experts, who were all at home with their families, and it was just possible that the story was true, most of the media ran the story anyway.

To show how timing can make news, or at least hugely improve the chances of a story getting covered, we just need to look at the importance of pictures. Our television news does not cover the main news stories of the day. Crucially, instead, it covers the top news stories of the day that we had pictures for by this bulletin. Deadlines are deadlines. Celebrities' agents, politicians and sports promoters all know this and time their announcements and key matches to fit with peak news bulletins and peak viewing times.

Finally, ask yourself can it be told simply? If the answer is no, then you have probably not got a news story. You may have a feature. Or a series. Or a fascinating magazine article. But not news. This is such an important point that former science editor Tim Radford used up two of his 25 commandments for journalists to cover it:

> Life is complicated, but journalism cannot be complicated. It is precisely because issues – medicine, politics, accountancy, the rules of Mornington Crescent – are complicated that readers turn to the *Guardian*, or the BBC, or the *Lancet*, or my old papers *Fish Selling* and *Self Service Times*, expecting to have them made simple.

So if an issue is tangled like a plate of spaghetti, then regard your story as just one strand of spaghetti, carefully drawn from the whole. Ideally with the oil, garlic and tomato sauce adhering to it. The reader will be grateful for being given the simple part, not the complicated whole. That is because (a) the reader knows life is complicated, but is grateful to have at least one strand explained clearly, and (b) nobody ever reads stories that say 'What follows is inexplicably complicated.'

Bad press releases

No one wants to write a bad press release deliberately, but all too often journalists receive things that have gone through some sort of committee stage for clearance, or which have been issued because senior staff insist on it, against the wishes, advice and tears of their press officers. Medical and science journalists collect the more spectacularly bad examples of these and share them among themselves with hollow laughter, or we use them in media training workshops. They fall into a few simple categories:

- **Jargon**: releases stuffed so full of technical jargon that they are meaningless to anyone not currently working in that scientific discipline.
- **Bland**: releases that are so hedged with qualifications and so afraid of making bold claims that they don't actually say anything newsworthy at all.
- **Vanity**: typical examples of vanity press releases are ones that say 'Prof Jones appointed to Stirling University department' or 'New chief executive promises to reach out by listening'. The correct place to send these is to the incumbent's family, or your own in-house newsletter, not busy medical reporters or news editors.
- **Grants**: you may be thrilled that you got £1,000, €10,000 or $100,000 but why should we be? We're interested in what you're going to do with the money and what difference it will make, not that your grant proposal was approved. Unless it's a spectacularly eye-watering amount, in the billions, or even more than a banker's bonus.
- **Collaboration**: you may also be thrilled that you'll be meeting colleagues in other disciplines for the first time ever. This is not news. We thought you shared useful information and techniques with other researchers as part of your normal skills and knowledge transfer. Similarly for working with colleagues in other countries. We're only interested in why this helps, or what new research avenues it will make possible for the first time.

Reference

1. Tim Radford's full list of 25 commandments can be found at: www.guardian.co.uk/science/blog/2011/jan/19/manifesto-simple-scribe-commandments-journalists.

6   Other types of health stories

Features

When you are trying to place a public relations story to gain positive media coverage, awareness of new products or treatments, or recognition for some outstanding new research, you need to think about the usual types of story you see in the media, and then match your story to the appropriate format to package and target it.

News stories are usually about current affairs, or a specific advance in the science (see Chapter 5 for examples of what makes health news and Chapter 4, 'Press release format' for writing in a news style). But overviews of the current state of research in a field, policy analysis and health system reorganisations, or stories with a strong human interest angle, may be better packaged as features or Sunday stories, which tend to allow more space for each item and include discussion and some context.

Several smaller stories, none of which is quite strong enough on its own to make a good news piece, may also be combined to make a successful feature article, radio programme or television documentary.

For example, two brief news releases, one about nanoparticles in paint that can kill germs when triggered by fluorescent light, and another about dyes used for painting surgical wounds that can be activated by ultraviolet light to disinfect the tissue, might be successfully combined into a feature about new approaches being taken to kill hospital superbugs.[1] Neither story would be quite strong enough on its own to generate much media coverage, but together they form the hook to convince a features editor that enough progress has been made that it's worth running another longer piece on hospital infections and drug-resistant bacteria. However, such a feature will usually need good pictures and some case histories of patients as well. You can think of the news style as 'facts, facts, context' told objectively, and the style of features as 'human interest, comment, analysis' from a more personal or subjective viewpoint.

The features format, rather than the news format, is often more successful for the type of story that requires explanation in addition to disclosure of information. For example, in the world's second worst nuclear incident after Chernobyl, at the Fukushima Japanese nuclear reactor, which was damaged by a tsunami and earthquake, the emerging story ran daily from 11 March 2011 for over a month, with the reactor flood, fire and radiation leak eventually being declared in the highest category of nuclear disaster.

As well as disclosing what was happening from day to day to control the fires, risks from the used fuel rods, melting core and the continuing battle to prevent further radiation leaks, the news media needed to explain the health consequences for workers and civilians in nearby cities. Even experienced public relations spokespeople and science journalists were struggling to clearly explain the distinction between amount of radiation dose and the rate of dose, which are not comparable.

Most media took a more features-oriented approach, with side boxes and digressions explaining the difference between short bursts of higher-dose radiation and longer-term but low-level exposures. These were compared and contrasted with doses received from medical X-rays, ordinary aeroplane flights and the background radiation from some types of rock such as granite.

Features are usually longer than news items, often from 1,000–3,000 words, so if they followed the rules of news writing, where the most important facts are put first and the text then gets progressively less important, few people would ever read them to the end. The news pages of a newspaper are usually at the front, and then further into the publication we get to longer, more thoughtful stories that analyse issues and also have comment pieces which are often accompanied by the photograph of the writer, confirming that this is someone's personal view rather than dispassionate news.

In practice, with the decline in readership of print versions of newspapers, this distinction is becoming slightly more blurred, as fewer news stories are being covered, those that are get slightly more space, and the stories usually now include some reaction or analysis from those most affected. This longer type of news story used to be a called a 'read' in journalist's jargon, as it is the type of story that people come back to later to enjoy when they have a little more time – you can imagine the readers sitting there with their feet up and a cup of coffee. However, it is useful when preparing and shaping your public relations activity to remember the traditional distinction between a news story and a feature.

In radio programmes we do this by having lighter, chattier items at different times of day such as mid-morning, during the afternoon or later evening, and the 'hard' news items are broadcast during the drivetime news bulletins at 07.30–09.00 hrs, lunchtime and 17.00–18.30 hrs, when people are commuting to and from work in their cars, listening to the radio. In TV this shows up most clearly as the difference between news headlines or news bulletins, and documentaries, current affairs and chat shows.

So broadcast and written features need a different type of structure from plain news. Features need variation, with highs and lows throughout the piece, more human interest, comment and analysis, but they still need a strong, gripping start.

Compared with news, which usually gets straight to the point and concentrates on the story's significant facts, features may even start with a dropped introduction, which acts as a hook to grab the audience's attention before coming to the main substance of the story. In a dropped introduction, the journalist often starts with a quirky phrase, a scene-setting description, poses a question or describes a problem before coming to the main point of the article. To hear good examples, or even just lots of examples, listen to Quentin Cooper, the presenter of BBC Radio 4's science programme *Material World*. But use them sparingly.

Dropped introductions

BBC Radio 4's *Material World* presenter Quentin Cooper once gave me the example of an article starting something like: 'I like bananas, because they have no bones, as the children's song says. Monkeys also like bananas, and they may be right as bananas are a good source of the phosphates which help make strong and healthy bones.'

This is a dropped introduction for an article that would go on to look at new medical or health research which discusses the importance of phosphates in babies' (and monkeys') diets. The danger with dropped introductions like this is that the story could cross the desk of a news or features editor who just reads the first few words and says 'Well I don't like bananas', and chucks the story in the bin without ever finding out about the important new research.

So dropped introductions should only really be used for news stories when the main focus of the story is so tedious sounding, or such a difficult concept to grasp, that it has to be sweetened with a more interesting hook at the start of the story. Data-processing stories may benefit from a dropped introduction.

Setting the scene, which does not mean giving a lot of background, is a legitimate tactic in feature stories. So a description of a place or landscape scene, or details from the daily life of a patient with a particular disease at the start, may help to raise emotional interest by describing a visual image, evoking a mood, or gaining sympathy and interest in the issue, before you come to the main thrust of the feature.

So how can we put these highs and lows, this variation and colour, into a longer feature story which will carry the reader along with us? The answer is often to use the same techniques that novelists or film-makers do, evoking a number of small scenes through descriptive anecdotes, all linked together by a narrative theme. If we can add in some exciting cliffhangers along the way, finishing each section in a similar way to the daily soap operas on television, your readers, listeners and viewers will be compelled to continue.

The television, film and other visual equivalents of the written feature story are current affairs programmes and documentaries. If your story has a very strong visual aspect then you should think about packaging and pitching it to attract the visual arts editors and producers as well as the written news media.

Narrative styles

Writers recognise at least five classic narrative styles or techniques for telling a story – and you can think of these as types of book, or different types of film you might go to see. You'll find that you are surprisingly familiar with the grammar, style and set pieces of the genre once you start writing in these forms instead of the classic research paper format (background, experiment, design, methods, results, discussion, conclusion), which you may struggle to wean career scientists away from:

- **Thesis**: this is probably the simplest style for a medical story. The facts are laid out in a manner that leads the audience from A to B to C as bits of evidence are logically piled up and therefore the conclusion must be D. You show the design of the research, how it supports your claims, what your findings were and how you knew what you had discovered, and how significant it was when you discovered it.
- **Problem**: this style lays out the facts as a problem – have you ever wondered what is happening when your car fails to start in the morning? Well your arms, legs and other parts of your body need good electrical connections in exactly the same way as the lights, indicators and other electrical components of a car do. If the insulation has become worn around a wire through rubbing, acid spills or damage, the metal core of the wire could be exposed. You can have a short circuit and the car may not work, or the wrong indictor comes on when you hit the switch ...
- **Disaster** (or thriller, or horror if you insist): in this narrative style you evoke a possible or real impending or unfolding danger or threat and follow its implications. A pandemic starts, a volcano could erupt, a tsunami arrives or a band of murderers may be loose in the street. You show how your new work, technique or protocol can predict, avert, minimise or help people to recover from the impending disaster.
- **Detective** (including medical drama): this is probably the most fun style to write in, and currently the most popular form of storytelling in our society if you actually analyse the current programmes on television or look at book sales. At the time of writing the highest paid actor in America, Hugh Laurie, was the eponymous hero of a medical drama *House*, a cranky but brilliant and slightly reclusive US physician who (and the clue is in the name, Dr Watson), after studying the patient's symptoms and discarding the impossible, usually arrives at the correct diagnosis, however improbable. In this genre you show how you were hunting for a solution and found a clue. That led you to another one, you realised that you had a mystery on your hands, and eventually after a series of red herrings and blind alleys you finally uncovered the truth and exposed the culprit.
- **Quest**: this style takes its name from the legend of King Arthur and his Knights of the Round Table, who lurch apparently at random from one extraordinary encounter or anecdote to another as they make their way on their journeys.

The only theme which links the different strands of the stories, each of which exposes some new aspect of the struggle between law and order on the one hand, and chaos and the forces of magic (think Monkey, another anarchic tale if you want the Eastern equivalent) on the other, is that Arthur and his knights are involved in them all. This style often works well for pure research findings (as opposed to applied research, when something useful has actually been discovered). We set off on a journey into the unknown ...

Reference

1. *Evening Herald*, Ireland, 11 September 2008.

7 New media

How it all started

The development of the internet, a worldwide group of computers all connected to each other via telecommunications systems and able to exchange information through a standard set of protocols, has changed the way we all work, and the task of managing public relations in the 21st century.

The internet is a metanet, or network of networks, linking private individuals, companies, charities, special interest groups and governments around the world, allowing them to exchange information in standardised forms such as electronic mail or email, and the hypertext documents of the World Wide Web (web or www).

The World Wide Web was invented by British computer scientist Sir Tim Berners-Lee in 1990 while working with colleagues at CERN, the multi-country-owned particle physics research facility in Geneva, Switzerland, as a way of identifying and sharing documents between scientists through the internet. Each document has a unique web page address and users can navigate between them using a web browser via hyperlinks written in hypertext.

Although previous file-sharing systems and email had been invented by the 1970s, Berners-Lee joined together the two technologies of hypertext and the internet by inventing three key new aspects: the Uniform Resource Locator (URL), which identifies each document; a publishing language called Hypertext Mark-up Language (HTML); and a standardised way of exchanging data called the Hypertext Transfer Protocol (HTTP).

A domain name defines a particular area of control of the internet, and follows set rules, enabling people to send messages to each other's addresses and host information pages or websites. The common and well-known top-level domains such as .net, .org and .com are primarily used by commercial organisations and private individuals; .gov is used by government organisations, and .ac is used by universities and academic organisations, with some US-based ones using .edu. In addition there are top-level country code domains such as .uk for the United Kingdom or .cz for the Czech Republic. There are then second-level domain names below these, such as .co.uk where the .co part is the second level, and so on. Most organisations choose and register domain names that will make them easy to remember or suggest something about their activity.

There is no legal rule that says which country's domain you have to use for your own website or email address, and in 2000 Tuvalu, the small pacific island, negotiated a substantial commercial deal to lease .tv domains, which are particularly attractive because the country code is also the abbreviation for television. Some agencies can now arrange to set up a branded television company for your exclusive video broadcasts.

As well as buying up and controlling the commercial domain addresses linked to your organisation's name (for example health.org.uk is a domain owned by the Health Foundation, a charity) some organisations have tried to buy up and control the negative names associated with it, in case they ever spark criticism or protest (such as healthsucks.org.uk in the example above). However, there are potentially so many of these that it is very expensive, if not impossible.

The internet has speeded up communications around the globe, allowing online shopping, social networking and instant messaging in various forms. The phenomenal increase in the power of computers over the last 20 years, their shrinking size and cost, wireless technologies making them portable, and the sheer volume of traffic and messaging now carried by the internet has hugely expanded the knowledge and information available to anyone, sometimes leading to an information overload.

But this traffic increase has also made the internet virtually impossible to police, monitor or control. This makes information management today a very different task from the practice of public relations using traditional media, and has allowed individual citizens to redefine the way they interact with each other and with traditional forms of authority. The absolute independence of the internet and the anarchic or piratical views of some of its fiercest and most prolific users have contributed to an internet culture that resists censorship, authority and any attempts at central control.

Perceived government interference, or calls by authorities and multinational companies who attempt to crack down on the freedom of expression in the internet, are likely to invite flaming attacks of angry messages; the attention of hackers who may try to break into your secure communications and computer files; and even denial of service bombardments that attempt to shut down or crash the authority or organisation's core computer systems or servers.

Problems

The cheap and ubiquitous availability of email has given rise to four particular problems that threaten its normal function and use for users:

- **Information overload**, where an individual or organisation is so overwhelmed with the volume of emails and other information arriving that they cease to function effectively and therefore become unable to take any useful action in response to what may be urgent messages. A simple example might be imagined where a medical researcher has apparently claimed to have cured cancer in a radio interview. The next day all the telephone lines and email inboxes of local family doctors are jammed with desperate relatives of cancer sufferers who wish to get hold of this new treatment, unaware that it takes ten years to typically get from lab bench to clinic. Other important messages might go unnoticed in the general email noise. The doctors may be unable to phone out and sick patients seeking to make appointments may be unable to get through to their local clinic as all the telephone lines are engaged and the receptionists tied up with the cancer enquiries.

- **Spamming** is the practice of sending unsolicited emails to large lists of potential contacts or just randomly to any email addresses. Because it costs virtually nothing to send millions of emails to a computer-generated list in the hope that one person will respond, ordinary people and business users now have a serious spam problem. Their email inboxes are getting clogged up with unwanted spam, the electronic equivalent of direct mail or leaflet drops. From a public relations point of view, spam is such a serious problem for most people – and creates so much bad feeling and anger towards the organisation generating the spam – that it is a tactical mistake to use agencies to send unsolicited emails on your behalf, as you will simply enrage almost all of the recipients. Even if one or two people do respond positively, you may gain such notoriety or negative feeling from the thousands or millions of others that it is a self-defeating activity. Because of the spam problem, many people now have anti-spam filters on their computers, which may cut out some useful messages as well as the many unwanted ones. For press officers using email lists to deliver press releases to target journalists this is also a problem, since press releases may be blocked as potential spam by the filters. In addition, emailed press releases that do get through may not get read unless the subject line is clearly labelled and the sender recognised as a reliable news source. Most people, and therefore most journalists, now delete the majority of their emails unread. Steve Connor, the science editor of the *Independent* newspaper, famously has his forcibly removed from his inbox every few months by the IT department and handed to him on disks, as their sheer volume slows the newspaper's activity down. And finally, emailed press releases that do get through and get opened by the journalists or other target audience need to be exceptionally well written and exceptionally well targeted to that particular journalist. A journalist or key decision-maker will resent any time wasted in opening and reading an irrelevant press release, and may treat all future releases from you as spam, taking out some of the anger and frustration generated by general spamming onto your organisation in particular.
- **Viruses, worms** and **trojans**. Viruses are small computer programs passed by emails and file-sharing that can infect your systems. They then multiply and spread to other computers by infecting your own communications, in a way similar to the spread of viruses in nature as they infect, multiply and pass between bacteria, animals and plants. Worms and trojans (named after the Trojan Horse of Greek mythology) are malicious programs that exploit security loopholes in your computer software to infect your systems and spread automatically through any networked computers. They can also spread via USB

flash drives, which are small portable data storage devices which combine flash memory with a Universal Serial Bus port connection. A trojan appears to be a safe file or application, but disguises a malicious application. These programs may spy on data held in your system, corrupt it, delete it or otherwise affect your computer's performance. Some simply replicate themselves and do no other harm. Your computer systems need to include constantly updated anti-virus software protection programs to avoid you accidentally passing viruses and other malicious programs to your contacts, customers, colleagues or the media, as they will not appreciate the cost and trouble of getting their infected computers cleaned up.

- **Phishing** is a form of identity theft, and is the practice of attempting to gain security data such as passwords and user identity details, or gain access to bank details or credit card numbers, by sending fake emails or other electronic messages that direct people to false websites or other places where the personal data can be harvested. Phishing sites often look very similar to the authentic websites they are mimicking, tricking users of social networks, online banking systems or electronic auctions into entering their financial details and then using these for fraud or theft. Press offices that send branded and formatted press releases, with embedded logos and complicated picture file attachments, may find that their messages are blocked, intercepted or destroyed by the recipient's security software. The software cannot tell between these genuine messages and malicious fake emails that contain phishing programs, or other viruses and worms, without first risking opening them.

A further problem, which has not arisen in Europe yet, but which governments are salivating over, is the plan to extend government surveillance powers to give security service officials access to every email, text message, phone call and record of websites visited as a matter of routine, as proposed by the UK Home Secretary Theresa May in April 2012. Civil liberties groups are strongly opposed, citing examples of censorship such as Chinese websites closed by their government for posting sensitive content.

Meanwhile UK government ministers and their civil servants are resisting the release of private memos, texts and emails that relate to government business after Christopher Graham, the UK Information Commissioner, ruled in November 2011 that simply using a private email address to send the communication did not exempt it from transparency legislation. He suggested that deliberately using private email addresses for sensitive messages to get round the law may be illegal. This has implications for all publicly funded and even arm's-length government bodies, as worst case scenarios, public relations crisis planning and risk registers should all become publicly available.

As late as April 2012, the UK government and Department of Health were still successfully resisting releasing the risk register assessments of potential threats to the National Health Service, if the 2012 Health and Social Care Act was passed, as it was in March 2012. This was in spite of instructions from the Information Tribunal in March 2012 to release the details.[1] A leaked partial copy later slipped out.

Online piracy or copyright infringement by users of social media is also being tested in law, with media firm Viacom in the US claiming $1bn from the YouTube website owners for allowing users to post clips from their hit television shows. Two New York appeal judges ruled in April 2012 that a case could be heard, overturning earlier decisions in 2010 in favour of YouTube, on a charge that was first brought in 2007.

Computer hackers, or hacking into social media, is a separate privacy problem, which Facebook, among other platforms, has addressed by rewarding hackers who successfully penetrate its firewalls. The hackers are thanked in Facebook's White Hat page, and can earn thousands of dollars from the company for owning up to their actions.[2]

Types of social media

According to Wikipedia, itself an extraordinarily successful example of new media, there are six distinct types of social media, as defined by Andreas Kaplan and Michael Haenlein in an article for *Business Horizons* magazine[3] in 2010:

1 **Collaborative projects** such as Wikipedia, the crowdsourced online encyclopaedia.
2 **Blogs** and **microblogs** such as Twitter, which allows users to make the 140-character posts known as tweets.
3 **Content communities** such as YouTube, the video-sharing site; Pinterest, the pinboard-style photo, ideas and image posting site; AlphaGalileo, the science media website for publishing news releases; TED, for spreading ideas on technology, entertainment and design by giving short talks.
4 **Social networking sites** such as Facebook, which gives you or your organisation a dedicated diary space to post comments and interact with 'friends'; Linked-In, the business contacts site that hosts professional discussion groups for a wide range of different subjects including ones covering public relations and science communication.
5 **Virtual worlds** such as World of Warcraft, an interactive video game.
6 **Virtual social worlds** such as Second Life, in which you can imagine a perfect existence and create an avatar to meet with other people, trade and share interests and experiences.

By 2012 the main impact that these types of social media have had on health and medical public relations practice has been in the first four types, although some larger companies and organisations have also established virtual presences in Second Life, even hosting virtual art exhibitions or science festivals which can be attended by avatars.

TED is an example of a social media publishing site that simply could not have existed before the age of the internet. Its mission as a not-for-profit foundation is to share ideas worth spreading, founded in 1984 as a conference bringing together people from the worlds of technology, entertainment and design. Alongside its website giving free access to hundreds of talks it runs two annual conferences in California, US, and Edinburgh, Scotland, every year. Inspirational TED talks[4] are posted in English or with English subtitles and last 18 minutes or less.

The collaborative encyclopaedia, Wikipedia, has tempted some public relations practitioners to edit entries relating to their own organisation or area of work, and even to subvert entries relating to their critics or competitors. As noted in this book's introduction, Jane Wilson, chief executive of the Chartered Institute of Public Relations, says:

> An encyclopaedia should not be leveraged for competitive advantage, whatever your perspective, or point of view. Those wishing to interact with the Wikipedia community must first understand it. Public relations professionals must be clear about its aims and ambitions, and before engaging they need to adopt its etiquette. You do not have to accept mistakes or misunderstandings on Wikipedia, but you do not have the right to edit the content so that it reflects what you want it to say.[5]

Similarly newspaper corrections and clarifications columns are also attracting increasing attention from online commentators, and inevitably from public relations staff on behalf of their organisations, seeking to get mistakes corrected or posts taken down as quickly as possible. But asking for matters of fact, or misspellings of names to be changed, does not also give you the right to ask for journalistic opinions or tone to be altered to favour the viewpoint of your organisation. In June 2012, the UK Chartered Institute of Public Relations closed its member consultation on guidelines for public relations users of Wikipedia, and issued formal advice.[6]

An internet etiquette, or netiquette, has grown up as different people from different cultures all interact using the internet, World Wide Web and the various social networks. As an example, writing in capitals is now considered shouting by most users of email or in internet posts.

As the person responsible in your organisation for managing its reputation, you may want to circulate or publish an online style guide for your staff, similar to the style guides used by newspapers and magazines to ensure consistency of house style in writing by their journalists. The style should cover typical standardised spellings, use of capitals, and also lay down easily accepted rules for maintaining the difference between personal postings and emails and official ones.[7]

Some joking and banter is unavoidable, but racist, homophobic, ageist or sexist comments, even those meant in jest, may be completely unacceptable to other users and recipients, especially among ill or bereaved people. If you have not laid down what is friendly and acceptable, and what is not, you may be unable to act officially when the consequences of one person's banter backfires on your organisation.

An unacceptable form of internet behaviour is trolling, where a user posts deliberately upsetting, rude or inflammatory comments, or simply ignores the topic under discussion and posts off-topic comments in the thread instead. Internet debates often get heated, and this can descend into exchanges of personal insults or flaming, but this is considered more acceptable, unless the flamer has specifically joined the discussion to provoke a flame war.

For discussion forums owned or operated by your organisation, such as blogs and websites inviting feedback, especially for controversial proposals, you will need to make sure that the discussion has a moderator employed by your organisation. The moderator can make sure that offensive or unacceptable posts are taken down as quickly as possible. But your moderator does need to understand netiquette, as removing troll posts should not be mistaken for censoring genuine users' feedback and comments, or the online community will rebel. In the online world, you are trying to engage and interact with your audiences and so inevitably they will sometimes express opinions that are detrimental to your organisation or which you will disagree with.

The internet and social media have also enabled new types of collaborative and interactive projects, such as the Big Knits. The food company Innocent Smoothies has run a Big Knit in association with the charity Age UK for several years – volunteer knitters make and send in tiny woolly hats for smoothie bottles, and for every hatted bottle sold, 25p is donated to the charity Age UK to help make winter warmer for older people.

A different Big Knit was run in 2011 by the British Society for Immunology to highlight multiple sclerosis. Knitters were asked to make individual parts of a collaborative woollyart installation, to engage people with science and raise awareness of the disease via the social nature of knitting. Knitters worked on brain cells, DNA and sunshine, to make the parts of three woolly tableaux depicting the nature of the disease, the role of genetics and the impact of the environment. Scientists were encouraged to join knitting groups to learn to knit, and to talk about their work in an informal chatty environment, exchanging skills and information as both student and teacher. The finished artwork was assembled and exhibited at the Cheltenham Science Festival in 2011.

Many universities' and organisations' websites now include blogs from researchers, or staff who have been on expeditions to interesting places to carry out their work. These may be backed up with podcasts, or short radio clips in which the scientist talks through an audio diary, or is interviewed by a professional journalist, or vidcasts, which are similar video clips. These all add to the richness and interactivity of your online presence.

For tips about blogs, research and communicating science generally, have a look at the Thesis Whisperer, the hugely influential newspaper-style blog dedicated to helping research students everywhere. It is edited by Dr Inger Mewburn of RMIT University, Melbourne, Australia.[8]

Even if English is not your first language, the English translation of your press releases, articles and blogs needs to be accurate and in colloquial language. According to David Belios[9] in his book *Is That a Fish in your Ear? Translation and the Meaning of Everything*, UNESCO says that one tenth of all translated books are into English, but two thirds are translated from English into other languages, putting English into use three-quarters of the time in translations. English is now the language of international competition, the language of visibility.

So when preparing press releases or public statements, English – and the good Anglo-Saxon English of English-speaking people, not the mangled English of academics – is the key you should be concentrating on. When you publish your organisation's latest research or announcements on the international science media website AlphaGalileo, remember this. The Romance languages of Spanish, Italian, French and Portuguese have very different cultural conventions, for instance shunning the repetition of words, and using more flowery descriptions, so a direct translation simply will not do.

The more collaborative the internet becomes the more the distinctions between content communities and social networking become blurred. As an example of social media, Mumsnet[10] is free to join, sends out emails on child development and pregnancy, has a weekly round-up of parenting news, suggests interesting talks, offers shopping discounts from partner organisations and acts as a pressure group on issues that members are concerned about.

Previously, in the UK, the equivalent organisation and the only way of contacting large numbers of women in a cascade communication model would have been through the Women's Institute. The WI has a strong interest in science, chooses, researches, takes on and debates science, medical and ethical issues such as the best system for organ donation. It then votes on two of these every year, delivering the results to the relevant organisation such as a central government department. Some village WIs are now closing their branches as younger users and mothers turn to Mumsnet, village community websites and the wider internet instead.

The widespread availability and falling cost of smartphones – and, to a lesser extent, tablets and laptops – is encouraging public access to social media. Smartphone owners are bombarded with newly developed, cheap and easy to download applications, or apps, allowing people to access their social media while on the move, and enabling them to post information as citizen journalists. Apps can now convert their phones into a whole range of useful gadgets from GPS trackers to currency converters, and in the world of health, to virtual stethoscopes or heart monitors.

A backlash from the public and bloggers is arising as the owners of popular sites attempt to cash in their public goodwill for hard currency by floating their companies on the stock markets, or selling directly to existing social media giants such as Facebook. Where owners of copyright were happy for individuals to post short clips and images on their personal parts of sites, as a form of viral publicity, it becomes a different issue when a media outlet such as the *Huffington Post*, which did not pay its blogging contributors, suddenly becomes worth millions of pounds. Should the content providers also have a share of the advertising value generated by the millions of clicks as users worldwide access their articles? If your organisation is hosting a chat forum, can you realistically check that everything posted is copyright free?

Analysis tools

Measuring the impact, reach and share of your social media outreach programme is incredibly difficult since so many social media conversations take place in essentially private places such as on individual Facebook pages or tweeted threads, which may get relabelled as they trend.

Google, as part of its onward march to world domination, offers some free analytical tools with self-explanatory names such as Google Analytics, Google Insights for Search, Google Keywords Tool and Google Alerts. Facebook Insights and YouTube Analytics let you see who is viewing your material and how they are using it (as an administrator). Other free digital tools are offered by Namechk which lets you test a name against 150 different web services, and Peerindex analyses Twitter lists. HootSuite allows you to manage multiple accounts from one webpage and Buffer App lets you schedule and upload updates at times when people are most likely to read them, while Bit.ly lets you know whether people click your link and where they are. All these analytical tools were recommended in April 2012 by Mark Pack, head of digital at MHP Communications, a US consultancy, via the online magazine *PR Daily*, and were shared through one of the useful PR groups of Linked-In, which recommends today's top news that you might be interested in and delivers tips directly to you via a daily feed.

In my experience so far, about half of the posted links, threads or discussion topics on Linked-In groups are simply people shamelessly plugging themselves and their consultancies, but the other half contains some real gems, such as Mark Pack's list. So if you want to check out whether you are using the latest or the most effective tools, and get some peer-reviewed feedback on them, then I suggest that you sign up to some of these social groups, as new services and new facilities within these services are coming online almost every day, and any printed book section will become out-of-date even before it is published.

References

1. *Daily Telegraph*, 5 April 2012.
2. *Guardian*, 4 May 2012.
3. Andreas M. Kaplan & Michael Haenlein, 'Users of the world, unite! The challenges and opportunities of social media', *Business Horizons* 53 (2010), 59–68.
4. Find TED talks at www.ted.com.
5. *Huffington Post*, 6 February 2012.
6. CIPR Member Newsletter, 30 May 2012
7. Associated Press Social Media Guidelines for example at www.ap.org/Images/Social-Media-Guidelines-7-24-2012_tcm28-8378.pdf.
8. Thesis Whisperer at http://thesiswhisperer.com.
9. David Belios, *Is That a Fish in your Ear? Translation and the Meaning of Everything*, Particular Books, 2011.
10. www.mumsnet.com.

8 Journals

Peer-reviewed journals

Peer-reviewed journals are a vital but problematic part of the process of transferring academic research from the lab bench and notebook to clinical practice or commercial development of medicines, and eventually into treating health and medical problems.

All qualified doctors and postgraduate researchers must have undertaken some personal research and need to understand the process of how research is carried out. Posing and testing a hypothesis, collecting and establishing facts, analysing the facts and making sure that results are repeatable, and interpreting discoveries are all valid aims in research.

The final output of a piece of research is the conclusion, which is then offered up for discussion and verification among the scientific community or establishment. A good piece of research will be new, or novel as scientists insist on saying, in the sense that no one has ever done quite this before, even if it is simply to design a different approach to check or repeat already known results, or to rule out possible misinterpretations or errors caused by faulty equipment, measuring methods or statistical bias.

This analytical process becomes such second nature to people working in the fields of health and medical research that they are constantly surprised when dodgy pseudoscientific claims are taken up by the media and believed by the public. Typical tricks in pseudoscience include claims that the observed effect is not open to repetition or analysis (for instance, getting messages from the afterlife through a medium); or using a whole suite of statistical tests so that one shows a statistically positive result simply by chance; or cherry-picking data, and even cherry-picking trials because if enough are carried out, one will inevitably show positive results.

The core test of a new piece of genuine research is whether the author can get it accepted and printed as a paper in a reputable peer-reviewed journal. Science and medical journalists do not check the facts of papers published in journals (in spite of early advice to journalists in a leaflet from the Science Media Centre, which suggested that we should). As journalists we do look at which journal the paper is published in, and perhaps look at the timescale of the trial, the sample size and the statistical confidence that this is a genuine result not an artefact. From a public relations point of view, you therefore need to know which journals are the most prestigious, and therefore which academic papers are most likely to get picked up and publicised by the mainstream media.

The top academic journals, especially those which cover many disciplines, themselves issue press releases every week to the science and medical media, highlighting and summarising the key papers that they think will be of interest to the wider public. Thus they gain themselves publicity which reinforces their pre-eminent position as a leading journal.

Most mainstream media does not like to report on other competing media – a *Guardian* article which started 'in the *Sunday Times* yesterday' would be unusual. However, this prejudice does not extend to the peer-reviewed journals, as publication of a paper in these is taken as a measure of veracity or trustworthiness. The only UK exception to this is *New Scientist* magazine, which serious scientists view as a light comic written for mass audience consumption, but which behaves as though it is a peer-reviewed journal, even to the extent of issuing press releases to other media about its weekly contents.

The top international journals are now all in the English language, and include *Nature, Science, Cell, Lancet, British Medical Journal* and the *New England Journal of Medicine* (plus, of course, *New Scientist*). Getting an academic paper published in one of these journals is the goal and lifeblood of all working scientists. You also need to know about a few others, including some in other languages, particularly in German for medical research, but your senior staff will be able to tell you which ones are the most relevant for your own organisation. Their own international prestige, the prestige of their department, their institution, and even the research funds that flow into your organisation depend crucially on these publications.

To a slightly lesser extent, scientific advances are also shared via academic conferences, where scientists read their papers to the audience present rather than publishing them. But since publicising their results widely in advance can prejudice their chances of getting a paper accepted by a journal, which usually only takes new work, most scientists only release their full results at conferences after a paper has been accepted by a journal, and is either recently published or coming out within the next couple of days (otherwise it could be withdrawn).

Since getting a paper accepted by a conference will usually involve having to disclose some of the results, in practice many conference presentations have already been published, or are so preliminary or partial that they are too inconclusive for your public relations department to issue a press release about them.

So that gives you two good chances of publicising a piece of academic research – when it is coming out in a peer-reviewed journal, in which case you need to abide by the journal's own embargo; or a second chance slightly later, when the work is being presented subsequently at a conference, in which case you need to abide by the conference's embargoes. The third chance comes when your own in-house magazine or annual report is published, as previously missed research results can still get picked up then by the mainstream media. A fourth and rarer chance comes when the authors pick up a Nobel Prize or other award for the work.

High impact factor

The more prestigious the peer-reviewed journal, the greater the likelihood of achieving wide press coverage, or citations by other authors for your paper, which is one measure of academic worth, commonly called impact factor. Curiously, the more prestigious the journal, the more likely the research is to actually have a wider social impact as well. Since the top journals are multidisciplinary or cross-disciplinary, to be accepted by one this particular piece of research has to have implications outside the author's own narrow field of work, or be such a significant advance that it simply cannot be ignored.

According to Claudia Wiedemann, chief editor of *Nature Reviews Neuroscience*, speaking at a science communication residential seminar with me in Solden, Austria, in 2009, a top journal paper is accepted because it is new and has wide implications, so the most important thing is not to be mainstream. To design research which is likely to achieve you a *Nature* paper, think laterally. Read and know the literature in your field and the fields immediately connected to it. Find an exciting new angle, don't be safe. Be enthusiastic about what you are doing.

What *Nature* wants

The *Nature* journals want:

- Technically solid work
- Correct controls
- Conclusions supported by the data
- Good quality data
- Importance to the field
- Conceptual rather than incremental advances
- Depth of findings for mechanisms, physiological relevance, generalism
- Settling a controversy
- A community resource
- Interest to a wide scientific audience
- Findings that are not straightforward
- The story attached to the work, not just the findings
- Some indication of the extent of the advance
- Some indication of the impact this is likely to have on the field of research

Public access to research

Some 20 years ago, when I was director of the Research for Health Charities Group, I suggested that major charity-funded research should be published publicly, so that donors could see where their money went. And so that the public could see how animals were needed for basic medical research, rather than just used in drug-safety testing, as the more radical activist groups seemed to believe.

Even though the Wellcome Trust does not rely on public donations for its funds (it is a charitable foundation based solely upon the original ownership of pharmaceutical company shares, long since sold out to GlaxoSmithKline), I recommended that as their chief executive was chairing our charity group, its research should also be made publicly available, possibly through allowing open access on its website.

I was told then that the dangers to researchers using animals were too great, as they would be individually targeted by extremists, and that unfortunately the research careers of scientists rested upon their being published in top-flight peer-reviewed journals, which all restrict access to work to their subscribers.

One of my concerns about the Wellcome Trust's moral position then was that its funding powers were so great compared with all other medical research bodies in the UK and Europe that they unwittingly distorted research priorities, with no public accountability, and that open-access publishing would go some way towards redressing this by increasing transparency.

I have recently discovered that one of the more forward-looking Research for Health Charities Group chief executives at the time, Prof Gordon McVie, now based in Milan, Italy, but formerly chief executive of the Cancer Research Campaign, has gone on to found an online open access journal, ecancer.org, published monthly from Bristol, England, and read by 40,000 oncologists in 190 countries.

Ten years later I was arguing for open access again when debating science ethics with researchers, while running the programme of science communication work-shops that I had designed for the public funding body the Natural Environment Research Council. Again, I was told that although the idea was sound in principle, and even though the public had paid for the work, the UK Research Councils and other public bodies all allocate funds to university departments and institutions based upon the findings of the Higher Education Funding Councils' Research Assessment Exercise (now rebranded the Research Excellence Framework for 2014).

This was, among other criteria, a much feared periodic count of how many peer-reviewed academic papers a department's top few staff had managed to get published since the last exercise. It was assumed to be a reflection of the research output quality of that department, as the catchphrase 'publish or perish' neatly summed up.

The importance that scientists attach to publication and subsequent citation has been highlighted by what may be the first case of journal paper retraction for attempting to manipulate the citation index, a measure of how important other scientists think a particular scientific paper, or a journal, is.

Two papers in the *Scientific World Journal* were alleged to have cited other papers published in another journal, *Cell Transplantation*, which in turn included papers that cited other journals which shared the same board members, thus arti-ficially boosting these journals' credibility (and the scientific standing of the board members). The *Scientific World Journal* papers were retracted after the allegations were exposed, and the authors banned from publication for the next three years in other journals owned by the same publishers, according to a Retraction Watch[1] blog posting in May 2012 by medical journalist Ivan Oransky, who is also executive editor of *Reuters Health*.

This seems to have been an extreme example of the banned practice of self-citation, in which articles in a journal cite previous articles in the same journal in an attempt to boost its impact factor, as measured by citations in the last two years, which can lead to journals losing their impact factor as awarded by Thomson-Reuters Journal Citation Reports.

While running their media workshops, one of my persistent concerns was the inconsistency of the UK Research Councils' position. The Councils each said that they wanted their staff and researchers to carry out public outreach, talk to the media, and generally disseminate the importance of their research work to wider audiences, including industry which could actually use some of the findings to improve our lives. But the only measure of the researchers' worth that the Councils counted and funded was to see how many peer-reviewed papers they had published. To see why this didn't work well, you just had to follow the money.

Our workshop discussions became so heated during the 13 years that I ran the programme of science communication and media training for NERC that eventually the then head of communications, Sheila Anderson, took the initiative to codify our discussions into an Ethics Policy. And then at great personal effort she pushed it through all the Natural Environment Research Council's committees until they became the first publicly funded research council in the world to formally adopt an Ethics Policy in June 2005.

This Ethics Policy was in turn so well received that Sir David King, the UK Government Chief Scientist at the time, suggested that all research councils and all science bodies should adopt similar policies. Unfortunately, against my advice, the NERC Ethics Policy was only adopted as an 'aspiration' rather than a strict guideline that people must work to. And it excluded any mention of open access to research findings for the public, only mentioning 'Have open and explicit relationships with government, the public, the private sector and other funders'.

The UK Research Councils do encourage their funded researchers to disseminate their findings as widely as possible – after all if no one ever finds out about a piece of work then it was wasted money. But as yet they do not go so far as to require publication in one of the free access and online Public Library of Science Journals which have sprung up since 2003, trying to break the big publishing houses' stranglehold over academic publication. The driving force behind the PLoS journals were a group of US cancer, genetics, biochemistry and medical researchers who wanted to make sure that the latest potentially life-saving research findings were freely and widely available as quickly as possible. They were backed by 34,000 scientists from 180 countries who signed an open letter of support in the year 2000.

Ten years on again, and a Cambridge mathematician, Tim Gowers, finally got so fed up with the rising cost of academic journals, which can easily be as much as £15,000 a year for a single journal subscription per institution, soaking up almost a tenth of public research funding money in the UK, that he wrote an article on his blog[2] in January 2012 declaring that he would no longer submit papers to any Elsevier titles, the world's largest journal publisher, or review other researchers' work for them.

According to Alok Jha, writing in the *Guardian* newspaper on 10 April 2012, Gowers was not expecting what happened next.[3] Thousands of people read his post and hundreds left supportive comments. The next day a supporters' website, The Cost of Knowledge, was allowing academics to register their protests. By April the Wellcome Trust director Sir Mark Walport was announcing the 'academic spring' and throwing its weight behind a campaign to allow all research papers to be shared online, within six months of first publication. As one of the world's largest medical research funders, if the Wellcome Trust requires it as a condition of getting future funding, it will be so.

The Wellcome Trust has subsequently founded a new open access journal *eLife*, which started accepting academic papers in July 2012.[4] In July 2012, at this book's final copy deadline, the European Commission announced that from 2014 all research articles produced through the €80m Horizon 2020 programme will have to be freely available, and the goal is for 60 per cent of European Commission funded research to be publicly available through open access by 2016. 'Taxpayers should not have to pay twice for scientific research and they need seamless access to raw data,' said Neelie Kroes, European Commission vice-president for the Digital Agenda.

The commission's move follows support from the UK government for a switch to open access and recent news that the European medicines regulator will open its data vaults to allow independent researchers to scrutinise results from drug companies' trials. 'The EU's decision to adopt a similar policy to that of the UK will mean that the transition time from subscription-based to open-access publishing will be substantially reduced,' said Professor Adam Tickell, who was involved in a recent UK government-commissioned report on the issue, to the Reuters[5] news agency (see also Chapter 11, 'Academic research issues: open access publishing', p 147).

As a final note on the issue of open access, the enormous cost of academic journal subscriptions and single-view charges can stop public relations agencies and freelances, and in non-academic institutions, even some in-house staff, from checking the basis of stories. The importance given to citations by the academic community means that the way something was discovered becomes a story we simply have to take on trust, and eventually part of the narrative of science itself.

Most biomedical scientists know that Rosalind Franklin (1920–1958) made the key advance, X-ray Photo 51, which led directly to James Watson (born 1928) and Francis Crick's (1916–2004) discovery of the helical structure of DNA in 1953. But as a woman, and dying of ovarian cancer at 37, history tends to overlook her (as did the Nobel Prize committee), and her radiographer Freda Ticehurst who took the picture. It was a visual image, a picture, once again, which made all the difference.

As another example, most people believe that the basis of genetics was uncovered for the first time by the monk Gregor Mendel (1822–1884), working in his monastery at Brno, now part of the Czech Republic, when he grew long and short, green and yellow peas, with extraordinarily accurate results which exactly matched the later theoretical predictions for dominant and recessive genes.

I am grateful to Prof John Bryant of Exeter University, England, for pointing out to me that around the time that Gregor Mendel was born, in 1824, a Devon smallholder called John Goss published an article in the *Transactions of the Horticultural Society of London*[6] detailing the patterns of daughter plants from his experiments in crossing long and short, green and yellow peas. I am equally grateful to legendary *Guardian* science editor Tim Radford for knowing who John Goss was. The journal *Horticultural Transactions* was available in the library of the club Mendel was staying at in London while studying for a degree, so in the absence of other social media, he probably read something during the evenings. So who discovered genetics?

References

1. http://retractionwatch.wordpress.com.
2. More on Elsevier's downfall in Tim Gowers blog at http://gowers.wordpress.com/2012/01/21/elsevier-my-part-in-its-downfall.
3. *Guardian*, 10 April 2012.
4. http://wellcometrust.wordpress.com/2011/11/07/elife-a-journal-by-scientists-for-scientists.
5. Reuters, 17 July 2012.
6. John Goss, 'On Variation in the Colour of Peas, occasioned by Cross Impregnation', 1824, Horticultural *Transactions* (Series 1) Vol 5 (1824): 234–237.

Part III

Communicating health in theory and practice

9 Health and medical public relations planning

Before we come to the way that you need to plan campaigns, or even why you might want to plan PR campaigns, you may like to pause for a moment and consider what you expect to happen when you run your campaign. We appear to be hard-wired to believe in cause and effect. So if a bush rustles suspiciously, we immediately wonder whether a sabre-toothed tiger is lurking unseen inside it, just waiting to pounce, and we watch it carefully or stay well away from it.

This tendency to ascribe purposeful action, or physical agents such as tigers, even if unseen, to possibly random stirrings of the wind or pure chance, is a useful survival mechanism for humans. We are weak soft-shelled beings in a nasty and brutish world, so anticipating calamities before they happen and assuming that random events have a meaningful cause is probably a good strategy for members of our clever, big-brained but fragile species.

This gives us many advantages, but also can lead us up blind alleys, in the belief that Cause A and Effect B are directly connected, just because we happen to have noticed that they usually happen together, or very quickly, one after the other. It is the basis of the science of epidemiology – which allows us to make meaningful deductions from large numbers of seemingly random observations and events.

It also causes people to believe in plausible but wrong explanations for what are actually spontaneous or apparently random events, which are actually being driven by unseen or so far undiscovered rules. So it is easier to hypothesise that a giant invisible person (a god, for example) exists who makes everything from scratch, than it is to notice and then understand a simple but incredibly slow process such as evolution.

We believe that things have causes, and on the whole they stay the same. So if you put a book, *War and Peace*, down on the table, it is still the same book by the same author when you pick it up again tomorrow, it has not evolved into something else, such as Shakespeare's Sonnets or a hatstand. But when we are dealing with complex systems with many interconnections and many nested layers working to different timescales, it is easy to make mistakes. So people believe peculiar things about health, such as that homeopathy is effective.

Many public relations people, especially in agencies, are asked to help change attitudes or behaviours, often by running a campaign. There is very little firm evidence that this is actually possible or, perhaps more accurately, frequently successful. Any change may not be for the reasons that drove the campaign in the first place, and distressingly often even the most well-intentioned campaigns seem to have a negative or unwanted effect.

We have all seen an advertisement that we found funny and clever the first time, but on the hundredth time that it interrupts our favourite television programme we start shouting at the screen, and vow never to use the product or service being offered, ever again, ever. So the anti-heroin campaigns of the late 1990s famously presented wasted-looking stick-thin models. And many young men and women thought, that's a cool look.

The more complex the interactions and the system that you are trying to tamper with, the more we run the risk of unforeseen consequences, or even of accidentally causing exactly the opposite behaviours to those that you desired. Many actions have built-in feedback loops that either magnify the original action, causing it to spiral out of control, or dampen it down, restoring calm or equilibrium. But if you don't know, or have not visualised, how the systems that you are tampering with work, you cannot take feedback effects into consideration. All models are a poor and overly simple representation of what is actually happening in our complex world.

If you are not familiar with systems thinking, then I can heartily recommend *Thinking in Systems*, the seminal 2009 posthumous book of Donatella H. Meadows' writings, edited by Diana Wright.[1] In Chapter 7, page 175, under the subheading 'Pay attention to what is important not just what is quantifiable', she writes:

> Our culture, obsessed with numbers, has given us the idea that what we can measure is more important than what we can't measure. It means that we make quantity more important than quality. If quantity forms the goal of our feedback loops, if quantity is the center of our language and intuitions, if we motivate ourselves, rate ourselves and reward ourselves on our ability to produce quantity, then quantity will be the result.

So as you design, propose or plan your campaign, ask yourselves – is quantity or quality the defining characteristic of the world you want to live in; the world you are trying to create by exercising your skills and influence?

Planning a health or medical public relations campaign

Planning is critical for successful public relations just as it is to all forms of organised, strategic activity. As a context, which frames and restricts PR activity, there are laws and rules that legally govern some of the things you can do and say when making health claims about products and services. There are also specific laws and rules that govern the marketing and sale of medicines to members of the public – as distinct from those affecting sales to medical professionals – in the UK, Europe and the US. The pharmaceutical industry also abides by its own codes of self-regulation.

But planning for public relations activities still follows the same basic planning principles as any other campaigns undertaken by organisations, whether you are representing a commercial company, a university or research institute department, or a medical or welfare charity.

My colleague Jon Cope, when leading the public relations degree course at University College Falmouth, and drawing upon his extensive knowledge of the existing academic literature, distinguished between campaigns, programmes and projects in public relations:

- **Campaigns** are made up of groups of activities designed to cause change by either making something happen, or preventing a change which would otherwise happen. They may address a range of publics on a particular issue, possibly in an exciting newsworthy way.
- **Programmes** are continuing activities targeted at a particular public to achieve a particular set of aims, often linked to long-term changes of attitude.
- **Projects** are essentially shorter-term activities.

According to Cope, planned PR activity works alongside, but may also incorporate, linked disciplines including marketing, sales promotion, advertising, sponsorship, community relations and lobbying. This means that it is seldom, if ever, possible to plan any public relations activity without a full picture of everything else that your organisation is doing to achieve its aims.

He also says that, in practice, the terms 'campaign' and 'programme' tend to be used interchangeably to describe any type of planned PR activity, and that it is the planning aspect which is important, as distinct from reactive PR activity undertaken in response to unforeseen events such as unwelcome media enquiries.

In a planned PR campaign, project or programme, you may be trying to get recognition and therefore usually some media coverage for a brilliant and sustained research programme, possibly with the intention of attracting the best postdoctoral students, research staff and other workers from around the world, or to signal your availability and capacity for international collaboration and grant proposals.

Or you could be trying to draw attention to your charity's research funding work, which will in turn encourage more donations from the public, allowing your work to continue. Or you are trying to change public opinion, challenge stereotypes, get government support for legislation, mobilise patient support and pressure groups, or change other practices through your campaign. Or you are supporting your brand and product awareness by trying to build relationships, reputation and trust through corporate social responsibility activities, sponsorship and voluntary actions. Whatever your aims, you should be planning your campaigns, not randomly undertaking one-off projects and sporadic activities in the hope that they may help you achieve your goals.

When you are planning a public relations campaign, hoping to change opinions, proposing a programme of activities and work to your superiors, board and trustees, or trying to build brand awareness for a new product or service, you can usefully prepare your plan by running through a simple checklist. This will help you present your proposition in a coherent manner, make sure that you don't miss any major elements of the programme and enable you to budget for the time and resources needed. It should also help you to measure the success of your work so that you can improve future campaigns.

There are lots of different elements to a planned campaign and several good models and checklists are covered in the general public relations literature, especially books by Prof Anne Gregory; see *Planning and Managing Public Relations Campaigns: A Strategic Approach: A Step-by-step Guide (PR In Practice)*.[2]

Most of the academic literature checklists are very similar to our standard template, which has served us well for many years and that I will describe here.

Your plan also provides a benchmark so that if unexpected extra work arises you can quickly identify with your superiors and finance department the elements of the planned works that you will have to abandon if you are to take on extra responsibilities without extra assistance.

Some of the elements on our checklist may not all be needed for your campaign plan or appropriate for every campaign, but running through it may prevent you from missing obvious aspects. Academic and theoretical campaign models throughout the growing public relations literature sometimes suggest that you should plan by identifying all the elements of your campaign and then present these to your superiors and finance departments, outlining the budget needed to complete the works. And the decision-makers will then assess the proposal and either release the appropriate funds, ask for modifications or reject the campaign concept.

In practice this is rarely the way the real world works. In the vast majority of cases, especially if you are working for a publicly funded charity or academic organisation, the budget is the overriding factor. So you will find it much less work, and more likely to be successful, if in the first stage of your campaign planning you discover how much money is available, and then build a realistic campaign around that sum. Effective campaigns can be run for €1,000, £10,000 or $100,000, but you will only know it was successful if you plan it in advance and you somehow measure the outcome.

Elements of a health or medical public relations campaign

The first thing you need to ask yourself therefore, when planning any public relations activity, is what is your aim, or for more complex campaigns hoping for several outcomes, what are your aims? Will it contribute to your organisation's overall mission? Are you trying to raise awareness of a new treatment, an unusual disease, change public behaviour or attitudes? Do you have a specific goal in mind, such as recruiting patients for a health study or is it a wider and more general aim such as improving your media relations?

15 Points for campaign planning

1. Aims
2. Objectives
3. Background
4. Scoping or research
5. Target audiences
6. Strategy or plan
7. Tactics or methods
8. Messages
9. Resources
10. Budget
11. Timetable
12. Monitoring
13. Feedback
14. Evaluation
15. Review

Once you have identified your broad strategic aim you need to consider your objectives. These are the specific goal or goals that you need to achieve in order to reach your overall aim. For example, if your overall aim is to prevent the spread of hospital acquired infections, your objectives might include:

- raising the number of people who know that hand-washing is an effective way to prevent the spread of hospital acquired infections;
- reducing the number of people who fail to wash or sanitise their hands upon entering and leaving a hospital ward;
- improving the accuracy and frequency of media coverage about how hospital acquired infections can be prevented.

Your objectives need to be effective and appropriate. According to Jon Cope, this often falls down at the evaluation stage. He quotes Tom Watson and Paul Noble's 2007 book *Evaluating Public Relations*:[3]

> The bedrock of the effective evaluation of public relations programmes and activities is setting appropriate and effective objectives. All too often, PR campaign objectives are poorly articulated, impossible to measure or simply not achievable within permitted time or budgetary constraints. To avoid your campaign objectives meeting a similar fate be aware of the difference between types of objective. Objectives are typically classified in relation to either outputs, outtakes or outcomes:

- **Outputs** are physical things and organised events such as press releases, press briefings, booklets, posters and stickers.

- **Outtakes** are what your target audiences 'take' from your campaign's outputs. Does the audience understand what you are trying to communicate?
- **Outcomes** are the measurable things that have changed as a result of your PR activities in their knowledge, attitudes or behaviour.

When you come to evaluating what your campaign has achieved, you should make sure that each of your defined objectives is being evaluated so that you can measure your success. Which means that when you are defining your specific objectives, you should make sure that everything that you choose can realistically be measured and evaluated.

Obviously your commissioning client or in-house senior colleagues will have a good idea of the current context and, hopefully, why your public relations campaign is being run. But it is still a good idea to include a section on background to make sure that everyone understands the reasons for it, the remit of your brief and why resources should be spent on this activity. Keep this section short, it's not a PhD literature review or definitive historical document, but it should help to define the current situation as it is now and focus attention on what needs changing.

If you are dealing with commercial clients rather than academic ones they may expect this background section to include a SWOT analysis – a brief table identifying the strengths, weaknesses, opportunities and threats that are currently available or relevant to your campaign. In crisis planning this is obviously much more important than in everyday press liaison, but even so, you are supposed to be the expert advisor within your organisation, so it may be wise to do a quick analysis for even the simplest projects.

If you do not know everything that you need to before you start the campaign, or if your project has not arisen as an idea out of some survey results that need addressing, then you are going to have to do some research or carry out a scoping exercise.

A scoping or framing exercise seeks to find out which particular aspects of an issue need to be addressed and are a way of identifying key concerns at an early stage in planning your campaigns or actions. Most public relations campaigns are not trying to address a long-running or slow-burning sensitive issue, so do not need major scoping exercises first. For simple campaigns some basic background research should suffice.

Of course, background research for a medical or health campaign is different from the research you might carry out to support the marketing effort for an ordinary commercial product. No one but an idiot would imagine that you could research the market to find out how many people suffer from hay fever and then simply design a new medicine with fewer side effects that would target that lucrative market. That's not how drugs are developed.

But you may need to find out which decision-makers sit on which parliamentary committees, how many people suffer from a specific disease every year or what the public and relevant pressure groups think about a subject such as stem cell therapy. You may also want to find out how people – especially the stakeholders – view the current situation, how happy they are with the way things are at the moment and what reactions you are likely to get if you try to change things. In these circumstances, a scoping exercise should show up any particular concerns that you have missed, as the way your audiences understand an issue may not be at all the same as the way your organisation does.

Once you have worked out the context of your campaign you can start to identify the various target audiences that different aspects of your activities will need to address and influence. If you do not already know who your audiences are then your research should have helped to identify them. Who are you trying to communicate with? Is there a special interest group for patients? Who are the decision-makers?

Target audiences

For simplicity's sake, you may want to classify your target audiences into three relevant groups:

- **Known Don't Knows**: people who have a problem but don't really know about it, such as young people at risk from sexually transmitted diseases.
- **Known Knows**: those who know about the problem and are concerned, but don't know what to do, such as family doctors, parents and teachers.
- **Knowers**: those that are actively involved in the issue and are trying to do something about it, such as family planning clinics.
- **Unknowns**: if we followed the logic of Donald Rumsfeld's famous saying about known knowns, we could also identify a fourth group whom we don't know have the problem and for whom we can't do anything. But it's fairly pointless to commit your resources to targeting this group, especially as you won't be able to measure any outcomes.

In addition to each group you are specifically trying to reach and influence, you should also consider who the other stakeholders are who may be engaged in this issue or who need to have their feelings and views taken into consideration. Do you have internal audiences as well as external ones that you need to reach? Do particular specialisms among nurses or doctors have a view on your issue? Will they be upset by the things you intend to say? What do patients and users know? What does the media think? Most campaigns will involve targeting several different audiences with several different strands of activity.

Your next creative step is to work out how you are going to achieve your aims and therefore what strategy you will use. Strategy is the overall big picture or framework that enables you to achieve your aims, compared with the tactics, or methods, which are the everyday activities you will need to do such as writing and issuing press releases.

Strategy is therefore a plan that helps you decide how to achieve your objectives, and also helps you to decide how to prioritise your target audiences and activities when you have limited budgets or resources. Without a well-thought-out strategy, any activities you undertake are just random efforts to do something or look busy, without any clear aim which will let you know what you have achieved and when you have achieved it.

Organ transplants

Example campaign: Our campaign aim is to provide the best and cheapest treatment for some severely ill patients. Our objective is to increase the number of hearts, kidneys and other organs available for transplants each year. The background is that we need more organs for transplants in the UK than we currently have every year, with many patients dying on the waiting lists.

From research we already know that some countries in Europe have higher donor rates than others, which may be due to different laws about organ donation and different systems of gaining consent to remove organs for transplants. But we also know that some areas of the UK successfully get more organs per million residents than other parts of the country, and the highest donation rates are comparable with the highest rates in Europe, so it cannot just be the law that makes the difference.

To achieve better donation rates we may decide on a strategy of targeting NHS staff, focusing on doctors and nurses in intensive care units. From our investigation and research, we know that ICUs are the key places where potential organ donors sometimes die while on artificial ventilators, thus making their organs medically suitable for retrieval.

Our specific tactic may be to disseminate to the target audience of ICU doctors and nurses the message that bereaved families get comfort from organ donation – which can save the lives of up to seven other sick patients – especially at a time of their own family tragedy. Our strategy is aimed at reducing any reluctance from ICU staff to offer the option of organ donation to distressed relatives at a critical time, and when the staff are themselves upset because their own efforts have failed and their patient has died.

The remainder of your campaign planning will involve working out the best, most sensitive and most convincing way of delivering your key message to ICU staff. Where do they get information? Is there any prejudice and resistance to organ donation which will need to be addressed first?

What resources will you need? Will you need to get personal testimonies and perhaps help with site visits from donor families to explain the comfort that they got? Will you need personal testimonies and site visits from organ recipients to show how successful transplants are? Have any celebrities had transplants, and would they be prepared to help? How long should your campaign run for? Are there enough donors every year for any statistical analysis to be significant?

So once you have identified a suitable strategy for your own campaign, you now need to get down to deciding the most practical and realistic way of carrying it out by identifying the methods or tactics that you will use. Tactics could include mobilising social media such as blogs, RSS feeds (really simple syndication, a way of receiving constantly updated information from selected websites by using a news reader program), chatrooms, Twitter and the main social media sites, developing a website, issuing press releases or starting a newsletter for supporters and patients. Or simply take the three key decision-makers to lunch.

Analyses

Commercial clients may expect the tactics or background section of your campaign plan to include a **PEST analysis** or its closely related cousin a **STEER analysis.** PEST identifies the current politico-legal, economic, socio-cultural and technological factors affecting your target audiences, the environment in which you will be operating and your own technical capabilities relevant to your campaign. STEER looks at similar factors such as socio-cultural, technological, environmental (usually understood in the green, eco sense), economic and regulatory issues. Choose the one that best suits your issue. There are several similar mnemonics covering other types of analyses and also similar shorter versions of our planning checklist including ROSIE – research, objectives, strategy, influence, evaluation. But be careful as acronyms often mean different things to different audiences. ROSIE was also a drug-treatment-effectiveness study, known as the Research Outcomes Study in Ireland, published in 2009. Keep it simple, stick to the better-known ones like SWOT and PEST until you find what works best for you. **PEST** factors:

- **Politico-legal** issues such as whether the current government is likely to pass new laws or change regulations that will affect your aims or your audiences, and how stable the current political situation is – so don't embark on a major new campaign two weeks before a general election.
- **Economic** will include factors that could affect your campaign such as rising interest rates, insurance costs or changing currency exchange rates if you are running an international campaign.
- **Socio-cultural** influences vary from place to place and between town and countryside, from country to country, and from one continent or world region to another. They will include the influences of differing religions, languages and gender roles within societies. What proportion of income is spent on medicine and healthcare and does everyone have equal access to aid? What is their life expectancy and their attitude to the elderly or disabled? Does society have a concept of risk and hazard and what weight does it give to green or environmental issues such as pollution, clean air and water? Will you need to pay commissions (or bribes)

to middlemen? How popular is business, and do people support wealth creation or consumer products and services provided by business and industry? Do consumers favour conventional medicines or is there a big market for alternative remedies?

- **Technological** factors such as internet access and mobile phones may make research cheaper and easier or message communication faster and simpler. Can you get products and services developed and delivered faster, cheaper or more efficiently thanks to superior technology? Can you now communicate with your target audiences in new and exciting ways which will give you an advantage over rival organisations or competing interests? Do your customers now expect you to have new interactive or internet-based services to support your operations?

Returning to our checklist for campaign planning, this is now a soundbite-sized world, so you have to work out what your key messages are. Start building them into every single communication activity, whether it is talking to decision-makers, issuing press releases or having your representatives speaking on the radio or in podcasts on your website.

By key messages we do not mean the bland pap that passes for mission statements in local councils such as 'Dullsville, a lovely place to work' or 'Boringtown, a great place to plan to visit other places from'. We mean useful, constructive or meaningful statements such as 'one in four people on the transplant waiting list die before they can get a new heart'. If you are planning to use Twitter, or hoping to be retweeted, then does your key message fit into 140 characters?

Logically, the next item on the checklist should be budgets, but before you start estimating how much money this campaign is likely to cost in cash terms, it is worth working out what it is also going to cost in terms of time and effort. So the next item needs to be resources.

You will need two sorts of resources for your campaign, whether you are working in-house or in a consultancy for a client: you may need equipment such as data projectors, voice recorders and exhibition stands. And you will certainly need client input (if you are working in-house this will be some senior management time from your specialists and spokespeople, and your own time to manage the project aside from all your other normal duties).

It is absolutely no use at all to put in all the effort needed to set up and launch a project or campaign if your client or your senior staff are not going to have time to carry out their part of the project. If you make it explicit from the start what resources you will need then you will be in a much better position to negotiate if things later go wrong or budgets are cut. Properly assessing the resources you need will also make sure that you do not find yourself overstretched and unable to do your own part of the work.

Now that you know what is needed for your campaign you can set out a realistic budget, which should include at least 10 per cent margin for contingencies.

However, if you overprice your project and cannot demonstrate that it offers value for money, then senior staff and finance departments are likely to veto it. Or worse, if you are in a consultancy, your competitors are likely to win the contract instead of you.

In academic and medical charity work, from personal experience, we estimate that about half the campaigns that get agreed start from knowing a maximum possible budget (including any overspend on contingencies) and are then developed backwards as a realistic possibility of what can be achieved for that much money. In a public relations consultancy you will need to distinguish between fees to cover your time and disbursements which will be the costs of the campaign, and on top of which your agency will expect to make a further profit margin. If you are working in-house, will you need extra help from specialists from an agency?

The next item on our checklist for planning a campaign is the timetable. You need to work out how much time each aspect of your strategy is going to take and when the significant milestones will need to be completed. You may have discovered during your research that there is a designated week of activities which is relevant to your campaign, such as National Transplant Week, which you will either want to avoid clashing with to save confusion, or coincide with to enhance media coverage.

Timetables

For something as simple as sending out a press release to make an announcement during your campaign you will need at least a month of preparation:

- arranging to interview the senior people that you will quote, or researching the human interest, and then writing the thing can take one week;
- getting your draft text checked by senior staff or clients and making the revisions needed takes another week;
- getting the text signed off, formatted and posted on a science media website or out to journalists through emailing lists takes a third week;
- journalists themselves want a final week to prepare their stories, interview stakeholders and publish their articles or compile their broadcast packages to hit the embargo deadline, so that everyone is making the announcement at the same time.

These days there is a day, week, month or possibly a year for just about every conceivable disease, charity or cause, from Alzheimer's disease to zoology departments promoting National Science Week. Even the public relations industry's own professional body, the Chartered Institute of Public Relations, still can't decide whether they actually work or not, or whether there are now too many of them to be effective. But for journalists they are often an easy option on quiet news days or as a peg to hang a feature idea on. Technically these dedicated periods, like National Transplant Week, are known as cause-related events and their promotion is called cause-related marketing, which has spawned a whole branch of the public relations industry.

The next difficult decision you are going to have to make is about monitoring your progress. How are you going to track the success of your campaign? If you are trying to alert patients to the idea that clinical trials or further research into their disease is going to start shortly, you can judge success by the number of enquiries you get to a response number or on a website. For all types of campaign you will have needed to think about the way you hope to monitor success or track your progress when you originally defined your objectives.

Every single objective you chose must be measurable and achievable in a realistic way within your project, and you will need to have set cut-off times or limits within which that success needs to be achieved. For many campaign objectives, such as changing public opinion on an issue, raising awareness of a problem, product or service, you will have to carry out further research during or after your campaign to see how opinions are changing, and possibly at a set time in the future as well, to see whether the effect was long-lasting.

But if your campaign includes media activities then you have a much harder task to track all the published articles, news broadcasts and internet mentions gained by your project. Often this is precisely the information that your senior managers or clients will want when judging the financial cost of a campaign against its economic returns.

It is possible to pick up and get copies of most of the national newspaper press cuttings and national news broadcasts in Europe over a short period through media monitoring companies, although this will often almost double the costs of a campaign. Some companies even claim to be able to track all appearances of your campaign's issues, organisation's name, spokespeople and keywords on the internet websites and blogs. But a huge proportion of these internet mentions will simply be word-for-word reprints or 'cut-and-pastes' of your press release on bulletins and blogs designed to attract advertising revenues, which are desperate for vaguely relevant new content that is also likely to attract search engines looking for key words. They will have simply downloaded and published your press release and news statements from the international science media websites.

If you try to monitor regional or local newspapers, regional television and radio, feature articles and magazines, as well as national ones, your costs will almost certainly exceed your budget for everything else needed to run the campaign, including your own time, and that of your chief executive (and her pension).

It is simply not usually realistic to try to monitor all instances of a press release's take-up, so you should also keep a careful record of all enquiries from journalists. Drum into your colleagues and any of your senior staff and researchers who are likely to be approached as spokespeople that they need to do the same so that you can later check whether that media outlet used the piece.

Your campaign also needs a feedback mechanism built in, so that if it starts misfiring or going horribly wrong you can correct it before too much damage is done. Very few campaigns are ever designed perfectly from the start, so for campaigns wishing to change public opinions you may want to consider holding pilot projects or tests on a small scale or focus groups (see Chapter 10, 'Surveys', p.104) before you launch the main thrust of your project.

A little like film or theatre companies testing their stage productions and movies out in the provinces before embarking on a major and expensive national run, you should analyse the early media mentions that you get for content as well as size and quality of coverage. Are the media commentators broadly supportive, and do any criticisms they make really matter? If you can pick up problems early and have built in a method of altering your approach to respond to public or professional opinion, then you have a useful feedback mechanism.

The last stage of most campaigns is the evaluation. How are you intending to measure the value of what you have achieved? Designing effective evaluation will present almost as many challenges as monitoring your campaign. What do you count as a success?

For a media campaign are you simply measuring volume of coverage, or weighting it for quality, or also analysing the content for positive and negative reactions? You need to think about how you will define the way you are going to evaluate your success for every one of your objectives at the time when you set them – or at least make sure that you only choose objectives that can be measured.

Finally, and this is the step that is missed more often than any other, you need to build a review stage into your campaign plan at the very start so that things that go wrong can be avoided next time, lessons that need to be learned are brought out, and so that your successes are recognised. If you don't insist on this from the start you will find that reviews are only carried out when things have gone horribly, horribly wrong and senior management are looking for a scapegoat to blame. You.

You need to have a review after every campaign, especially the successful ones, to make sure that you come to your superiors' or clients' attention whenever things have gone right to counterbalance the hopefully rare times when things have gone wrong. It also gives you a good opportunity to pitch your next idea to the key decision-makers.

References

1. Donatella H. Meadows (ed. Diana Wright), *Thinking in Systems*, Earthscan, 2009.
2. Anne Gregory, *Planning and Managing Public Relations Campaigns: A Strategic Approach: A Step-by-step Guide (PR In Practice)*, Chartered Institute of Public Relations, 1996.
3. Tom Watson & Paul Noble, *Evaluating Public Relations*, published by Kogan Page in association with the CIPR's PR in Practice series, 2007.

10 Communication, consultation and access

In the previous chapters we have looked at the nuts and bolts of public relations practice, the craft techniques that you will need if you are going to try to communicate your clients' messages and manage their reputations. From here and into the following chapters we will stray into areas of opinion and issues, where the crucial points to take into consideration before planning your actions become a matter of personal judgement rather than an easy to follow set of rules.

You are free to accept or reject my opinion as you choose, and indeed for many applications, my reading of the right course or response to a situation might be considered inappropriate – it all depends upon what you want. So if it is important to you personally to uphold the highest ethical principles then you may follow one route, but if you simply want to chalk up a quick win, then other options will be available to you and you will be able to ignore some issues that I would consider important.

I suggest that you treat the following chapters as a discussion with many possible outcomes. If you find yourself disagreeing with me, then that is fine, so long as you can articulate why you disagree and, if it came to a public debate, could muster a strong argument to support your view and rebut my submission instead. Sometimes when we are drafting a speech, strategy or press release, it is helpful to do a quick draft for internal use and put it up for discussion with the decision-makers, who can then see what they don't like, which makes it easier to clarify what you and they are trying to say instead.

Communication theory

Where and how do we learn our ideas, memes or methods of working? I have had 30 years of practice at speaking without notes, and too often over the years have outlined or drafted the nearly-final-version of speeches, lectures and conference or seminar presentations at the airport and on the aeroplane, while on the way to give the talk. I figure that I will remember most of the important stuff that I want to say and that anything I forget was simply not that important. Do not copy this.

I do know that I have crowdsourced much of my in-service learning from the thousands of postgraduate students, postdocs, senior executives, politicians, scientists, doctors, engineers, nurses, midwives, press officers and academic lecturers whom I have had the enormous pleasure of working with, meeting and teaching on media training, issue management and science communication workshops over the past 30 years.

Consequently, although I know that it is absolutely sacrosanct for academics to credit their sources, and I agree with this generous impulse in principle, all too often it is impossible for me to pin down exactly where I first heard something, or indeed to properly credit it to its original published source. We seem to just absorb some information out of the ether, and in practice, it is only when trying to write a formal journal paper, report or other publication that is itself likely to be cited that we tend to go back and try to find and credit the original source.

The accumulated public relations literature today contains a lot of discussion about mass communication theories, which sadly I have never had enough time to read thoroughly, learn and internalise. The only useful diagram on communication flow that I have seen, I first saw demonstrated by Martin Taylor when he was a senior tutor for the Joint Training Services of the UK Research Councils and speaking at the science communication workshops I designed and ran for the Natural Environment Research Council. A well-read reviewer has since informed me that this communications model was developed by Shannon and Weaver.[1] This is the simplified version I was shown:

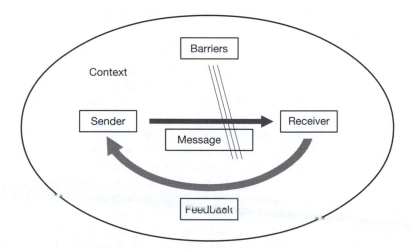

Figure 10.1 Communication. The flow diagram represents any **communication** action, or **message**, which is sent from one person or organisation, the **sender**, to another, the **receiver**, via a **medium**, which could be by speaking, sending a letter, email, or through the press, broadcast or social media, and across any other **barriers** which it has to pass through before being received. Often the sender will then get some **feedback** indicating that the message has been received and in some way **interpreted**. In order to pass through the medium the message first needs to be **encoded** by the sender and then **decoded** by the receiver. All of this activity happens within a **context** of time, place, the relationships between the sender and receiver, and any other socio-political influences which affect the interpretation of this message. And this happens for every single communication activity that you undertake.

So if we want public relations activities that communicate our key messages to our audiences, or indeed if we want to get feedback or reaction to our proposals from a group of our stakeholders, then we need to find a context in which those messages can be sent and received. In addition, we need to consider the way that our audiences want to receive those messages, the context in which they are likely to hear them and the types and content of messages that they will accept. As my first public relations head of department, Tony Court, said way back in 1980: 'It's not what we want to say to people, it's what they can hear that matters.'

Instead of having one-way communications with our audiences, today we try to have two-way dialogues, or even more meaningful interactions. The internet, World Wide Web and the rise of social media has changed forever the way organisations and their publics relate to each other. It is no longer good enough to just tell people things that we think they need to know; now we need to consult them, interact with them, make them feel valued and perhaps even reassure them that our organisations are part of their lives. And in these days of social media, that may mean being a part of their social lives as well as their business dealings. Different audiences have different expectations, but many will now seek to interact or engage with your organisation in previously unimaginable ways.

Consultation, public dialogue and independent scrutiny

In June 2010, Professor Brian Wynne of Lancaster University, one of the UK government's senior advisors and an expert on public consultation, resigned as vice-chair of the Food Standards Agency's genetically modified food dialogue steering group. The steering group was about to undertake a £500,000 research exercise into public opinion on GM food in response to widespread health and environmental concerns.

Wynne alleged that the planned consultation was 'biased in favour of the GM technology and was little more than propaganda for the industry', according to a *Guardian* newspaper article.[2] He also suggested to *Country Smallholding* magazine that to have a proper dialogue about GM concerns any consultation exercise should be in two or three phases.[3] First, checking public opinion about GM foods and crops; then consideration and a response from government; then further public consultations and a final response from government so that all decisions were taken openly and accountably and people could clearly see why they were being made.

Anti-GM pressure group Friends of the Earth gleefully reported that Professor Wynne's departure followed the resignation of another steering group member, Dr Helen Wallace, who alleged that one of the contractors shortlisted to facilitate the dialogue – Ipsos Mori – was also engaged in reputation management for the GM industry. The *Guardian* newspaper report[4] quoted her as stating: 'Taxpayers' money should not be wasted on a PR exercise for the GM industry.'

While the GM consultation was still being framed, the new Environment Secretary in the Conservative–Liberal Democrat coalition government's Department for Environment Food and Rural Affairs, Caroline Spelman, herself a former biotechnology lobbyist, announced that she backed the commercial growing of GM crops.

The resignations of Wynne and Wallace highlighted the growing cynicism towards consultation processes undertaken by government departments. Both of these senior scientists seemed concerned that the consultation's purpose was not to establish the public mood on a controversial issue, GM foods, but rather to boost the reputation or credibility of the GM industry by publicising an apparently well-intentioned, but in fact meaningless, interaction with the general public.

By 2010, public and pressure group confidence in public consultations, and therefore in the public relations industry that conducts them, appeared to have reached a new low due to a string of similar sham dialogues in which the results may have been decided before the consultation was complete.

In October 2008, Greenpeace announced that the Marketing Standards Board, which sets the standard for opinion research, found that the UK government's market research company had breached the Code of Conduct in its second public consultation on nuclear power.[5] Greenpeace claimed that the board found information inaccurately or misleadingly presented, or imbalanced, which gave rise to a material risk of respondents being led towards a particular answer. This second consultation was commissioned after Greenpeace won a High Court ruling in 2007 that overturned the government's first public consultation on nuclear power, which the judge had ruled manifestly unfair and unlawful, according to Greenpeace's website.

These examples do at least show how far we, and decision-makers, moved in the past 20 years, that these consultation exercises were even considered.

Genetic modification

It was a major blow for the biotechnology industries when Greenpeace, Friends of the Earth, the Soil Association and other influential lobby groups first mounted a sustained and ultimately successful public campaign against GM foods in the UK and most of Europe in the early 1990s.

New medical discoveries, the function of specific genes for diseases such as cystic fibrosis, cancer and muscular dystrophy, and new cell transformation and genetic manipulation technology were being announced almost every day. At the time it seemed inevitable that major biotechnology companies would be allowed to move from laboratory experiments on tissues, or induced models of diseases in animals, into GM animals as better models for these and other genetically determined or inherited medical diseases. And at the same time into producing GM crops, which could be made tolerant of commercially available herbicides and pesticides, killing all competition from weeds and insect infestations, and therefore increasing our food yields at the expense of pest biodiversity.

In 1990, some research scientists who had been personally targeted, the UK Medical Research Council, the pharmaceutical industry and medical charities (who formed the Research for Health Charities Group, with me as its director from 1991 until it merged with the Association of Medical Research Charities in 1997) were already coping with and responding to a revived and increasingly vocal animal rights movement, which had in turn evolved from the anti-hunting lobby of the 1970s.

By 1995, UK Research Councils, and some industry and academic experts, were predicting that the public were only concerned about suffering in animals and would not be unduly worried about GM manipulation of plants. I disagreed, as I could see the parallels with the animal rights movement, and the scale of the funds opposing GM. They had underestimated the tenacity, creativity and wealth of the big international pressure groups. They had also underestimated the public's concern about health threats from food.

Government ministers and their advisers, and academic medical and veterinary experts, were also distracted from the GM foods debate by new health challenges. These were posed by the unexpected spread of Aids and HIV from the homosexual community into heterosexual drug users and then the wider public; the revival of tuberculosis in cities; and the emergence of new and frightening diseases such as bovine spongiform encephalopathy under its media-friendly name of mad cow disease, and its human version, new variant Creutzfeldt–Jakob disease (CJD). It was not until 2010 that the government felt confident enough to test the waters of public opinion again in a public GM opinion poll. A new era of response-driven public consultation had been born after Greenpeace's GM success.

Public consultation is a form of information-gathering or informal regulation in which the general public and groups representing various specific publics or special interests are invited to comment on matters affecting them, usually because the government is considering some major or controversial change in current practices, laws and regulations.

Consultation aims to improve the transparency of decision-making and gain legitimacy for the proposed change by involving the public in major projects, policies and legal changes. In the case of scientific research, consultations may be designed to reinforce science's licence to practise, especially in controversial areas, for example in stem cell research or cloning.

The battle for public opinion and media attention is still being constantly fought by pressure groups, industry, academics and politicians over an increasingly wide range of concerns. Today these include GM technology in medicine, crops and food, stem cell research, abortion, euthanasia and the right to die, animal experiments, nanotechnology, intellectual property and patents among other issues.

Without public support for a policy or course of action, politicians expect that voters, and especially taxpayers, who are opposed to any new policy or diversion of funds, will resent public money being spent on these projects and may punish the perceived architects of this change at the next election. Public consultation attempts to assess the prevailing mood and also identify potential problems that may be unforeseen by legislators but are obvious to particular special interest groups who will be affected by the proposed change.

Public consultation therefore usually starts with notification of the proposed topic that is being consulted upon. This may be in an informal consultation document, prompting a two-way flow of information and opinion exchange which may or may not be widely publicised. Or it may be made more formally through a government Green Paper, which is a first discussion paper or government proposal without any commitment to subsequent action. This may then lead to a White Paper, which is understood as a clear intention that a government is proposing to pass a new law or amend an existing one.

In Europe, according to the European Commission's own europa.eu web portal, European Commission White Papers[6] are documents that propose European Union action in a specific legislative area, and may follow a Green Paper, which was published to launch the consultation process at European level. Green Papers are published to stimulate discussion on a particular topic. They invite individuals or relevant bodies to participate in a consultation process and debate on the basis of the proposals put forward. Green Papers may eventually lead to proposed legal changes, which are then outlined in more detail in White Papers.

The term 'white paper', previously confined to government and legislative activities, is starting to leak into commercial marketing activities as well. A commercial white paper is aimed at raising market awareness of a new product, technology or service, generating sales leads or suggesting a solution to a problem. The commercial white paper will contain details of particular research and carefully chosen facts that support the specific product or service supplied by the company. In that sense it is very like a physician's drug information sheet or, allegedly, the published versions of a report on clinical trials when sponsored by a pharmaceutical company.

When I was running the public relations office at UK Transplant Service in the early 1980s, I once made the mistake of trying to advise the Department of Health civil servant responsible for our organisation. This was in the days before UK Transplant Service became a Special Health Authority, and when it was still funded directly from the Health Minister's own budget, which tended to make us unpopular when we overspent by finding homes for spare organs and therefore assisting with too many transplants, freeing up dialysis machines and allowing more patients to get treatment.

I was senior enough to be attending and reporting on my actions to the UK Transplant Service Management Committee meetings, and naïvely assumed that the responsible civil servant would be interested in my ideas to help publicise the desperate need for more kidneys, hearts and livers. So I suggested some patients' charities and medical research organisations that we could usefully debate with publicly, and then cooperate with to raise interest in and jointly promote organ donation. This would avoid the department's need to stump up all the cash, and attempt to shift the focus from the widely held but erroneous view that the

UK used an opting-in system based on donor cards, which actually made almost no practical difference to a person's chances of becoming a donor.

The civil service mandarin listened to me gravely and then said: 'Myc, we don't just work with or even talk to other organisations. When planning something we divide NGOs into three groups: those we inform; those we consult and those we cooperate with. We do not have public disagreements.'

Today the language has changed but the sentiment remains. You may find yourself dividing your friends, rivals and your critics among the NGOs, academics, public bodies, commercial organisations or even members of the general public as those your organisation wishes to simply inform (or tell, as we journalists say); those you consult, advise or engage with; and those you cooperate, collaborate or participate in joint ventures with. You may even have a special group of those you wish to be Linked-In to, Facebook friends with, Pinterested in or tweeting about.

Surveys

If you want to survey or take the temperature of public opinion (or sound out expert opinion) then you may wish to do it by using one particular way or even several different methods. The different ways of surveying opinion each tell you slightly different things and their costs vary hugely, depending upon the size of samples you consult. If you are later going to claim statistical accuracy, base a press announcement or major policy change on your findings, then we strongly recommend that you use a reputable opinion polling company or other recognised and independent academic expert to carry out your research for you.

Unless you have an information science qualification or are used to academic statistical analysis, then if you try to construct the survey yourselves you will almost certainly find it impossible to avoid observer bias or leading questions in the way you elicit your responses. This can lead to charges of propaganda or sham consultations, as identified at the beginning of this chapter by Prof Wynne in the GM public consultation case.

Some typical methods of consultation surveys:

- **Opinion polls**: Public opinion research is often used to find out what issues and proposals mean to people, sometimes using in-depth or unstructured interview questions with fairly small samples as qualitative research. The key factor in these is often the way the responses are interpreted by the interviewer. Opinion polls can also be used to mean a larger sample, typically now contacted through an internet survey, where the sample is weighted or constructed to represent the general population. The term 'opinion poll' often specifically refers to a political survey, designed to find out how people intend to vote on an issue. In any poll the responses are prone to bias because some groups of people will choose not to be interviewed, and some may give answers designed to please the questioner.

- **Questionnaires** or **surveys**: Research in which fairly large numbers of people are asked a standard set of questions, posed in exactly the same way, often with multiple-choice answers. The numerical data gained can be analysed, often by computer, and collated as quantitative research. The results are usually interpreted using statistical analyses. This type of research can be conducted by telephone or be internet-based, but is prone to bias and errors caused by the way the questions are phrased, the order they are asked in or the different groups of people who choose to respond. People with very strong views are more likely to express them, as are people who oppose the proposition.

- **Focus groups**: A form of group interview. In the focus group, a random or specifically chosen selection of people who might be expected to represent the target audience of your proposal, or simply the general public, are invited (often by paying a small fee to them and providing refreshments) to come to a neutral place such as an hotel conference room. They are briefed about the aims of the group exercise, then shown the idea (for instance a new information leaflet design or a proposal for cervical smears) and asked to consider it and then comment on it in a structured exercise. They may then be encouraged to discuss the project as a group and answer a set of specific questions using a preprepared questionnaire (giving some quantitative feedback as they all answer the same questions), and also make free-form comments (giving some qualitative feedback about their personal feelings). The findings may either form a simple statistical reaction to the proposal, or may be interpreted further by an expert to try to understand the reaction to the topic or issue in the respondent's own terms.[7]

- **Delphi groups**: A way of assessing expert opinion on a subject, named from its 'consulting the oracle' associations, sometimes known as a consensus method. The participants in a Delphi group are either specifically selected for their range and expertise by the interviewers, or some issues may be recommended by the group members themselves. You could for instance initially ask one or two recognised experts in a field, especially those from opposing viewpoints or areas such as industry, NGOs, academia and government, who they think are the key thinkers and experts in this field. The second group are then asked in turn to list who they think the recognised experts are, and any expert listed by three or more of these people, or by people from two different areas, is invited to participate in the Delphi group. Delphi group members may sometimes not know who the other participants are. In any case, because of the problems of getting a group of busy experts together at the same time in the same place, Delphi group consultations are often conducted by email (previously we used letters and questionnaires), circulated in several stages. Members are invited to comment on an initial proposal, and then circulated with all of the comments from the group, so that they further respond to and comment on each other's ideas and assessments.[8]

Other survey methods are available. In the UK, the Association for Qualitative Research, founded in 1980 as the Association of Qualitative Research

Practitioners, can suggest suitable methods of consultation and provide a list of association members. It does not yet appear to have Chartered Institute status. As a test of the power of public relations, and your understanding of professionalism, you should now decide whether it is simply a loose trade association or whether the qualifications for membership constitute a suitable professional recommendation. Or you could ask a responsible social science academic.

Medical, health and science communicators

Some time back, senior scientists, the pharmaceutical industry and policymakers realised that the public were losing confidence in science generally and did not necessarily have a rational response to health scares such as flesh-eating superbugs, mad cow disease or combined measles, mumps and rubella (MMR) vaccines. They decided that something had to be done to improve the public understanding of science, accidentally spawning an entirely new branch of the public relations industry – science communication.

This discipline has quickly gained its own specialists, called science communicators, who may be seconded from industry, from backgrounds in medical or science journalism, from charities and non-governmental organisations or from academic research.

In the UK, the British Science Association now runs an annual two-day Science Communication Conference; in 2012 the theme was 'Impact'. Europe has a biennial Euroscience Open Forum, one of the largest international conferences aimed specifically at science communicators. It was founded by five European foundations: Compagnia di San Paolo, Fondazione Cariplo, Riksbankens Jubileumsfond, Robert Bosch Stiftung GmbH and Stifterverband für die Deutsche Wissenschaft, in partnership with Euroscience, based in Strasbourg. The 2014 Euroscience Open Forum will be in Copenhagen, Sweden.

For visual and interactive ways of communicating science, including biomedical disciplines, some of the best examples from more than 25 countries are shown at the biennial European science teaching festival Science on Stage. This festival was originally started with European Commission funding by the seven major science facilities, including CERN, the European Space Agency and the European Molecular Biology Laboratory. Together they make up the EIROforum. Science on Stage is now organised by a consortium of national committees from offices in Berlin, Germany. It presents the European Science Teacher of the Year Awards, for which I was one of the judges at CERN in 2005, and I have hosted the Highlights shows there and main stage events at the three subsequent festivals in Grenoble, Berlin and Copenhagen, and have been asked to host the 2013 joint Polish and German festival, so I may be a little biased.

Deficit, dialogue and upstream engagement

The deficit model of science communication is based on an assumption that the public doesn't care enough about science and therefore doesn't support scientific and medical research, simply because most people don't know about it.

So, the theory goes, if they just knew more, they would support it more. Under this model, experts such as senior doctors, industry specialists and academics would just need to pass their own information down through the supply chain, and the public will magically start supporting science. This in turn will make the public accept animal experiments, GM manipulation, stem cell research, increased science funding, higher salaries for researchers and any other issues that people currently and unaccountably oppose because of their present ignorance.

As you will appreciate, this didn't work too well. The more senior, revered and august the scientist, the more they were assumed to know by the scientific community. So the great, the good and the frankly geriatric were wheeled out to make definitive pronouncements about their fields of science. The classic deficit model delivery is sometimes known today as 'death by Powerpoint'.

Ordinary people and pressure groups objected to being hectored as though they were stupid, and became even more resentful and suspicious of arrogant scientific experts who appeared totally divorced from the everyday concerns of people who were worried about our increasing technological ability to tamper with nature and natural processes. For an example of deficit model communication you could have a look at the slides for 'Exploring the different careers in science', a Science Council presentation at the University of Leicester in February 2012.[9]

Back in the real world, the scientific community retreated, licked its wounds and rethought its approach. Suddenly in the 1990s the buzzword became public dialogue rather than communicating science *to* the public. The new concept was to enter into a two-way discussion with the public about issues of concern, rather than simply telling people what they should think. You could visualise this as an advance similar to moving from the stone age to the bronze age. People didn't abandon all their stone tools and suddenly start using metal implements. It was a slow, gradual but jerky shift at different speeds and in different places.

In April 1993, the government published the White Paper 'Realising Our Potential: A Strategy for Science Engineering and Technology'.[10] This was preceded by an extensive consultation exercise, leading to some proposed reforms. Amongst the four main purposes set out in the White Paper was an aim to 'develop greater understanding and appreciation of science, engineering and technology by the British public'. The way the White Paper proposed to achieve this was through 'a new campaign to spread the understanding of science through schools and amongst the public'. This wording was interpreted by some of the existing publicly funded science communicators as a call to step up their deficit model activities. It was interpreted by a few others as time to move into genuine dialogue.

In his final address as President of the Royal Society in December 1995, Sir Michael Atiyah said:

> Science now occupies too important a position in modern life to turn the clock back. The question we scientists face now is how to conduct our relations with government and industry so as to regain the confidence of the public. It is no use complaining that the public is simply ill-informed. We have

The answer, I later discovered, was that some of the scientists conducting the trials had wished to, but that was not what they had been funded to research. If the public had been allowed to set the remit of the trials, the questions it was designed to answer, they almost certainly would have insisted on this three-way comparison. It still raises the question, if research is being carried out in the wider public interest, with public funds, should the public be allowed (or trusted) to have a closer hand in commissioning it?

By 2004, this concept of an early agenda setting role for the public in such proposals was being named 'upstream engagement', a term picked up, or even possibly invented, by the Demos think tank in its publication,[14] by James Wilsdon and Rebecca Willis, of 'See-through Science: Why Public Engagement Needs to Move Upstream'. This excellent and stimulating discussion pamphlet seems to have been prompted by rising concerns about future public acceptance of nano-technology, amid fears that the debate would follow the same route as the public rejection of GM foods and crops.

The deficit model of science communications can be thought of as push technology, where information is pushed out from an organisation in the hope that people will accept and use it. Dialogue and upstream engagement can be thought of as pull technologies, where once they are aware of an issue, audiences who wish for further information actively seek it out and therefore create a demand for more. The most successful providers of Web 2.0 or social media are fostering pull communications.

Given all this careful thought about the need to fully understand your audiences, targeting them with specifically chosen messages and engaging them with the sorts of information that they are specifically interested in, it is extraordinary to discover how many press officers still just randomly send out, email or post press releases on media websites without tailoring them to their target journalists and publications.

Petitions, protests and marches

Petitions have been a longstanding way of expressing public or grassroots disquiet to authority figures, mainly those in government and local planners. Governments do take note of the numbers of people signing them, but 1,000 individual letters (and not simply duplicated form versions) will carry more weight with decision-makers than a single petition with 1,000 signatures, as the suspicion is that many people do not know quite what they are signing and that signatures may be duplicated or faked. The UK government has brought in an e-petition facility, with the suggestion that issues that attract more than 100,000 signatures may get presented to parliament for debate. But not necessarily.

Independent online forums such as 38 Degrees have also sprung up, becoming especially popular during the Occupy protest movements of 2011. As skiers and snowboarders know, 38 degrees is the angle at which avalanches happen, and the website's mission is to enable enough people to act together to create an avalanche for change. The group has a relatively democratic method of asking

So, the theory goes, if they just knew more, they would support it more. Under this model, experts such as senior doctors, industry specialists and academics would just need to pass their own information down through the supply chain, and the public will magically start supporting science. This in turn will make the public accept animal experiments, GM manipulation, stem cell research, increased science funding, higher salaries for researchers and any other issues that people currently and unaccountably oppose because of their present ignorance.

As you will appreciate, this didn't work too well. The more senior, revered and august the scientist, the more they were assumed to know by the scientific community. So the great, the good and the frankly geriatric were wheeled out to make definitive pronouncements about their fields of science. The classic deficit model delivery is sometimes known today as 'death by Powerpoint'.

Ordinary people and pressure groups objected to being hectored as though they were stupid, and became even more resentful and suspicious of arrogant scientific experts who appeared totally divorced from the everyday concerns of people who were worried about our increasing technological ability to tamper with nature and natural processes. For an example of deficit model communication you could have a look at the slides for 'Exploring the different careers in science', a Science Council presentation at the University of Leicester in February 2012.[9]

Back in the real world, the scientific community retreated, licked its wounds and rethought its approach. Suddenly in the 1990s the buzzword became public dialogue rather than communicating science *to* the public. The new concept was to enter into a two-way discussion with the public about issues of concern, rather than simply telling people what they should think. You could visualise this as an advance similar to moving from the stone age to the bronze age. People didn't abandon all their stone tools and suddenly start using metal implements. It was a slow, gradual but jerky shift at different speeds and in different places.

In April 1993, the government published the White Paper 'Realising Our Potential: A Strategy for Science Engineering and Technology'.[10] This was preceded by an extensive consultation exercise, leading to some proposed reforms. Amongst the four main purposes set out in the White Paper was an aim to 'develop greater understanding and appreciation of science, engineering and technology by the British public'. The way the White Paper proposed to achieve this was through 'a new campaign to spread the understanding of science through schools and amongst the public'. This wording was interpreted by some of the existing publicly funded science communicators as a call to step up their deficit model activities. It was interpreted by a few others as time to move into genuine dialogue.

In his final address as President of the Royal Society in December 1995, Sir Michael Atiyah said:

> Science now occupies too important a position in modern life to turn the clock back. The question we scientists face now is how to conduct our relations with government and industry so as to regain the confidence of the public. It is no use complaining that the public is simply ill-informed. We have

to examine our own position to see whether any of the criticisms levelled against us are valid.

Quoting Atiyah two years later in an article 'The pressure group problem' for the Royal Society and British Association for the Advancement of Science journal *Science and Public Affairs*,[11] I wrote:

> Precious little has changed in the two years since … [it is] scientists themselves who now have to justify their actions. They have worked their way into this position by being terrible communicators and by not recognising the validity of the criticisms levelled against them.

The same day that this article appeared, I was one of the invited speakers at Newcastle-upon-Tyne University in the first formal session of the British Association Science Festival's newly established Science Communicators Forum.

In April 2000, the Parliamentary Select Committee on Science and Technology decided to examine the impact of 'Realising Our Potential', but was forestalled by the government releasing a new White Paper in July 2000 called 'Excellence and Opportunity: A Science and Innovation Policy for the 21st Century'. This second White Paper surprisingly made no mention of the 1993 one, but identified three main objectives, of which one was 'to restore public confidence in science'.

The House of Commons Select Committee's Sixth Report, eventually published in March 2001, considered both these earlier government White Papers and other relevant initiatives. Amongst its recommendations it says: 'There needs to be a better dialogue between scientists and the public.' It also noted: 'We welcome the increasing use of the term "Science and Society" or, even better, "Science for Society", to describe activities to promote dialogue and mutual understanding between the scientific community and the public.'[12]

This was a clear call for publicly funded bodies to move from deficit models of science communication to a more two-way communication process. Suddenly academic chairs appeared. And then changed from being a Professor of the Public Understanding of Science, with the first UK appointments of Kathy Sykes at Bristol University in 2002 as a part-time post and full-time since 2006, and evolutionary biologist and atheist Richard Dawkins at Oxford University from 1995–2008, to being a Professor of Public Engagement in Science, with physicist and TV presenter Jim Al-Khalili at Surrey University in 2006. And most recently, on 1 February 2012, with the first medical incumbent, clinical anatomist Alice Roberts, best known as an archaeological bone expert in the long-running Channel 4 television programme *Time Team*, taking the chair at Birmingham University.

The vogue for dialogue has moved from academic science and research funding bodies through to medical charities and clinical practice, with physicians and nurses now expected to listen to their patients as well as telling them information. And of course into government consultation, or the hastily convened NHS Future Forum listening exercise, as the 2011 foray by the Coalition Government was termed, as it paused in its restructuring (some say privatisation) of the UK National Health Service in the face of overwhelming opposition from patients' groups and medical royal colleges.

The concept behind public dialogue and community engagement is a good one – instead of just telling the target audience what you think they need to know, you are attempting to find out what they actually hear, and then addressing their concerns as they come up. It allows for a much deeper level of mutual understanding, and so comes closer to the more recent definitions of public relations that we saw in Chapter 1. However, it is still arguably a process philosophically based on the original deficit model of communications, which claimed that if people just knew more they would agree with the proposals.

By the early 2000s, the debate, especially within my own speciality of not-for-profit sector issue management, had moved further and several of us, unhappy with the narrow remit of some public consultations and research projects, were advocating a shift from dialogue to real consultation that sought to find out what people wanted before any proposals were framed.

In some fields this was interpreted as needing to carry out scoping exercises, to see what aspects of an issue had to be addressed, or as a way of identifying key concerns at an early stage in planning any campaigns or actions. For an example see the snappily titled 2002 report: 'Young men and suicide prevention: a scoping exercise for a review of the effectiveness of health promotion interventions of relevance to suicide prevention in young men (aged 19–34)' by the Evidence for Policy and Practice Information and Co-ordinating Centre, University of London, commissioned by the Department of Health.[13]

In my view at the time, by the end of the 1990s, the move from dialogue to genuine public involvement needed to go even further, especially where public funds were concerned, allowing the public to be the main drivers of some research in areas of public concern. I discussed this concept as part of ethics and issues sessions with the 20–30 groups of medical researchers and scientists on the media training and science communication workshops I was running at the time for universities, research councils and medical charities every year. In general they supported the concept, but could not see how the funds would be channelled to allow it.

As an example of failing to involve the public in remit setting, the UK publicly funded research bodies, the Natural Environment Research Council and the Biotechnology and Biological Sciences Research Councils published the results of their Farm Scale GM Crop Trials in 2003. This compared the effects on biodiversity and the environment of three conventionally grown versus three GM varieties of the same crops.

I was present at the press launch and first public announcement of the results of the Farm Scale GM Crop Trials at the 2003 British Association Science Festival, which I was covering that year as a science journalist. The immediate reaction from journalists and special interest groups was to question why the UK's largest and most comprehensive crop trials ever had not included a comparison with organic crops at the same time.

Lords or the House of Commons were about to make. As defined by the UK Parliament official website, the Division Lobbies are the corridors where members of both Houses go to vote. In the House of Commons the division lobbies are either side of the main debating chamber and are called the 'ayes' lobby and the 'nos' lobby; in the Lords one is for 'content' and the other 'not content'. Both Houses vote by dividing, and simply tally the number of members in each lobby after the vote is called by the Speaker announcing 'Clear the Lobbies', or in the Lords by calling 'Clear the Bar', which always seems much more apposite.

People wishing to influence parliamentary legislation would hang about in the corridors nearby, hoping to persuade the politicians to go into their preferred one of the two division lobbies to be counted, hence lobbying.

Formal and informal lobbying, or parliamentary liaison, often as a job called public affairs in public relations jargon, is a form of advocacy now carried out by a very wide range of organisations including ordinary members of the public. Lobbyists include companies, public sector and local government representative bodies, trade unions, pressure groups or special interest groups. Lobbyists may even include members of parliament or the Lords. Lobbyists for medical and health issues include the pharmaceutical, commercial care and insurance industries, patients' bodies, research charities, academic interest groups and representatives of the various medical, nursing and allied professions.

Successful lobbying means getting access to key politicians, with ministers and especially Ministers of State or Cabinet Ministers the biggest prize of all. Access to ministers is guarded more or less successfully by their civil servants, mainly due to the time constraints and the necessity of weeding out supplicants, so that the few successful people who do gain access are of particular relevance or personal interest to the particular politician being targeted.

One of the ethical problems of successful lobbying is that once one side or particular interest starts doing it, all the other sides of the issue and competing interests also need to spend time and money, and the politician's time, seeking to put their differing or opposing view to make sure that any subsequent legislation or change in rules is fair. Consequently for example medical charities and patients' groups will lobby on issues such as the price or access to particular medicines, which the uninitiated might imagine should be the interest of the pharmaceutical companies, health insurance companies and the National Health Service budget-holders alone.

Some people even feel that all lobbying is intrinsically wrong, and should be banned or at least much more tightly regulated. In 2009, the UK House of Commons Public Administration Select Committee said that lobbying to influence decisions is a necessary and legitimate part of democracy. People wish to influence decisions that affect them and the government needs their knowledge and views. However, it also recommended setting up a statutory register of lobbyists because of concerns about conflicts of interest and undue influence.[15] By which we may understand that the temptation to attempt to suborn or bribe politicians is just too great. Not that any of our politicians today would accept money, or favours or even the promise of future jobs for themselves or members of their families in exchange for looking favourably on certain propositions.

To promote transparency, and in the expectation of regulations, the UK Public Affairs Council has set up a register of public affairs lobbyists and it is a condition of membership of the Chartered Institute of Public Relations that if you meet the UKPAC definition of a lobbyist, then you must register with them. The Public Relations Consultants Association also requires members to register.

In 1994, a 'cash for questions' scandal rocked the UK when allegations leaked out that a parliamentary lobbyist had paid two members of parliament £2,000 each to ask formal questions on his behalf in the House of Commons. The subsequent scandal prompted the Prime Minister at the time, John Major, to set up the Nolan Committee to investigate Standards in Public Life.

The ramifications and declarations of interest have had a substantial impact on all levels of UK government, down to even the Parish Council level, its lowest tier. In the spirit of Nolan, I should here declare that I was a Parish Council chairman for five years, and a member of my District Council Standards Committee, and am currently an Independent Person for a National Park Authority Standards Committee, hearing cases alleging breaches of the Code of Conduct.

In March 2012, the Prime Minister, David Cameron, was caught up in a scandal in which it was alleged that he had been riding a retired police horse at the country estate of a racehorse trainer friend of his, Charlie Brooks, who happened to also be the husband of Rebekah Brooks, disgraced former chief executive of News International, publishers of many UK national daily newspapers, some now defunct, who was herself embroiled at the time in a highly politically charged phone-hacking scandal. A scandal that had already forced the Prime Minister's press chief to resign.

While this 'Horsegate' twist was still playing out in the media, a Conservative party treasurer and fundraiser Peter Cruddas was caught up in a new scandal in which it was claimed that major financial donors to his political party were treated to exclusive dinners at 10 Downing Street, the Prime Minister's official residence, and Chequers, the official country residence. This 'cash for access' or 'dinners for donors' scandal was prompted when undercover reporters from the *Sunday Times* released secretly recorded video footage of Cruddas offering 'premier league' dinners with the Prime Minister and Chancellor of the Exchequer in exchange for donations of £250,000.[16]

Such privileged access to the top two decision-makers in government would obviously allow unparalleled lobbying opportunities for donors from industry or other special interests. To promote transparency, parliament called for the names of donors who had been entertained to such dinners to be released to the public.

By the Monday morning the Prime Minister was facing calls for an independent public enquiry into the suggestion that wealthy donors could buy audiences with him, and a complaint had been made to the Metropolitan Police, who were considering whether to start a criminal enquiry.[17]

The donor list was released on Monday 26 March 2012, and the following evening a second list of 'forgotten donors' who had been left off the first list was also released. Among this second group, according to newspaper reports,[18] was the name of Sir Christopher Gent, chairman of GlaxoSmithKline, the biggest UK and world's third largest pharmaceutical company and the fifth largest company in any sector listed on the London Stock Exchange at the end of 2011.

Personal donations to the UK Conservative Party made by Sir Christopher Gent apparently total more than £100,000 between 2005 and 2012. He was appointed as a member of the government's economic recovery committee in 2009, and one initiative being discussed in 2011 was the suggestion that patient data should be made available to drug companies, in spite of fears about individual confidentiality. Fortunately GlaxoSmithKline has a corporate responsibility committee that oversees such ethical issues, whose members included Gent himself, and James Murdoch, who featured so prominently in the 2011 *News of the World* phone-hacking scandal.[19]

In a press release[20] on 26 March 2012, the Public Relations Consultants Association said:

> The PRCA view remains the same as it did before yesterday's story. The Government needs to establish a credible, independent body to hold a register of lobbyists. That register must cover all who lobby – whether they work for multi-client agencies, in-house teams, legal or accountancy firms, trade unions, charities or business groups. The Government should waste no more time in establishing this wide-reaching body. Separately, it should also address the effectiveness of the current codes that cover Ministers and the laws that cover donations.

In a further exposure of lobbying and access,[21] the *Guardian* newspaper revealed on 11 April 2012 that parliamentary all-party groups had received perks worth £1.8m in the previous year, including sponsorship, free gifts, funding and trips abroad. There are more than 300 of these semi-official groups of members of parliament and Lords, and the all-party group on health had received contributions of more than £117,000 for the purchase of 'associate memberships' at £8,400 each from companies including pharmaceutical giants AstraZeneca and GlaxoSmithKline; and that MPs and Lords were also offered free memberships through the all-party groups supporting Slimming World and Weight Watchers.

Lobbying activities, or directly seeking to influence government and decision-makers' opinions through confidential briefings, can be viewed as covert or indirect actions, carried out in relative secrecy. As the Freedom of Information Act (2000), aimed at promoting transparency in decision-making, becomes more widely used, and further clarified by the law courts and the Information Commissioners Office, we may start to see more briefing documents submitted as part of such lobbying campaigns becoming exposed to public scrutiny, which will obviously in future affect their contents.

According to DirectGov, the UK government information website, the Freedom of Information Act confers the right to see a wide range of public information. It gives you the right to ask any public body for all the information they have on any subject you choose. Unless there's a good reason, the organisation must provide the information within 20 working days.

The Act covers England, Wales and Northern Ireland; Scotland has a similar Act.

As an example of sensitive documents becoming public (or not) as a result of Freedom of Information requests, students of public relations should consider the UK government's prolonged resistance to releasing the NHS risk register, a briefing document routinely prepared for ministers by civil servants, which allegedly contains the details of potential areas of concern should the 2012 restructuring of the Health Service go ahead as planned.

The Information Commissioners Office and a later tribunal both ruled that the documents should be released, as being of public interest. Ministers resisted on the grounds that to do so would prevent civil servants giving candid advice to ministers in future, and that the public might confuse worst case scenario planning with actual or realistic risks. Opponents argued successfully that parliament was being asked to vote on legislation to transform the NHS without access to relevant information about the risks posed and therefore without being fully briefed and able to make reasoned decisions.

In spite of leaks, the Coalition Government managed to delay publication until after the Health and Social Care Act was passed by parliament in March 2012. During the 19-month campaign to get the risk register released, campaigners failed to make the distinction between the transition risk register on specific and predictable threats, and the strategic risk register, covering threats outside government control, according to the Shadow Secretary of State for Health Andy Burnham.[22] In May 2012, cabinet ministers exercised their right to veto the release of documents under the Freedom of Information Act for only the third time in ten years, citing 'exceptional' circumstances.

A more subtle form of lobbying are the policy reports released by thinktanks, which are frequently reported in the media as though they were independent opinions from experts in a field. Usually, but not always, the proposals, and your concerns, will relate to the economics or politics of proposed actions. If your organisation welcomes a thinktank's proposals, then you should make sure that you have found out in advance who, as individuals, or which particular organisations fund the thinktank, as you may find a hidden agenda that you are unwittingly supporting. Conversely, if a thinktank proposes a policy that your organisation opposes, then you may wish to expose its funding sources as a way of demonstrating its true agenda. No thinktanks are neutral.

Access: interns, secondments, spads, moles and revolving doors

As we move further into the murky world of just who is paying, for what access, to whom, we start moving away from public relations and public affairs activities into marketing and sponsorship. The lines are becoming increasingly blurred. As a public relations practitioner, you certainly need to be aware of the ways that favours can be exchanged and influence and access can be bought by your competitors, your critics, your colleagues in other organisations and sometimes even by your own company or charity without your knowledge.

Having these activities exposed unexpectedly, or indeed, exposing those of your competitors in the dog-eats-dog political fight for economic advantage, media coverage, government influence and public opinion, can precipitate a full-blown crisis. And crises most certainly are within the remit and responsibility of public relations offices, so you probably need to know what's going on.

Government ministers, members of parliament, charities and special interest or activist groups are all notoriously short-handed and short of funds and will often welcome the offer of extra help. This help can be given through core funding, sponsorship of specific activities or temporary staff positions and, possibly most controversially, offering more senior staff on secondment. A military strategist might view this as embedding some undercover agents or moles in the enemy camp.

The argument for secondment of senior staff is that it benefits both parties. It widens their own experience, for instance by allowing a senior civil servant an opportunity to leave her office for six months and actually work in the industry she is regulating, gaining valuable first-hand experience of trade practices and the realities of the job. In return for a little hospitality, the company gains someone with a genuine understanding of the difficulties it faces, and a friendly ear in a position of responsibility when the civil servant returns to her full-time post (or promotion).

Or equally likely a civil servant may be seconded to a charity to gain first-hand experience of dealing with drug users, anorexics or other vulnerable users of public services. While there, offering his management experience, he may also help the charity to understand the minister's current thinking on outreach and delivery of services and, crucially, how to successfully apply for new grant funding streams that have become available. In the financial squeeze of 2012, many of these civil servants were recalled to their original departments, to do the jobs that they were originally hired to perform, assuming that such a need exists.

A further ethical issue arises if after leaving her post (and satisfying the regulatory period of waiting), the civil servant is offered a job by one of the relevant industry bodies that she has been responsible for regulating or monitoring. Even while still sitting as a member of parliament, some politicians take well-paid speaking engagements, advisory posts or executive directorships with industry bodies.

In some cases politicians may have previously worked in industry and will have close personal ties and financial interests in commercial practices that they are now responsible for regulating. This type of revolving door switch between regulators, officials and the industries and practices that they are regulating are becoming increasingly controversial, subject to media and activist scrutiny, and may need to be declared under registers of interests.

It becomes similarly controversial when a company, charity, faith organisation or other special interest group sponsors an intern, providing a low-ranking member of staff who will typically carry out menial or repetitive tasks for the host person or organisation. The intern may be nominally working for a government minister, member of parliament or charity, but where do his loyalties really lie? Is the intern also collecting commercially or politically valuable intelligence?

Another similarly controversial issue at the moment is the practice by government ministers of appointing special advisors, or spads, who are embedded within the civil service and may even have real civil servants reporting to them. The role of a spad is to bring in specialist expertise to assist the minister, as a loyal personal advisor.

Unless something goes wrong, as happened to Culture Secretary Jeremy Hunt, whose spad Adam Smith resigned in April 2012 over allegations that he had given inside information, or acted as a back channel to Rupert Murdoch and News Corporation over their attempted takeover of television channel BSkyB, and exposed by the parliamentary Leveson Inquiry into media standards.[23]

If a minister chooses to ignore the proper civil service channels for conducting business, and his spad makes unwise decisions or leaks instead, the minister should take full personal responsibility for the spad's actions. If your organisation is thinking of embedding spads in government departments, make sure that you have thought through the PR implications of any actions.

In all these incidences, if evidence of undue influence, unexplained payments, success in winning contracts, or controversial access become public then the reputation of both parties may be damaged and public trust and confidence is lost.

Sponsorship

In the 1990s, hospital consultants, general practitioners and other senior medical and nursing staff came in for similar criticism when it emerged publicly that pharmaceutical and laboratory equipment manufacturers and other suppliers were routinely sponsoring them.

As drug companies developed new medicines and treatments, so they needed to inform already qualified doctors of the latest products available. And so they commissioned drug representatives, as a modern equivalent of travelling salesmen, to visit the doctors, GPs and other purchasers in their surgeries and clinics. Busy doctors and senior staff did not have sufficient time, or inclination, to see all the possible drug reps from different companies who wanted to see them, especially during normal hours.

So the drug reps concentrated on building personal relationships with the consultants, doctors and GPs, taking them out for meals, funding their trips to relevant academic conferences, and even, in some cases, paying for them and their families to go on holiday.

If the doctor had carried out research or clinical trials on the efficacy of a new drug, then obviously it was in the pharmaceutical company's interest to make sure that the doctor could attend as many relevant conferences as possible, worldwide. She would deliver papers on her findings, boosting confidence in the results, and so create demand for the new drug, even if only on a named patient basis. So doctors were routinely paid to attend conferences (in the parlance, given small honoraria) and had their travel and accommodation expenses covered.

Most GPs and hospital doctors simply had no other way, or source of funds, to attend the conferences, which were seen as vital for them to keep up-to-date with their fields, and share their experiences with their colleagues. At the conference the drug reps, who had accompanied the sponsored doctors, manned their own exhibition stands in the sponsors' areas and would typically host dinners in the evenings for their own speaker, the chairman of the session and any other influential leaders in the discipline that they could attract.

The learned societies, university research departments and other organisers of the academic conferences also needed sponsorship to cover the costs of mounting the event in the first place. So they raised further funds directly from the pharmaceutical companies, either as overall conference sponsors, or in return for stand space in the exhibition areas where tea, coffee and refreshments were served at breaks and lunchtime. Typically a session chairman would announce a reminder for delegates to visit the sponsors' stands as the session was closing, in recognition of the vital role that the companies played in allowing the conferences to continue.

In a further development of these relationships, some pharmaceutical companies (or their PR consultancies) even allegedly organised their own mini-conferences and study sessions, inviting carefully selected key thinkers and influential people from a particular field of medicine.

A typical all expenses paid mini-conference or long weekend break could be held at a ski-resort or other attractive destination, with conference sessions held from 08.00–09.30 hrs and 17.00–19.00 hrs or perhaps shorter sessions, allowing the delegates the rest of the day free to ski. Understandably some journalists and regulators became concerned about the impartiality of some of the doctors who were routinely invited.

I was assured recently that these practices, which may have been widespread until ten years ago, are now banned in the UK and US, and that there are very strict rules in place both for healthcare professionals and pharmaceutical companies to restrict freebies offered to doctors. Sir Richard Sykes, former chairman of GlaxoSmithKline, told the *Guardian* newspaper in July 2012 that he did not have a clue about the details of a $3bn settlement paid to US regulatory authorities after revelations of entertainment and holidays offered to doctors to encourage the prescription of antidepressants to children, payments for positive articles in medical journals, and hiring doctors as cheerleaders to promote their treatments. Although this was a large fine, the three drugs involved, two antidepressants and an asthma treatment, made combined sales worth $28bn during the miss-selling years according to the allegations.[24]

Drug company sponsorship also extended into university and hospital medical research at every level from tissue and animal models up to clinical trials, with medical researchers receiving more generous budgets to carry out their work than public funds sometimes allowed. In this 'publish or perish' culture, where academic reputations, senior posts and even departmental funding awarded through the Research Assessment Exercise, depended solely on peer-reviewed publications, everyone needed to get as many academic papers published in as many prestigious journals as they could.

Doctors and scientists found it difficult to resist the lure of easy research funding with few restraints, apart possibly from the funders' right to delay publication of some key data or even whole papers if unpalatable facts, lack of results or unwelcome side effects were discovered. In a world in which positive results are much more likely to get published in a major journal than results that show no effective pharmacological action, the academic literature, and therefore the apparent effects if all published trials were taken into account, became increasingly skewed.

Critics of the system, such as GP Ben Goldacre who wrote the Bad Science Columns for the *Guardian* newspaper for many years, and the well-respected journalist Nigel Hawkes, former health editor of *The Times* newspaper, who is now the director of pressure group Straight Statistics, have suggested that to be accepted as evidence all drug trials should be numbered and pre-registered, with all the trial subjects named to avoid the same patient being included in several different study papers. And with all the interventions, dosage regimes, timescales, comparisons and outcomes defined, so that independent observers can verify the efficacy claimed for the product. And every single trial should be published, especially those that are statistically inconclusive or fail. This would prevent cherry-picking of data and even cherry-picking of entire trials.

This transparency should also similarly extend to interventions announced, commissioned or made by government departments and their agents in public health and education initiatives. Popular announcements such as programmes to reduce drug dependency, lower childhood obesity or cut smoking rates should be audited. The initiatives should have a set and clearly stated aim, targets and timescales, thereby showing which initiatives offer value for money and effective results, and which ones are simply a sop to public outrage or a vain hope that something is being done.

Increasing regulation in the UK, US and European countries, and ethical concerns about the safety of patients enrolled in drug trials, which has led to ever greater difficulty in properly gaining consent, has driven many multinational pharmaceutical companies to run their drug trials in developing countries. Some critics say that this is because regulation is more lax, and commercial companies can have freer access to patients and hospital clinics, with less pressure to publish unfavourable results.

In response, pharmaceutical company supporters point out that developing countries now have the highest rates of untreated disease, and therefore that these are the places where new medicines need to be targeted. In addition, developing countries often have very few effective drugs available and insufficient funds to treat many diseases. Therefore running medical trials, even of drugs that turn out to be less effective than existing alternatives, still offers substantial benefits to patients who would otherwise go completely untreated. Finally and perhaps crucially, drugs that work on well-fed, literate, Western citizens with easy access to clean water, may not work in the heat, diet, genetic traits and other environmental circumstances of the countries where they will ultimately be needed.

References

1. The classic communications model can be found at http://en.wikipedia.org/wiki/Shannon%E2%80%93Weaver_model or Claude Shannon & Warren Weaver, *The Mathematical Theory of Communication*, Urbana IL: University of Illinois Press, 1949, page 5.
2. *Guardian*, 2 June 2010.
3. *Country Smallholding*, August 2010.
4. *Guardian*, 2 June 2010.
5. Fixed nuclear consultation, see http://www.greenpeace.org.uk/blog/nuclear/breaking-news-another-nuclear-consultation-was-fixed-20081016.
6. European White Papers and Green Papers, see http://europa.eu/documentation/faq/index_en.htm.
7. For more on focus groups see Jenny Kitzinger, 'Qualitative research', *British Medical Journal*, 311 (29 July 1995).
8. For an example of a Delphi Group see Stephen Campbell, 'How do stakeholder groups vary in a Delphi technique … ', *Quality and Safety in Health Care* 8 (2004): 428–434. This journal is now called *BMJ Quality and Safety*.
9. Deficit model communication at the University of Leicester, see www2.le.ac.uk/departments/gradschool/news/garnham-lecture/slides.pdf.
10. 'Realising Our Potential' 1993 full text is available at the National Archives at www.official-documents.gov.uk/document/cm22/2250/2250.asp.
11. Myc Riggulsford, 'The pressure group problem', *Science and Public Affairs*, Autumn 1997: 40–43, published by the Royal Society and British Association for the Advancement of Science.
12. House of Commons Science and Technology Select Committee session 2000–2001 Sixth Report, 'Are we realising our potential?', paragraph 55, published 3 April 2001. For recommendation 28, see www.publications.parliament.uk/pa/cm200001/cmselect/cmsctech/200/20003.htm.
13. A. Harden, K. Sutcliffe and T. Lempert, 'Young men and suicide prevention: a scoping exercise for a review of the effectiveness of health promotion interventions of relevance to suicide prevention in young men (aged 19–34)', London: EPPI-Centre, Social Science Research Unit, Institute of Education, University of London, commissioned by the Department of Health (2002).
14. James Wilsdon & Rebecca Willis, 'See-through Science: Why Public Engagement Needs to Move Upstream', Demos, 2003.
15. Recommendation 41 (referring to paragraph 188), House of Commons Public Administration Select Committee, 'Lobbying: Access and Influence in Whitehall: Government Response to the Committee's First Report of Session 2008–2009', Eighth Special Report of Session, London, published 23 October 2009.
16. *Sunday Times*, 25 March 2012.
17. *Daily Telegraph*, 26 March 2012.
18. *Guardian*, 28 March 2012.
19. *Guardian*, diary, 9 December 2011.
20. Public Relations Consultants Association, press release, 26 March 2012.
21. *Guardian*, 11 April 2012.
22. *Guardian*, letters, 19 March 2012.
23. *Independent*, 26 April 2012.
24. *Guardian*, 4 & 5 July 2012.

Part IV

Health and medical PR in society

11 Politics, ethics and the media

In this chapter we look at some of the issues and concerns affecting the health and medical sector, consider some that have been successfully handled and some efforts that have been less successful, or are still continuing with no clear resolution in sight.

It would be impossible to cover all of the possible issues, and all of their ramifications, since we simply do not have the space, and also, health issues are unfolding in real time, so this book would never finish. I have chosen a few to discuss, either because they are good examples, particularly pressing concerns or because they are just quite interesting in themselves. Other issues may be available.

Once again I do not expect you to agree with me and accept my opinions on these unquestioningly – you have your own views, you will have a different political, cultural, religious and ethical standpoint, different background knowledge, and you may be trying to achieve particular outcomes in other arenas that will colour your interpretation of similar problems. So I simply offer the issues raised in this chapter as being up for discussion and debate, or as pointing to potential pitfalls that you should be ready for, not as solutions you should adopt or paths you should follow.

If you are a new student of public relations or a seasoned practitioner trying to wider your own knowledge and analytical abilities, then I suggest that you treat this chapter as a series of case study exercises. Adopt the viewpoint of one of the affected or interested groups active in the debate and analyse the issue from their point of view. What would you do? Now analyse the same issue from one of the opposing parties' viewpoints. Is this an issue requiring action or planning? What actions would you need to take to move the issue forward successfully? What key messages can you develop to support your position? What will the other players do and say, and what outcomes are they seeking? Who, realistically, is going to win?

Slow-burn issues

Doublethink, according to George Orwell in his novel *Nineteen Eighty-Four*, is the ability to hold simultaneously two opinions that cancel each other out, knowing them to be contradictory and believing in both of them. The equivalent postmodern malaise is cognitive dissonance, where two strongly held or cherished beliefs cause conflict and mental confusion. Or in the case of politicians, who suffer from a similar but subtly different syndrome, it is sometimes called hypocrisy.

Public relations practitioners are faced with a public, and therefore media and politicians, who sometimes try to hold or champion two logically incompatible beliefs at the same time. Experienced public relations people know that the public, and politicians, and the media, tend to vote with their hearts rather than just their minds. So your carefully briefed representatives can appear in a television debate, armed with all the best logic and facts that you could muster for them, and the public will choose the person or argument that they like best, not necessarily the most logical or legally valid position, even if this is against all rational science and their own best interests.

In disputes with animal rights activists in the late 1980s, some drug company representatives and industry bodies would state as justification that all animal experiments in the UK are granted Home Office licences regulating and permitting the experiments. Just because something is legal doesn't mean that it is right. Their argument did not convince the public.

Shortly after setting up our consultancy in 1991, I was contracted as the director of a group of major UK medical research charities, addressing why we need to use animals in research. I advised the clients that we should tackle the issue on ethical grounds rather than its legality, as ethics, pain and suffering were the major public concerns. I was originally told that if I did, the public would always side with animal rights activists, since they held the moral high ground. My view was that medical charities held a higher moral position, the desire to help suffering patients. Fortunately, the public generally agreed.

By addressing the ethical and emotional issues, as well as the rational, scientific and legal position, we were able to tease out in public debates some difference between the opposing views:

- The animal welfare charities' position, that animal experiments for human or veterinary research should be reduced, replaced or refined to cause less suffering and that, in particular, experiments causing severe suffering or using particularly sentient animals such as monkeys should be phased out.
- The pharmaceutical companies' position, that animal testing is a necessary part of efficacy studies in the early stages, and legally required toxicity testing in later safety tests, and that experiments are strictly governed by legal licensing, and conditions ensuring good laboratory animal welfare.
- The medical charities' and other funding bodies' position, that animal experiments are only used where no other suitable method could be, alongside tissue studies, computer modelling, population studies or epidemiology, human volunteer testing and studying patients in clinical trials, and that these techniques are not alternatives to each other but complementary forms of investigation.

- The animal rights groups' position, which is that animal experiments are completely unnecessary, do not work and that studying animals only tells you about animals since all species are fundamentally different (although all can suffer equally). Also, undercover infiltrations have always found evidence of animal abuse.
- The academic researchers' and medical professionals' position, that animal work has contributed to almost all modern medical advances and veterinary science, that it will be needed for the foreseeable future, and that it is in researchers' own interests to use the best possible technique to uncover the next piece of evidence in the search for answers to existing medical problems, in fundamental research, and in genetics.

Obviously the debate is much more complex than this oversimplification, with many more arguments used on each side. For instance many animal rights arguments rest on potential flaws in toxicity testing, but that is only a minor part of animal use. It is certainly true that if animal rights groups had not entered the debate alongside the welfare groups, then animal use would be much more poorly regulated, laboratory conditions worse and the suffering greater.

By identifying these core negotiating positions, we were able to hold more rational debates as members of the public and politicians came to understand that the issue was more complex than a simple right/wrong argument, with competing and not necessarily reconcilable costs, benefits and desires.

When thinking about other similar issues, it may help you to think of these types of position as a Venn diagram:

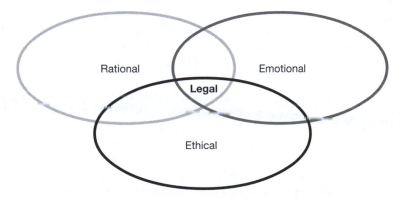

Figure 11.1 Intersection of rational, emotional, ethical and legal issues.

In these highly sensitive debates, all the different elements need to be addressed if public opinion is to go with you. By contrast, many academic and commercial interests are happiest addressing just the scientific or rational parts of the argument; and special interest and pressure groups tend to focus on the emotional and ethical aspects instead. Sometimes the participants do not even know the true legal position.

If you think that the emotion is all on the side of the bunny huggers and patients' groups, then take a look at the UK law governing animal research, the Animals (Scientific Procedures) Act 1986 (currently being revised).[1] It gives special protection to monkeys and other primates, because they have the self-aware capacity to suffer and because they are so closely related to us, their human cousins. It gives special protection to cats and dogs, because in Britain they are members of our households, living within our homes in a family relationship with our children and us. And having taken them in, we have special duties to care for them.

But it also gives special protection to horses. Why? Why not sheep, goats or ferrets? Or rats, which arguably have more complex social systems? It's simply that in the UK we like horses and are the only country in Europe that doesn't eat them. That's not a rational law. So why do you expect the politicians who made it, or the public who elected them, to behave as though it was?

Animal use in medical research is a classic example of a long-running debate, or what I have called for many years a slow-burn issue, which periodically blows up into a crisis at particular revelations of wrongdoing, animal cruelty, bomb threats and firebombs, and as other media stories break. But the underlying slow-burn issue is still simmering in the background. It was not then, and is not now, an issue that can be won or made to go away through a simple, clever public relations campaign by any one of the actors in the debate or by finding a killer argument. Animal use in research is always undesirable. It is often simply a question of doing the least harm possible.

In many ways, it is these slow-burn issues, such as the debates about abortion, stem cell research, nanotechnology or neuroethics, that make health and medical public relations such a fascinating field to work in, from whichever side of the debate your organisation stands. None of these issues have an absolute right or wrong position.

Nanotechnology is only just hitting the public consciousness, and is a sufficiently hot topic that it was on the front cover of *Nature* in November 2011. But the word formally entered the English language in 1974 when it was first listed by the *Oxford English Dictionary*. How much slower do you want your crisis to burn?

I made it an absolute condition of working on the animals issue that my clients at the time, the Wellcome Trust and other medical research charities, made sure that it became more difficult to use animals in research than to do similar work by any other method. So one of my most unpopular personal legacies as director of the Research for Health Charities Group is all the extra paperwork that researchers now have to fill in to gain grant committee funding and ethical committee approval.

For anyone specifically interested in the animals in medical research debate, the other legacy that I am particularly proud of was the establishment of the Boyd Group,[2] named neutrally after our mutually agreed and independent chairman, the ethicist Prof Kenneth Boyd. I do not wish to take any undue credit: all the main work was done by the other two founders, Prof Colin Blakemore of Oxford University, who was personally being targeted by animal activists at the time, and Les Ward, who was then director of the Scottish radical activist group Advocates for Animals, which had recently exposed serious wrongdoing in a university department by an elderly and academically revered researcher.

The Boyd Group is a round table discussion and consensus forum for animal activists, animal welfare charities, medical charities, funding bodies, academic researchers, patients' groups, laboratory animal technicians, pharmaceutical representatives and has Home Office observers.

The Boyd Group was founded when the three of us, Colin, Les and I, met for the first time in the *Kilroy* daytime television studios, during a debate that I had set up as the public relations launch of the Research for Health Charities Group in October 1991. From the extremely heated studio discussion, and a private talk afterwards, we realised that we had many views in common, such as a belief that cosmetic testing on animals was not justifiable, and from there the notion of setting up a consensual discussion away from the spotlight was born. The Boyd Group has since published many influential position papers and still exists 20 years later.

Most television debates set up by the media actually stifle rational discussion, because the participants are simply there to win this round, not to try to convince their implacable opponents. To move the animals debate forward at all, we had to find a different discussion forum, change the paradigm, find areas of consensus and remove the need for the grandiloquent posturing designed to establish each participant's position in the public's eyes.

As the public relations practitioner who deliberately set up the *Kilroy* debate, I didn't actually expect to win that one (although, on balance, we did). It was simply a vehicle for me to announce to the public that medical charities were now standing up to the cowards and bullies attacking their charity shops under cover of night. And crucially (for me) a quick way for me to hear the way all the main arguments were being phrased (so that I could deconstruct them later), and to personally meet the main players. I needed to see the whites of their eyes.

Today many PR people feel that it is their role to identify the key experts from their organisation to put up for debates, not to take to the barricades and trenches in the frontline themselves. In the UK, in war, only the air force still sends its officers into battle first while the other ranks wait behind. War was conducted more honourably when we used to send all our generals and admirals to the front line, leading by example. I'm a bit old-fashioned like that.

However, there is a good lesson in this. If you are bound to lose by playing fair and conventionally, then change the rules, change the paradigm. That was the secret of all my campaigning. That way at least you will briefly be in control, and stand a chance of winning your argument, even if the odds and public opinion are stacked firmly against you. One of the most seminal books that I ever read was James Gleick's *Chaos – Making A New Science*, published in 1988.[3] It changed my way of thinking forever.

I was reminded of it again this year, when I came across a key passage from Gleick quoted in Donatella Meadows' book, *Thinking in Systems*.[4] It's still as true today as it was in 1991 when I first read Gleick's words, just after I had set up the UK's first dedicated issue management consultancy for the not-for-profit sector:

> Linear relationships are easy to think about; the more the merrier. Linear equations are solvable, which makes them suitable for textbooks. Linear systems have an important modular virtue: you can take them apart and put them together again – the pieces add up.
>
> Nonlinear systems generally cannot be solved and cannot be added together. Nonlinearity means that the act of playing the game has a way of changing the rules. That twisted changeability makes nonlinearity hard to calculate, but it also creates rich kinds of behavior that never occur in linear systems.

Polarised debates

Television, radio and other public debates, even ones with more time allowed such as daytime television shows, are usually constructed to give the audience a choice between two competing positions, black versus white, in an attempt to simplify and clarify the argument for the public, and provide balance in a political debate, as the television operating charters demand.

In the UK this reflects our national parliament set-up, where we have the government, and on facing benches, the loyal opposition, whose job is specifically to disagree. But there is no 'loyal compromise' position, or 'woolly middle way'. As a politician, you are just there to win.

I have argued strongly that this results in media debates that are overly polarised, with producers choosing protagonists who represent the extreme ends of the spectrum of views, who trivialise and sensationalise it, rather than presenting these difficult subjects as a complex issue and multi-layered debate. A debate that could, should be held in public, as all of the technical experts from each side have no particular right or skill to make the moral and ethical judgements for the rest of us.

In my own work, I have been particularly interested in finding how to unpick the arguments being used, and in trying to help not-for-profit, charity and publicly funded organisations, who occupy the various middle grounds of these emotive and difficult debates, to get their voices heard in the media. And the academics. They can be tricky for anyone to understand.

The BBC has decided to change the way it covers science after an independent review chaired by Prof Steve Jones of University College London and analysis by Imperial College London found that the BBC was giving too much weight to fringe views and creating false balance in its science reporting (presumably to meet the terms of its charter, to provide 'balance' in political issues).

The BBC report[5] highlighted in particular the way issues such as climate change, GM crops and MMR vaccine were made apparently more controversial by giving airtime to fringe scientific viewpoints, putting them on a par with well-established scientific fact. It found that these minority views are often given almost equal weight to the broader scientific agreement. The BBC Trust now plans to make changes, supported by the BBC executive.[6]

The BBC's science coverage has to balance 'due impartiality' with giving 'due weight' to competing arguments, but should not rely so much on fringe views that can give the impression that scientific controversy exists where none actually does, in the face of general scientific consensus.

The charge of 'dumbing down' or trivialisation of science is most often blamed on the tabloid newspapers in the UK, especially when scientists discover during media training workshops that the tabloids have a reading age of nine years old. Actually, science reports in the popular press are often written very clearly and concisely, and surprisingly accurately, as they are one of the few remaining sectors of the media that still has the financial resources to do proper fact-checking.

Medical and health professionals who are sniffy about the tabloids would do well to remember that the term was originally invented as a meaningless word by the pharmaceutical company Burroughs Wellcome in the 1880s to refer to the compressed pills they produced, and attached to several other compressed products as a popular buzzword, before finally allowing their trademark protection to lapse. Much more about this fascinating early history can be found in the Wellcome Trust Library and its History of Medicine collection in London.

Emotions and icons

One of the biggest problems for public relations practitioners in the health and medical field, compared with most other areas of work (apart possibly from food), is the huge emotional investment that we all have in our own health and, more importantly, the health of our loved ones. We daily applaud desperate attempts to save lives or alleviate suffering and, in the UK in particular, the National Health Service has an iconic status and affection in our minds.

These icons are things that you tamper with at your peril, where the peril is normally in the form of infuriated backlash and wild arguments on every side, either when a change is suggested or when nothing seems to be being done to improve matters. Emotions can run so high that they may end in threats or violence. Health PR is rarely a win-win situation. It is intensely political.

You might expect the NHS to be able to afford some of the very best public relations staff to work in-house on its important public health education initiatives. And, on the few times when it would be inappropriate to use in-house staff, to clearly explain to taxpayers and parliament why outside assistance is needed from a particular specialist agency for this particular campaign.

When one of the last major NHS PR contracts was awarded, it was announced in a press release on 20 December 2011, buried in the news run-up to Christmas, when Freud PR won a £1m a year contract from Whitehall. The Department of Health announcement[7] that Freud PR had won all of its 'life course' communications work was based on the assumption that centralising services would save money and could be measured using objective targets.

Sheila Mitchell, Head of Marketing at the Department of Health, said:

> Freud Communications have some big ideas that we believe will not only promote good health, but will really change people's behaviour. Our public health social marketing strategy takes us to the next level, adopting a life-stage based approach, which will make our campaigns more effective and save money. Freud Communications will forego a percentage of their fee if they don't meet the targets set in their plans.

It is notoriously difficult to change people's behaviour or attitudes through health PR campaigns. If you think back to Chapter 9, 'Planning a health or medical public relations campaign', as a PR practitioner, what objective targets would you have offered as the pitching public relations agency? And as the Department of Health, what objective targets would you have demanded from your retained commercial agency? Now ask yourself how often you saw those targets met and publicised during the NHS reorganisation row of 2012, to show that Coalition Government policies were working. How much of its fee is the agency likely to have had to forgo?

According to NHS Choices, the UK National Health Service's own website, the NHS was created in July 1948 with three core principles:[8]

- that it meet the needs of everyone;
- that it be free at the point of delivery;
- that it be based on clinical need, not ability to pay.

This concept of 'free' has been at the root of much of the political and social debate about the way medical care is provided in the UK ever since. It does not seem to generate quite the same passionate feeling in other countries of Europe, where (sometimes compulsory) health insurance has usually funded individual care, with the state only providing core services and some infrastructure. The American view, from the lens of this side of the Atlantic, is simply incomprehensible. Or self-destructive. Or mad.

Clearly, however, in the UK, doctors, nurses, ambulance drivers, hospital clinic receptionists and all the other support staff who enable the NHS to function are paid their salaries, pensions, sick leave, holiday pay and all the other employment benefits that people expect in European society. Their desks, offices, operating theatres and all their other business premises are bought and paid for, not donated for free.

NHS staff have traditionally accepted slightly lower salaries and fewer benefits than they might expect in the equivalent jobs in the private sector, because in some way the work that they are doing is considered a social good and therefore fulfilling in job satisfaction. People enjoy helping other people, and health service workers are held in high social esteem. Compared with, for example, bankers, health workers are generally reckoned to be undervalued rather than overpaid, in spite of salaries that are often well above the national average.

The pay rates in the NHS are so much lower than the rates that a free market might support for life-saving interventions that physicians, surgeons and the other consultant-level senior staff, who had to be lured into the new nationalised system of healthcare, retained the right to practise private medicine in addition to their NHS work. Which immediately created a two-tier system of those who could afford to pay to jump queues by going private and those who had to wait. Inequity was built in from the start. But whatever, we still have a royal family as heads of state in the UK, we can live with this.

The pay row escalated in May 2012 when NHS doctors voted to strike over proposed pension reforms that would have left retired doctors in future on publicly funded pensions of only twice the national average wage. For the first time that I can remember, and in a particularly straitened economy, public sympathy started to shift away from doctors. As social commentator Deborah Orr wrote in her *Guardian* newspaper column in June 2012:

> One of the BMA's negotiators, Dr Simon Fradd, later told the BBC that GPs were so stunned by the generosity of the terms offered for out-of-hours opt-out that they thought it was a 'bit of a laugh'. But they accepted them anyway, in 2004. Doctors are hardly alone among professionals who made hay while the sun was shining, rather than mending the roof. They are hardly even chief among them. That dubious distinction goes to the bankers.[9]

The fat cat criticisms are not confined to just NHS employees, the public also resents suggestions that pharmaceutical companies are exploiting the public purse, so stories claiming that GlaxoSmithKline's chief executive Sir Andrew Witty is underpaid at £6.7m a year caused outrage in 2012, during the bankers' bonus scandals, when the company's remuneration committee raised his pay to £10.4m. GlaxoSmithKline was the first UK company to have its pay deals voted down in 2003.[10]

So, once we start looking at it, the notion that in some way the British have free healthcare and that the National Health Service is 'free' is just plain wrong. It could not function without paid staff, commercially developed medicines, the engineering wizardry that gives us our modern diagnostic machines and a whole system of medical research subsidy paid for by taxpayers, industry and charities.

Second, the notion that the pinnacle of NHS delivery, the consultants in the various disciplines, those who ultimately have to make life and death decisions every day, are in some way altruistic paragons unsoiled by the taint of money or power is also manifestly untrue. Today's NHS consultants were, on the whole, trained through medical school by the NHS, learned their craft in NHS hospitals and clinics, and have risen to positions where they can finally cash in with lucrative private practices if they so choose. All this simply through the experience afforded them by working within one of the world's most comprehensive healthcare systems. We no longer need to lure them in, so why do we still allow them to work privately?

This two-tier system would not of course be necessary or even economically viable on such a large scale if the NHS actually delivered free healthcare to all who needed it. The original funding concept was that as more people were treated for their long-term, chronic ailments, and got better, then the need for healthcare would gradually fall off. So costs would stay roughly the same for some time as the more intractable, expensive and difficult to identify illnesses were tackled. Then costs would eventually fall away to a new lower level as good health created by universal healthcare was enjoyed by all.

The reality has of course been somewhat different, with NHS costs spiralling out of control as more and more diseases become identified, or relatively widespread conditions such as depression, mild headaches or sporadic backache become medicalised, and the drugs and equipment needed become ever more specialised and expensive.

It didn't help that Europe had a baby boom in the 1950s and 1960s, creating a bulge in the population, and no one predicted the extraordinary increase in life expectancy that slightly better nutrition, housing, sanitation and medical treatment would bring. We now face a crisis of old age, with more people simply living much longer than expected, and therefore needing increasing care as they finally become infirm.

The NHS has never managed to treat everyone. Since its inception more than 60 years ago, treatment has effectively been rationed by failure to gain access, failures in diagnoses and by simple waiting lists. In addition, the NHS cannot afford to treat every possible patient with every possible drug or surgical intervention, the wealth of the nation is insufficient. Deep down inside, we all know this, but we choose to ignore it. Healthcare in the UK is intensely political, and no politician who suggested a truly equitable or rational system of health provision would ever get re-elected.

So in 2012, the furore surrounding the threatened 'privatisation' of the NHS through the Coalition Government's Health & Social Care Act – which finally passed through the House of Lords on 19 March 2012 – seems to embody a profound disconnection between the reality of delivery of UK healthcare, and the expectations and belief so firmly held by our various and general publics.

No previous health service reorganisation, apart possibly from the original founding of the NHS, has attracted so much debate and so much opposition from every side, including from within the Medical Royal Colleges, the official registration bodies of the various healthcare trades. Over the final year, from when the new act was first debated, we saw successive waves of public relations activity from different interest groups within the healthcare sector, both over the general principles and from specific disease interest groups or health specialities trying to make sure that their own area does not suffer cuts.

For the next few years at least, any perceived failure, any perceived digression, or change in services, or suspected profit motive, will probably be a public relations hot topic within UK healthcare and the wider media, sparking internet chatroom debates and news headlines. Managing reputation and public opinion, engaging the wider publics and holding real public dialogues on healthcare issues may become even more intensely scrutinised and extremely difficult, if not impossible.

Similarly in the US, healthcare has become one of the hottest political issues thanks to President Barack Obama's Patient Protection and Affordable Care Act, known locally as Obamacare, which was upheld as constitutional by the US Supreme Court on 28 June 2012. I was lucky enough to be given a brief analysis of the ruling by elegant philosopher and ethicist Prof Martha Nussbaum, with whom I shared a taxi from St Andrews to Edinburgh a couple of days later.

Nussbaum suggested that the legal challenge was based upon the idea that governments do not have the constitutional right to tell citizens how to spend their own money. President Obama won the day on the crucial vote of the usually conservative chief justice, John Roberts, who ruled in essence that everyone eventually needs healthcare at some point in their lives. Even if they do not have medical insurance, they will be treated when taken into hospital as an emergency, which pushes up insurance premium costs for everyone else.

So health insurance is not an optional service, it is a tax instead, fairly shared by everyone. As such the Obamacare measure, called the individual mandate, which now requires almost all Americans to buy insurance, is legal because it is a tax. The Republican challenger vowed to repeal the measure if he won the 2012 presidential election (for more on similar ethical debates see Martha Nussbaum's book, *The New Religious Intolerance: Overcoming the Politics of Fear in an Anxious Age*[11]).

So what types of issues are lurking out there, waiting to trip up the unwary or hasty public relations practitioner? In some cases, where you may wish to refer back to contemporary press reports as an analysis exercise, to look at the language used by journalists at the time, and to assess public mood, I have given indicative dates of media stories. I have usually only given one newspaper reference or example for each issue, but in most cases other print, broadcast and social media outlets will have carried similar reports on the same day, and there may even have been later commentaries in peer-reviewed journals, quite apart from any original scientific papers that prompted public interest in the issue in the first place. These are generally slow-burn issues, which have not yet been resolved, so more recent media reports will now exist, and the debate will have moved on.

NHS issues

Charges: hospitals in England make more than £100m every year from car parking charges, according to information provided by the NHS Information Centre, while car parking in Wales, Scotland and Northern Ireland is typically free. Volunteers driving relatives, friends and neighbours into hospital, and patients' visitors particularly, resent paying these costs in a supposedly free health service, and blame the need to drive in the first place on the closure of many local and cottage hospitals and centralisation of specialist services.[12]

Waiting lists and **targets:** waiting lists are a rationing system within the NHS. A proportion of medical problems will simply get better on their own if the patient waits; another small proportion will prove fatal and therefore also disappear; a small proportion will cease to worry the patient sufficiently to be pursued after a short wait; and a proportion of clinical appointments will be cancelled by patients for logistic reasons.

The NHS adopted targets so that patients should not have to wait more than 48 hours to see a family doctor, four hours in hospital accident and emergency departments, and 18 weeks after referral to see a consultant and start treatment. However, anecdotally, some people report that appointments are made within this referral time, to hit targets, and then cancelled; it then takes more time to get the consultant appointment rearranged, as a way of lengthening waiting times without apparently missing targets. Some published waiting times may not reflect the reality, with patients routinely waiting more than 18 weeks.

Hospitals, administrators and consultants bear the brunt of dissatisfaction in this issue, and therefore positive stories that celebrate some new advance by them may trigger a backlash asking why local waiting times were not reduced instead.

During one of the many NHS rationalisations in the 1980s, health regions and individual hospitals started being set targets or standards for a range of other services such as operations for glue ear or hip replacements, for example. This was an attempt to standardise treatment rates and prevent postcode lotteries, where patients in one part of the country were unable to access a treatment, while clinics in other parts might be undersubscribed.

Statisticians collected a wide range of data about different conditions and then worked out what the average rates of provision were, and these were used to calculate targets. Often targets were set at slightly above this average, although funding did not always match this. The targets therefore usually reflected average practice in the UK, rather than any need for such procedures. Please note that half the sample for anything will always be below average. Very little work was done on establishing what the right rate for each procedure was, or even whether the procedure itself was effective, as evidence-based medicine.

This should raise alarm bells for you as a public relations practitioner. If you are working on a medical condition, make sure that you have collected some genuine evidence about the real need for a treatment, rather than just the published target rates, as these may well be completely meaningless.

For example, you might find it easy to collect evidence about the proportion of people who go to their dentist for a regular check-up and tooth de-scale every six months, as recommended to prevent gum disease. But is there any evidence at all that having a dental check-up every six months, instead of every year or every month, is beneficial? There is evidence that visiting your dentist reduces gum disease, of course, but who set the frequency target? Dentists?

In 2010, a public consultation was opened to review NHS standards and targets, with the clinical watchdog for England, the National Institute for Health and Clinical Excellence, being asked to develop new standards in 150 areas of healthcare.[13] If you ever need to prepare a campaign based on risks and public perception I recommend that you first read *Superfreakonomics*, by Steven Levitt and Stephen Dubner.[14]

Self-harm and **addiction**: obesity, anorexia, smoking, drinking, taking drugs and other forms of self-harm are all conditions perceived by the public as being self-inflicted to a certain extent, and therefore possibly less deserving of urgent treatment or special resources than other medical conditions. In a rationed system, people presenting with these conditions may be resented by other patients. Positive stories announcing advances in these areas, either through research, new medicines or new treatment centres, may trigger a backlash asking why these patients get special treatment while others (implicitly more deserving) are ignored. The particularly vulnerable or fragile mental health of some patients presenting with these conditions means that public relations activity in these fields needs to be handled with special sensitivity.

In 2009, Prof David Nutt was sacked as chair of the UK government's Advisory Council on the Misuse of Drugs for saying that some drugs such as cannabis were less harmful than alcohol or tobacco. Several other members of the government committee resigned in protest over his sacking, leading to him setting up an independent advisory committee.

In 2012, David Nutt published a new book, *Drugs Without the Hot Air*,[15] claiming that bona fide drug research into the useful medical effects of illegal drugs on the brain, such as cannabis for pain relief or ecstasy for depression and schizophrenia, was being hampered by the government's insistence on their illegality, making medical research difficult, expensive and time-consuming. He also suggests that by 2030 it is likely that every child will have their DNA sequenced at birth, helping to avoid adverse drug side effects and predicting any tendency towards drug dependency.[16]

As an example of the type of medical advances that could be made if drug research was rationalised, non-addictive drugs derived from magic mushrooms could help people with depression or help users overcome other addictions.[17]

Any addicts using alcohol or illegal drugs who refuse treatment face having their welfare benefits cut from April 2013 under new proposals by the UK government. Work and pensions secretary Iain Duncan Smith announced this in a talk given to representatives from Alcoholics Anonymous organised in Parliament. Almost 40,000 people claiming incapacity benefits are diagnosed as having alcoholism, and 160,000 dependent drinkers receive some welfare benefits in the UK according to the Department of Work and Pensions.[18]

More recent research is starting to voice the opinion that sugar is as addictive and as dangerous a drug as alcohol, and is directly leading to the obesity epidemic threatening to overwhelm developed countries' health services. In 1806, Britain's fattest man, Daniel Lambert, had his portrait painted weighing 53 stones or 335kg. He made a career and his fortune at a freak show by charging people to see him. Today he would not be considered particularly unusual, according to Jacques Peretti, who has investigated the introduction of sugar and corn syrups as food additives and preservatives into our everyday diets.[19]

By blaming fat and fatty foods as the cause of rising rates of heart disease in the 1970s, the food industry was able to sell us a whole new range of low-fat health foods, in which fat had been replaced by sugars (since otherwise it would taste like cardboard). This led directly to the current obesity crisis, since sugar is addictive and does not trigger our natural defences that tell us when we are full, as exposed in a 2012 BBC2 programme, *The Men Who Made Us Fat.*[20]

When I last researched the subject for an agricultural story, the UK's biggest sugar company alone was receiving more than £120m a year in EU Common Agricultural Policy subsidies; subsidies that a trusting public fondly believes are there to help small family farms survive and protect our characteristic countryside.

Researchers from Oxford University have suggested that a 20 per cent 'fat tax' is needed to improve health, cut heart disease and reduce obesity, in a paper published in the *British Medical Journal* in May 2012. The study found that taxing a wide range of unhealthy foods or nutrients is likely to result in greater health benefits than narrow taxes, they say, although the strongest evidence base is for a tax on sugary drinks.[21]

This research raised the debate from a previous recommendation of a 10 per cent fat tax on sugary drinks, recommended in a study published in the *British Journal of Nutrition* in December 2011 by Prof Susan Jebb, the UK government's obesity adviser, and others. In October 2011, Denmark introduced a fat tax on foods containing more than 2.3 per cent saturated fat, and France has already adopted rules on salt, sugar and fat in food and drink in schools, cutting the proportion of overweight children.[22]

The word obesity, previously a value-neutral clinical description, is now being criticised as offensive to patients, and new official guidance suggests that it should be avoided. This can make discussing these important health-threatening issues in public very difficult for public relations departments, in a syndrome popularly known as political correctness gone mad.

The UK's National Institute for Health and Clinical Excellence, usually known as NICE, issued new draft guidance on 8 May 2012, 'Obesity – working with communities',[23] which had, among its key suggestions:

> [People] should carefully consider the type of language and media to use to communicate about obesity. For example, it might be better to refer to a 'healthier weight' rather than 'obesity' – and to talk more generally about health and wellbeing or specific community issues.

Perhaps all NHS public relations people should have responded by asking the NICE policy wonks to rewrite its draft guidance, completely avoiding the word obesity, to test whether this was a realistic or even meaningful suggestion. Certainly the science journalists mocked it.

Mental illness and **medicalisation:** increasing medicalisation of life, or defining as medical conditions things that most people would regard as within the range of normal behaviour, raises issues of stigma and prejudice about mental illness. It also raises questions of personal responsibility and blame if genetics or upbringing can cause such aberrant behaviour; and legal considerations such as whether a person meeting the clinical criteria for some syndrome involving impulsive behaviour or risk taking can be considered culpable and convicted of a crime such as theft (see neuroethics, p.145).

Fertility, gender reassignment, cosmetic surgery, implants: elective cosmetic surgery, gender reassignment and, to a lesser extent, fertility treatments (in an overpopulated world) are all seen as lifestyle choices by some groups or members of the public and therefore also perceived as less slightly deserving by placing an unnecessary and expensive burden upon the NHS.

As with self-harm, the particularly desperate, unhappy, vulnerable or fragile mental health of some patients presenting with these conditions means that public relations activity in these fields also needs to be handled with special sensitivity. Patients who have burns, surgical cancer treatments, congenital abnormalities or who have been involved in accidents that have left them needing cosmetic reconstruction may feel criticised, or resent being confused by the media with people who chose elective cosmetic surgery.

The media's fascination with the French breast implant manufacturers Poly Implant Prosthese, or PIP, in December 2011 and early 2012, who were found to have used inferior quality silicone gel, meant for mattresses rather than surgical-grade material, with a presumed greater risk of cancer, demonstrated a measure of schadenfreude mixed with genuine concern for the tens of thousands of women affected.

UK women who received their implants during reconstructive surgery on the NHS were offered free removal and replacement, while women who had elective surgery in private clinics were originally in many cases faced with further charges for removal or replacement by the clinics. It became a PR disaster for some private clinics, and eventually, in a press release on 15 March 2012, the NHS offered free removal for all women worried by their implants.

Because implants were in the news, stories about the possible cancer implications of artificial hips and other joints moved from medical discussion forums into the mainstream media. In February 2012, long-known findings from US and UK research into metal-on-metal hip replacements hit the news with suggestions that they could cause cancer or genetic damage. Two devices implanted into around 10,000 patients in the UK were taken off the market in 2010 due to safety concerns and high failure rates.[24] In the subsequent media discussions, science facts were misquoted such as a danger from toxic cadmium ions rather than the true risk from cobalt ions, and illustrations included X-rays of plastic replacements rather than metal ones.[25]

The issue of fertility treatment has come under similar public scrutiny and divided opinions in a cash-strapped health service. The National Institute for Health and Clinical Excellence issued a press release[26] in May 2012 announcing consultations on a new policy. This could see 'a broadening of the criteria for the provision of in-vitro fertilisation (IVF) to include some women aged 40 to 42', according to Dr Gill Leng, deputy chief executive of NICE.

To a public relations practitioner, stories about fertility present a challenge to tread the fine line between public sympathy for childless women and public censure for apparently feckless career women who may be perceived as having made the lifestyle choice to delay childbirth until too late to conceive naturally. Men, of course, rarely get any of the blame. Although male-dominated official bodies do seem to feel that they should make the decisions.

The language of medical intervention and public debate also often serves to hide the reality of commercial transactions carried out under the guise of compassion. There is nothing surrogate about a surrogate mother paid to sell a child, and a paid egg donor isn't a donor, according to bioethics expert Donna Dickenson.[27]

Abortions: women needing abortions, the counsellors advising on them and the medical teams providing them have all recently come under intensive criticism, intimidation and threats, mainly from faith-based groups. In the US, abortion doctors have even been shot. During 2012, UK faith campaigners mounted an intensive 40-day campaign of clinic doorstep protests in the religious Lent period, and were accused of intimidating women attending clinics. This followed recent UK government ministers' calls for the law to be changed to make getting an abortion harder.

Not-for-profit clinics providing abortions were branded as having vested interests and therefore as being unsuitable to provide unbiased counselling. A pregnancy advisory charity was replaced on a government consultation committee by a faith-based group. After undercover media investigations, clinics were subsequently subjected to extra official oversight, surprise visits and scrutiny in an effort to uncover wrongdoing, which could lead to abortion services being suspended.

Women's groups are concerned that young doctors are not seeking to train in abortion as a speciality because of the stigma and threats.[28] Campaigners on both sides choose emotive language to describe their position in the debate, such as pro-choice or pro-life. The right for women to control their own bodies is also seen as a feminist issue for many people. Special consideration needs to be given to any public relations activity, especially where it may concern women who have been subjected to criminal rape, physical abuse, incest, or when a girl was under consensual age for sex.

The Care Quality Commission has inspected abortion clinics as part of this recent clampdown, and the Royal College of Obstetricians and Gynaecologists responded with concerns that this extra scrutiny could deter doctors from performing them and deter women needing abortions. The Royal College suggested that the 1967 Abortion Act requirement for two doctors' signatures should be reduced to one. The annual statistics show that about 200,000 terminations a year are carried out in England.[29]

In a further exchange, a wide alliance of women's groups, including the Fawcett Society, UK Feminista and Marie Stopes (the UK's biggest abortion provider), responded to this by pointing out that the UK requirement for two doctors' signatures was introduced to provide legal protection for doctors, not as a guarantee of good care for women, and that it is the law, not doctors' practice, that should now be reviewed.[30]

Elsewhere, a law court in Spain has ordered a doctor who failed to terminate a pregnancy successfully to pay maintenance for the child until he is aged 25 years. The doctor was considered to have paid insufficient attention to an ultrasound scan two weeks later to check that the abortion had been successful, and by the time the mother realised that she was still pregnant she was well past the 22-week legal limit for abortions in Spain. The mother sued for damages, and was awarded €150,000 plus nearly €1,000 a month for 25 years.[31]

Data protection: campaigners are concerned about efforts to computerise NHS records, so that when a person changes area or has to go into hospital for an unrelated procedure, the attending doctors and nurses can see what other medications the patient is taking, and also see their life history. This may mean that some patients are stigmatised, and that their personal histories will be open to unauthorised access or leaks.

NHS efforts at computerisation have been claimed to be very expensive, wasteful and unworkable. The data produced by health authorities is also sometimes questionable. For instance researchers from Imperial College, London, found that during one year, 17,000 men were admitted to hospital for obstetric services, another 8,000 went to see a gynaecologist and 20,000 needed midwives. The 2009–2010 statistics also found 3,000 children who apparently needed geriatric services.[32] Given this inability of the NHS to accurately record the statistics and data that it already collects, it is hardly surprising that announcements of proposals for further sensitive data storage are met with less than enthusiastic responses.

In December 2011, the United States' Mayo Clinic launched a pilot study in proactive genomics, which will record the full genetic code of thousands of volunteers in an attempt to offer them personalised healthcare. The trial will allow doctors to see which drugs work best for which patients, who is likely to be unresponsive or suffer side effects, and whether an alternative drug would be likely to work better, based on the patient's genetic make-up. At present, expensive genetic tests are usually only commissioned once problems show up. Using genomics may also allow healthcare to become predictive, allowing doctors to advise on lifestyle, exercise or dietary changes that could help to stave off diseases identified as high risk for particular individuals.

Response in the UK to the Mayo Clinic's proposed trial focused on the data storage and security issues. Prof Tim Altman of Imperial College, London, interviewed by Ian Sample, the *Guardian* newspaper's science correspondent, said:[33]

> The questions that arise are who is going to store the information, how is it stored securely, who has access, and what are you going to do with information that you or the patient might not necessarily want to find out?

Mistakes and compensation: the rise of no-win, no-fee litigation in the UK has seen ambulance-chasing lawyers mounting expensive television advertising campaigns to seek clients and obtain compensation for patients damaged through medical negligence, mistakes and misunderstanding. The public relations position here is difficult if your organisation is involved. On the one hand, damaged patients may need extra care which incurs extra costs; on the other the other lawyers' fees and punitive compensation payments come out of the public purse, ultimately reducing the care and services that other NHS patients can be offered in a cash-strapped service.

Relatives naturally want to see someone pay for mistakes, or at least apologise; medical staff are warned that admitting any liability could increase compensation awards. Patients' pressure groups may also get involved, including Action Against Medical Accidents. Claims are handled by the NHS Litigation Authority.

Part of the public disconnect here is a feeling that the government should pay for mistakes, but forgetting that governments do not have their own money, it is all raised through taxes. As an example of the scale of this problem, consider newborn babies, who are especially vulnerable – and emotive – and we rightly pay a lot of attention to trying to give them the best possible care. In April 2012, NHS lawyers set aside £235m to pay 60 claims for compensation for brain damage to newborn babies, allegedly caused by midwives' and doctors' negligence in failing to adequately monitor blood sugar levels.[34]

Government attempts to cut legal costs by £350m a year and reform the way state subsidy through legal aid is offered in the UK came under fire in December 2011 when senior politicians including Lord Tebbit campaigned to save access to legal aid for children in medical negligence and compensation cases. Other clinical negligence cases for adults may still lose legal aid. Justice Secretary Kenneth Clarke criticised the current system for awarding lawyers costs that dwarf the damages they have won for their clients.[35]

The NHS paid out a record £1.2bn in litigation claims for clinical negligence compensation between 2011 and 2012 according to the NHS Litigation Authority, plus £52m for other non-clinical claims such as people slipping and hurting themselves on wet floors.[36]

MRSA and superbugs: a huge problem for hospitals and clinics, a source of real fear for patients, and a staple of media scare stories is the rise and spread of antibiotic-resistant bacteria, especially Methicillin-resistant *Staphylococcus aureus*, sometimes now known as multiple drug-resistant *Staphylococcus aureus*, or MRSA. There are now other bacterial species that are similarly resistant to antibiotics, but the terms MRSA, or superbug, have become a shorthand for them all.

We are now seeing these superbugs spread outside hospitals with new strains called community-acquired MRSA or community-associated MRSA. The bugs are often contracted through closed environments, such as prisons or sports centres, where people are in close personal contact.

Hospitals and doctors overprescribing antibiotics are routinely blamed for the spread and the bacteria's development in the first place, yet people with mild viruses or general aches and pains still turn up in GP clinics demanding antibiotics. And many patients, anecdotally, fail to complete their drug courses and may even save a few pills for future use, either by themselves or family members. Which is probably what caused the problem in the first place. See also synthetic life, p.147.

Ageism: as noted earlier in this chapter, we are now facing a crisis of old age, with more people living much longer than expected and needing increasing care as they become infirm. This need for care is becoming a major issue, as younger people may see it as a concentration of scarce resources on the elderly, which could breed resentment. Conversely, and in doublethink, many younger people, priced out of current housing markets and facing an uncertain financial future themselves, may be hoping for capital legacies from their parents and grandparents.

People want the government, by which they unconsciously mean 'the state' rather than 'taxpayers' or 'me', to fund care for the elderly without forcing them to use up all their assets by paying for personal care themselves. Governments meanwhile try to tread a fine budgetary line between funding proper nursing care for the elderly and sick, and avoiding paying for social care for the simply infirm, without drawing voter fire for imposing granny taxes. The public is quite capable of holding these two opposing and mutually exclusive opinions simultaneously.

The independent Commission on Funding of Care and Support, which reported to the UK government on 4 July 2011, known as the Dilnot Commission, suggested that state support for people with assets should be increased. It recommended a cap of £35,000 on care costs faced by any one person before receiving full state support, and an increase in the means-tested threshold to £100,000 from £23,250.

By contrast, the right-wing thinktank, the Centre for Social Justice, published a report *Transforming Social Care*, on 8 May 2012, calling for support to pensioners to be concentrated instead on the neediest, identified as those people completely dependent on state benefits, particularly the two-thirds of elderly people living in care homes who are funded by the state.[37]

In the UK, the financial crisis precipitated by the banking collapse has seen some private care homes running into problems, with major provider group Southern Cross collapsing in 2011 and its homes being sold off. In May 2012, Terra Firma, a private equity fund run by financier Guy Hands, purchased the UK's biggest care homes group Four Seasons for a reputed £820m and members of parliament called for a review of care home ownership, and the introduction of a fit and proper person test.[38]

Residents in care homes are considered especially vulnerable, and NHS officials have criticised GPs who are treating patients in care homes for putting 'do not resuscitate' or 'do not attempt resuscitation' notices on their notes without first discussing the action with residents themselves or their families. Even if the doctor considers that the patient does not have the capacity to make an informed decision, failing to consult the family could be considered to be a breach of human rights.[39]

As a public relations expert, you need to identify and examine any potential opportunities for unconscious ageism to creep into your organisation's communications and policies. The relationship between young and old, and the cut-off points for defining young and old, are in flux. If your organisation is suggesting that a new policy or proposal will harm or aid either the young or the old at the expense of other groups, then you need to make sure that you have sound basic data to support your underlying proposition, in addition to the data supporting the actual proposal. Is it true that the elderly are actually well-off compared with the young of today, or are you just echoing a popular myth? Where did you get your income distribution data?

In June 2012, the UK Home Secretary Theresa May announced that from October 2012, health treatment cannot be withheld on the grounds of age, under tighter discrimination laws.[40]

The *Guardian* newspaper's style guide suggests that only those over the age of 75 years should be described as elderly or older people, and never 'the elderly' to avoid defining someone by their age. Chris Elliott, the *Guardian*'s readers' editor, wrote that 'patently age is relevant in some stories: man runs marathon – so what? Centenarian runs marathon – a story'. Our ageing but more active population needs careful treatment.[41] 'The young' may be an equally touchy label.

Doctor-induced illness: first do no harm. Cancer treatment is probably the obvious example to take as an example of this issue since, generally speaking, cancer treatments target dividing cells and so they damage some healthy tissues as well as the rapidly multiplying cancerous tissue, or involve radical surgery that may or may not be successful. Cancerous cells not at the point of division may also get missed, requiring repeated treatments.

In recent research review findings, the harm caused to women from wrong diagnoses and damaging treatments after breast cancer screening appears greater than the good done for the small number of women's lives saved, according to a Cochrane Collaboration study published in Norway in January 2012, and a *British Medical Journal* paper in December 2011. Mammogram cancer screening saves one life for every 2,000 women screened, but harms ten others with needless breast surgery, radiotherapy, chemotherapy and other treatments, and false positives that cause mental distress.[42] NHS leaflets explaining screening have been criticised for exaggerating benefits and not spelling out the risks.[43]

The public probably does not attach as much importance (or, at least, pay as much attention) to Cochrane reviews as it does to dramatic but single research result stories from a well-known hospital group. This is even though the Cochrane reviews are much more statistically powerful, typically looking at all the available evidence, assessing the quality of the studies and aggregating findings from a wide variety of medical research and follow-up statistics, often across several countries, allowing overall patterns to emerge.

Pharmaceutical company issues

Side effects: all drugs have side effects. They are active and standardised pharmaceuticals designed to alter your body's chemistry. We are individuals. Hopefully the risk from the side effect is lower than the risk from the medicine, otherwise it would never have been licensed for general use. However, for individual patients, especially in the case of preventative medicines, some people will suffer adverse side effects who would never have contracted the disease they were trying to prevent. Whose fault is this?

For instance, commonly prescribed sleeping pills have been linked to a fourfold risk of death, according to a study published in the *British Medical Journal* Open journal in February 2012. In addition to an estimated half million extra deaths in the US every year, sleeping pill users were found to have a one-third increased risk of cancer, although as with the extra deaths, the relationship may not be directly causal, simply associated.[44] A survey for *Mixmag* magazine by Global Drug Survey in March 2012 found that weekend recreational drug users were using sleeping pills to help them get back to work on Monday, with more than half the drugs coming from friends or dealers rather than doctors.[45]

In addition to unforeseen side effects, medicine labels giving dosage regimes have been criticised as being too complicated for most patients to understand, especially those with poor literacy skills. In a paper published in the *British Medical Journal* in 2012, researchers from University College London found that a third of older people have an increased risk of dying because they do not understand the instructions on labels.[46]

We do not have a culture of risk assessment or risk intelligence in Europe, we naïvely expect things to be safe and may look for someone else to blame when they are not. For more on risks see *Risk Intelligence: How to Live with Uncertainty* by Dylan Evans.[47]

Fake drugs: like counterfeit currency, fake drugs are a high-value but small-sized commodity with a very large market, making them an attractive proposition for criminals and a serious problem for the pharmaceutical companies whose genuine products they undermine. In 2012, malaria experts writing in the *Malaria Journal* said that any hopes of the disease being controlled in Africa were being wrecked by criminals selling substandard and counterfeit drugs, risking millions of lives.

Fake drugs that contain low doses of the active ingredients are not only unlikely to save lives, they also risk spreading drug resistance from the surviving parasites, making the genuine medicines ineffective. Other fake drugs were found to contain mixtures of active ingredients, but the wrong ones, running the risk of causing dangerous side effects or interactions with other genuine medicines such as HIV treatments.[48]

Misrepresentation, fraud and **bribes**: claims that doctors are deliberately misled over the risks associated with a drug and are encouraged to prescribe medicines for groups they have not been licensed for, such as young children or patients suffering from different diseases, can lead to government and court fines in addition to loss of reputation. Medical device manufacturers are similarly alleged to have illegally paid doctors to implant their pacemakers and defibrillators, for example when US company Medtronic was fined $23.5m (for this and similar cases see Prof Allyson Pollock's 2004 book, *NHS plc: the Privatisation of Our Healthcare*[49]).

In 2012, the US company Johnson & Johnson was given a $1.1bn fine (£700m) by a US court under consumer protection laws, for misleading doctors over the risks posed by an anti-psychotic drug, by claiming that it was safer than rivals.[50] British pharmaceutical company GlaxoSmithKline paid $3bn to the US government in November 2011 to settle claims that it hid damaging findings, encouraged inappropriate or off-label use and used aggressive marketing tactics to persuade doctors to prescribe its drugs.[51]

Drug trials: pharmaceutical companies are criticised for cherry-picking drug trial data, failing to disclose the full results of all trials, comparing doses of their drugs with unrealistic doses of rival drugs and other manipulations that present their medicine in a better light than is really justified in order to gain drug licence permission and encourage widespread prescription by doctors. *Guardian* columnist and GP Ben Goldacre has written extensively about this in his Bad Science articles for many years, and available in book form since October 2008, although at least one chapter was held back for legal reasons until 2012.[52]

In a sidetrack to the question of dosages, there were calls for all drug guidelines to be reviewed as children and adults get heavier, in a discussion in the *British Medical Journal* in December 2011. For many years doctors have estimated that a big child's drug dose is half an adult's, a small child's half that, and a baby's dose is half that again, or an eighth of an adult's.[53] However, for drugs such as penicillin, which makes up three-quarters of all antibiotic prescriptions in the UK, the dosages are based on expected weight at particular ages, weights which have increased by 20 per cent since the guidelines were set in the 1960s.

Further problems with drug trials include getting ethical permission from regulatory committees and full consent from healthy volunteers who test drugs in some of the final stages before they are released. Volunteers should not be paid to take unnecessary risks, all fees paid are supposed to be token payments to cover the reasonable expenses and costs to volunteers for offering their help.

In practice, and anecdotally as presented at a conference I attended in 1996, the university students and other people who volunteer to test drugs almost all do it for the money, even though the amounts are very small, suggesting that drug testers should perhaps be paid properly for the work instead.

In cancer trials in particular, it is difficult to recruit sufficient controls in clinical trials, due to the known unpleasant side effects and toxicity of most chemotherapy drugs (for a case history example see Exeter pharmacist Libby Hardy, writing in *Daily Telegraph* letters[54]).

Sponsorship: drug companies have been criticised for sponsoring trips, meals, and conferences for doctors as these perks may be seen as trying to encourage doctors to prescribe expensive branded drugs rather than cheaper and equally effective alternatives. Pharmaceutical company AstraZeneca said in 2011 that it would no longer pay airfares and hotel bills for doctors attending medical conferences.[55] For more on this issue, and the $3bn fine levied on GlaxoSmithKline in 2012, see Chapter 10, 'Sponsorship', p.117, and widespread news reports from 4 and 5 July 2012.

Patents: many of our most effective medicines have been synthesised after finding active molecules in plants, whose action was first recognised in traditional cultures or as herbal medicines. Campaigners are concerned that these traditional remedies are becoming medicines that are now patented by international pharmaceutical companies and the resulting profits go to developed world investors, not the indigenous people who first recognised, owned and used the herb as medicine.

As an example the San Bushmen in the Kalahari desert have been using a local cactus-like plant, hoodia, to ward off hunger pangs and help mobilise fat reserves during their hunting trips for thousands of years. In 1995, an active ingredient from hoodia was isolated in South Africa, patented and licensed to Phytopharm, a British pharmaceutical company, to develop a safe appetite suppressant as a diet and weight loss pill. A fund was set up for the San to pay for waterholes, schools, hospitals and other medical care, reputedly giving them around 15 per cent of the profits from any commercial marketing of hoodia. This was allegedly the best deal that any indigenous people had ever managed to strike, and as such a credit to Phytopharm for recognising the San's intellectual rights.

As a public relations practitioner, could you defend 15 per cent? How about 10 per cent? Or 20 per cent? The sums involved are huge. Should it have been 15 per cent of the profits or 15 per cent of the gross income? Should the San have been given the patent outright? How can something that was based on their indigenous knowledge be patented by someone else in the first place?

Political, ethical and philosophical problems: neuroethics

Neuroethics is becoming a recognised and specialised branch of medical ethics due to concerns over mental health implications, mind-reading technologies and smart drugs in particular.

Smart drugs are medicines designed to boost intelligence or cognitive functions, especially in patients with early stages of Alzheimer's disease or Parkinson's, enabling them to go on functioning for longer and with better results, in some cases even reversing the effects of brain degeneration. These mood- and mind-altering drugs are understandably attractive for university students and others who wish to temporarily improve their memory or brain function while sitting exams, in spite of their side effects and known harmful or banned ingredients.

For example drugs used to treat attention deficit and hyperactivity disorder may improve concentration. The drugs are now turning up in some products for sale on the internet and marketed as natural or herbal according to Prof Mark Bellis of Liverpool John Moores University.[56]

Mind-reading machines, which can interpret brainwaves and allow locked-in patients to communicate for the first time with their carers, have now been successfully developed and are offering a huge improvement in quality of life to their users. Other mind-reading devices are now controlling prostheses or artificial limbs, with a woman paralysed 15 years earlier by a brain stem stroke recently managing to use a brain implant to move a robot arm to drink coffee.[57]

These same machines, and further developments leading from them, have the potential to be used as sophisticated lie detectors and could be used in criminal trials to decide someone's intention as well as whether they actually committed a criminal act, so-called thought crimes. In a sinister application of the same technology, soldiers could be plugged directly into their weapons in the future, and memory-wiping drugs could suppress any traumatic after-effects of their actions.[58]

Mental illness, diseases and impairments are becoming better understood as neuroscience advances, and it is apparent that people with any of a number of autism spectrum disorders and other mental challenges means that their responses are often not within the normal boundaries set by civil society. They are much more likely to be involved in accidents such as car crashes, or convicted of crimes such as theft and drug abuse, than are people found within the more average ranges of society. This may be because some people with autistic and attention deficit disorders are more likely to overestimate the rewards of an action and more likely to underestimate the risks, leading them to impulsive and potentially dangerous behaviours. These could include jumping red lights at traffic signals, trying addictive drugs such as heroin, or simply picking up a handful of cash on the counter in a bank.

These people are not usually malicious criminals, indeed many autistic people find it difficult to lie and so may make no attempt to hide their actions, leading to a much greater likelihood that they will be caught and prosecuted in a society that holds them personally responsible for their actions. Is this right? Will further neuroscience advances mean that even mild autism could become a successful legal defence? Remember, autism is a spectrum, which means that we are all on it somewhere.

As noted earlier in this chapter (p.136), increasing medicalisation of what many people would describe as normal if somewhat unacceptable behaviour is leading to a further blurring of the boundaries between culpability and behaviour that needs treatment, counselling or understanding rather than punishment. The latest edition of the psychiatrists' bible in the US, known as the *Diagnostic and Statistical Manual Edition 5*, or DSM-5, has raised concerns that hundreds of thousands of extra people could now be diagnosed as mentally ill in the UK alone, due to its widespread use as a reference tool and in research worldwide.

Because it gives names to specific conditions that many people might dismiss as ordinary mild anxiety, such as shyness in children or unhappiness after bereavement, pharmaceutical companies are able to generate funds by devising drugs to treat them, which healthcare insurers in the US are then obliged to pay for. The British Psychological Association has strongly criticised DSM-5.[59]

Similar arbitrary distinctions are being made by doctors about other potential hazards such as high blood pressure or cholesterol, with GPs often prescribing pills rather than recommending lifestyle changes, and patients content to take them rather than addressing the underlying lifestyle factors. This can lead to a succession of other medicines such as laxatives or eyedrops designed to solve problems created by the first ones.[60]

Drugs may not even be the best treatment for preventing mental illnesses according to research published on the *British Medical Journal* website in April 2012. A study led by the University of Manchester found that psychotic symptoms usually leading to more serious schizophrenia could be better reduced by counselling and cognitive therapy, often known as talking cures.[61]

Academic research issues

Source of funds: medical researchers have been criticised for accepting research funds from inappropriate bodies. Most notably in 1997, when one of my friends and a widely respected public relations colleague, the head of communications for the Medical Research Council in the UK, Mary Rice, was sacked for revealing to a journalist that a Medical Research Council institute had accepted tobacco company funding to carry out cancer research.

Acknowledgement and **equity:** it has been suggested that as part of their ethical codes, research groups should adopt feminist principles of research, in which all contributors to the research – such as indigenous peoples who have been studied or acted as native guides during a research trip – are acknowledged and properly rewarded for their part in the work, rather than just the developed country researchers who write up and publish the paper. Postgraduate students believe that they are badly paid; but students who temporarily lodge with a remote tribe are likely to be receiving far more money, however inadequate their stipend, than the tribal members.

More famously, arguably the most important woman in recent medical history, a poor black farmer called Henrietta Lacks, whose immortal cell line known as HeLa is used by almost every laboratory in the world, did not profit from her own cancer cells, nor did her family, while academic researchers built lucrative careers on her illness.[62]

Synthetic life and **bioterrorism:** the ability of research groups to construct synthetic life, as claimed by Craig Venter in May 2010,[63] or artificial bacteria, or insert a variety of genes into yeast and other simple organisms whose genomes have been decoded have raised real fears of bioterrorism. This has also prompted the suggestion that some research is too sensitive or dangerous to be published in mainstream academic journals.

Laboratory reports of a genetically engineered and easily transmissible version of bird flu, due to be published in the peer-reviewed journal *Nature*, were asked to be censored by US authorities in February 2012, although the papers were eventually published in full. The issue was debated at the New York Academy of Sciences by leading virus experts after two research groups successfully showed that the bird flu virus could be transmitted through the air.[64]

Open access publishing: the academic spring of 2012 has seen a wave of leading scientific institutions, universities and medical charities rebelling against the stranglehold of the big three scientific publishers by suggesting that publicly funded research should be available in open access journals rather than through the eye-wateringly expensive traditional journal system.

The revolt has been led by the Wellcome Trust, which put down a marker that researchers accepting its grants would have to also publish in open access forums within set time limits of first publication. Academics, conscious of their prestige, have grumbled about costs of reprints and expensive access for years, but then jumped at any chance of publishing in *Nature* or *Science*, widely regarded as the top two journals in the world.

The current system restricts readership of major scientific papers to academics working at the richest few institutions and unfairly excludes developing countries and independent researchers from keeping up to date with their field. In July 2012 following recommendations from Dame Janet Finch of Manchester University, the UK government unveiled plans to make publicly funded research available to anyone[65] (see also Chapter 8, 'Journals').

Plagiarism: the scientific practice of building on and referencing all previous work in a field, the academic pressure to publish and the system of peer review for both grants and published articles all mean that the fine dividing line between furnishing a thorough review of competing theories and advances; developing and following promising lines of thought; and outright copying are becoming increasingly blurred.

Universities routinely offer advice and guidance to postgraduates as they study for their degrees, and supervisors may even help with suggestions for rewriting sections to make findings clearer or recommending promising avenues for further enquiry. All of these teaching practices can increase the chances of the researcher, and therefore the department and supervisor, of getting a journal article accepted in a good publication.

The distinction between these legitimate aids to clarity, and charges of outright plagiarism or receiving unfair paid assistance, may be unclear in an increasingly globalised world where researchers often move across continents and into different cultures, where different traditions of respect and imitation apply. Research groups from the same narrow field who are asked to review other groups' grant proposals, and who then decide in future to explore similar lines of enquiry, may also find themselves criticised for copying, or even be suspected of stealing ideas (see Chapter 8, 'Public access to research', p.81, for Rosalind Franklin and Freda Ticehurst's parts in the discovery of DNA structure).

Scientific fraud: deliberate academic fraud undermines the fundamental purpose of doing science, which is arguably to increase the sum of human knowledge. Fraud can send other research groups off on wild goose chases, delaying the successful developments of treatments; it can divert precious research funds into pointless avenues; and most importantly, it undermines public trust in research. Fortunately it is fairly rare. Or at least, exposing it is fairly rare.

One of the most recent, public and controversial cases of academic fraud came to its close in May 2006 when BBC News covered the story of South Korean stem-cell researcher Hwang Woo-suk, whose groundbreaking work on producing stem-cell lines from cloned human embryos was exposed as a fake, and he was subsequently charged with breaking bioethics laws, fraud and embezzlement of millions of dollars in grants.[66]

Such major cases of deliberate academic fraud appear to be infrequent, and likely to be exposed in the longer term when other research groups discover that they cannot replicate an academic research paper's findings or published techniques. However, cherry-picking results, using multiple statistical tests or excluding anomalous findings from a larger study to achieve statistical significance, are all lesser tweaks to data that may ultimately skew findings and enable an author to get a successful research paper published in a prestigious journal.

Epigenetics and **junk DNA:** epigenetics is a strange concept to those of us who grew up in the days of nature versus nurture or evolution versus environment debates, rigorously taught in an orthodoxy that said that your genetic material is fixed, has evolved through survival of the fittest, and it is this which makes you what you are, as first proposed by Charles Darwin (1809–1882) in *On the Origin of Species* in 1859, and Alfred Russel Wallace (1823–1913) who independently proposed evolution by natural selection. The phrase 'nature versus nurture' itself was later popularised by Charles Darwin's cousin, Sir Francis Galton (1822–1911).

The now discredited contrasting theory, transmutation of species, based on natural changes in species due to the ability to pass on learned traits, or acquired characteristics gained during your life, was proposed by French naturalist Jean-Baptiste Lamarck (1744–1829) in his *Theory of Inheritance and Acquired Characteristics* in 1801. Lamarck suggested that if an animal needed a particular ability to survive, such as a giraffe which stretched its neck to reach food at the tops of trees during times of sparse food, then it would pass this ability on to its offspring to ensure their survival too. Rudyard Kipling's (1865–1936) *Just-So Stories for Little Children* of 1902 are Lamarckian fables.

In a simplified form, the Darwinian explanation is that only those animals with naturally slightly longer necks (later shown to be due to their genetic mix), giving them an advantage during the prevailing conditions, would be likely to survive, mate successfully and pass on the genes for the slightly different characteristics. This long slow process eventually leads to distinct species as prevailing conditions in one area select for particular characteristics, compared with the conditions elsewhere which might favour a different set of characteristics. Or so several generations were taught at school and university (unless you attended a faith school, in which case scientific explanations for evolution are themselves fabulous).

Unfortunately epigenetics is showing that the simple evolutionary assumption of one gene, one action, is proving to be harder to justify than the mainstream scientific community thought. It now appears that some learned characteristics can be inherited, and that the inherited effects can last for several generations, through the action of switching on or off particular genes. Prof Tim Spector of King's College London has studied twins who have identical genes, but different abilities. Different experiences can make measurable differences to our brains and bodies as natural chemicals turn on some genes or expand and strengthen some areas at the expense of others. But the weird thing is that these differences appear to be able to be passed on to future generations, just as the *Just-So Stories* claimed.

Our genes code for proteins, not traits, and it is the proteins, working and interacting with the thousands of others within our bodies, which give us our abilities, often after thousands of hours of continued use. And it is those hours of use, using some gene products, or proteins and pathways, and not others, which leave a mark on our body systems, even as our cells divide and multiply. Many family traits have a surprisingly small original genetic component, perhaps only 1–2 per cent, others such as autism or a belief in God have as much as 50 per cent.[67]

The critical switches that turn genes on and off may be hidden in the 98 per cent of our DNA that previously geneticists have called junk DNA, after discovering through the Human Genome project (see http://genome.wellcome.ac.uk/) that we have far fewer genes than expected. Hundreds of researchers across the world in the Encyclopedia of DNA Elements or Encode project have been studying our junk DNA since 2003, and their results can be found on the website of the journal *Nature*.[68]

Genetics, gene therapy, stem cells: gene therapy, which can be seen as tampering with nature, and using stem cells (especially those derived from embryos) to treat diseases, are both seen as major ethical issues in medical research. The public may know that gene therapy and stem cells are controversial, thanks to anti-science campaigns by faith groups opposed to their use, but probably do not know why such therapies are considered unacceptable or what would constitute non-controversial treatments instead.

For nerve degenerative diseases such as Parkinson's, for replacement organs in transplants, repairing other tissues or even regrowing whole limbs, and to treat a wide range of genetic diseases, stem cells and gene therapy are seen as offering some of the most promising long-term solutions by researchers. At present, because of the widespread interest, these treatments are still seen as newsworthy in their own right, just as organ transplants or the identification of new gene functions were 20 years ago.

Doctors at Great Ormond Street Hospital in London announced in March 2012 that a 16-year-old boy born with a genetic immune deficiency, Chronic Granulomatous Disorder, had become the first patient to be given a new type of gene therapy while waiting for a more permanent cure from a bone marrow transplant.[69]

In February 2012, Japanese doctors from the Nippon Dental University in Tokyo announced that stem cells taken from tooth pulp obtained through routine extractions had been successfully converted into liver cells.[70]

US researchers from the Memorial Sloan-Kettering Cancer Center in New York successfully made dopamine-producing brain cells from stem cells, to reverse Parkinson's disease, and transplanted them into monkey brains in 2011 in a study published in the journal *Nature*.[71]

In a further development of genetic treatments, and in an attempt to consider ethical problems before treatments have caught up with research ambitions, science is now considering the possibility of so-called three-parent babies. These could avoid mitochondrial diseases caused when faulty DNA in the mitochondria or cell powerhouses, which is quite separate from the DNA in the cell nucleus, is passed on by the mother during cell division leading to egg formation. Around 1:6,500 children are affected by severe mitochondrial diseases in the UK every year, covering about 50 different genetic disorders.

One proposed solution would be to use techniques developed for in vitro fertilisation, to take an egg donated by a healthy person and insert the fertilised nucleus from the affected couple, so that the resulting child grows up with the healthy mitochondria inherited from the donor egg. Only mitochondrial DNA from the mother is passed on in normal fertilisation, so any genetic defects are also inherited and cannot be corrected by the father's mitochondrial DNA.

A Nuffield Council on Bioethics working group report concludes:

> Due to the health and social benefits to individuals and families living free from mitochondrial disorders, and where potential parents express a preference to have genetically related children, on balance we believe that if these novel techniques are adequately proven to be acceptably safe and effective as treatments, it would be ethical for families to use them, if they wish to do so and have been offered the appropriate level of information and support. Given the above and subject to the appropriate oversight, we believe that as a research objective it is ethical to gather further information about pronuclear transfer and maternal spindle transfer in order that they can be considered for treatment use.[72]

The concept of three-parent babies is opposed by activist faith groups such as the Christian Medical Fellowship.[73]

Charities, Churches and NGOs

Chuggers: rather than having volunteers collecting money in street collections, larger charities have sought to maximise their income by employing agencies with armies of paid street collectors, the so-called charity muggers or chuggers.

In addition to soliciting ordinary donations, chuggers typically get paid extra, or have targets, for signing up members of the public to monthly direct debits or other regular payments from their bank accounts. This provides the charity with a more regular source of income and allows it to reclaim the tax as well, increasing the value of the donations at no apparent extra expense to the donors. Because cancelling a bank order takes effort, the donor is more likely to allow it to continue for longer, resulting in more money for the charity over a longer period.

However, from a public relations point of view, using chuggers can be a reputational mistake as many people resent paid collectors, cherishing a notion that charitable work should be done free, and also strongly resent the aggressive tactics and dogged persistence used by some chuggers to solicit bank details on the street or in evening doorstep visits. So much so that people have now started crossing the road to avoid confrontations after spotting chuggers in action.

This came to a head for the Macmillan Cancer Charity in April 2012 when its own fundraisers in Aldeburgh, England, voted to boycott the charity after 30 years of support because of the agency fundraisers being used by the charity.[74] A government-commissioned report, 'Trusted and Independent: Giving Charity Back to Charities', chaired by Lord Hodgson and published in July 2012, recommended that if charities failed to regulate their agency chuggers, then laws should be passed to rein in bad behaviour. It suggests that the complaints system should be strengthened and simplified, replacing those currently operated by the three different regulatory bodies, the Fundraising Standards Board, the Public Fundraising Regulatory Association and the Institute of Fundraising.[75]

National versus local fundraising: the Great Ormond Street Hospital in London, formerly known as the Hospital for Sick Children, was famously supported and funded by the author and playwright J.M. Barrie, who donated the copyright and proceeds from his work *Peter Pan* to the hospital in 1929. In 1987, a major appeal, the Wishing Well, turned it in the public consciousness from a London-based good cause into a national charity, and it has since continued with a £300m fundraising effort to refurbish and update the facilities and continue its research work.

Local charities can suffer when major national charities are so successful in raising their public profile in this way that groups which formerly might have supported their local hospice or air ambulance decide that this year they will adopt a national charity instead. The local charities often have few other sources of support, so if several of their key fundraising groups such as local darts teams, rugby players or supermarkets decide to adopt a national cause for a change, they can run into severe financial difficulties.

Non-charities: if people see a street collection, information stalls and other evidence of activity normally associated with charities, they assume that the organisation involved is a registered charity, governed by the regulations of the Charity Commission in the UK.

Many local councils, which have to give permission for street collections, limit the number of days they will allow collections, to minimise nuisance to the public. They have some regular days such as Remembrance Day, 11 November every year in the UK, set aside for specific charities and appeals, but otherwise often take applications on a first come, first served basis. Crucially, many of these local authorities do not have a set policy for what constitutes an acceptable organisation to be allowed a street collection.

This has enabled many activist groups to successfully gain permission for street collections by mimicking charities. For example some animal rights groups are regarded as political entities by the Charity Commission and therefore denied charitable status for their main activities. But they still apply for street collections.

This has several advantages for the NGOs. It raises their public profile. It makes them appear to be charitable and reputable by mimicking charity activities, and therefore gains them credibility. It allows them to raise funds and it can allow them to distribute political literature, sometimes making unsupported claims, which would not be allowed from a genuine charity. And lastly it deprives a genuine medical or otherwise charitable cause the opportunity to use that day for their own street collections. Win, win, win.

Faith groups: probably the biggest faith issue is population control. The Catholic Church has consistently campaigned against contraception, even though rising population is now recognised as one of the major threats facing world health. A UK Royal Society report chaired by the Wellcome Trust's Nobel Prize-winning biologist Sir John Sulston, published in April 2012, warned that population must be controlled if the world's 9 billion people expected in 2012 are to live long and healthy lives.[76] The report says that all women who want it should be offered contraception. For abortion, see p.138.

Faith schools were still putting teenage girls' health at risk in July 2012 by denying them routine cervical cancer vaccines on religious grounds, according to an investigation by Marina Soteriou for *GP* magazine. Some UK schools have opted out of the human papillomavirus vaccination programme on religious grounds, citing a ban on sex outside marriage, but were not informing the pupils' GPs, so that alternative vaccine protection could be offered through their clinics.[77]

Euthanasia, assisted dying, eugenics: another set of no-go issues for faith groups. Almost anything to do with them is controversial, see Chapter 12, p.174, 'Dead and undead'.

Homosexuality: meanwhile homosexuality has consistently been portrayed by the Christian Churches, especially Catholics, as a transient illness that can be treated and cured, rather than a permanent, legitimate and natural part of the identity of some human personalities. Not everyone agrees with this position. Opposition to the concept of gay marriages may cause the Church of England to lose its state function in performing legally recognised marriages.

Wealth: the main faiths appear to be supremely relaxed about eye-watering wealth, in spite of several of the more well-regarded religious texts specifically warning against its dangers. Still, perhaps the faith groups will get to financial inequality once they have solved the problems of homosexuality and birth control.

Complementary and alternative medicine, placebos

Homeopathy, alternative and **complementary therapies:** there is no convincing evidence that homeopathy works, and it is probably a placebo effect (which is a very powerful effect indeed). I took part in an annual debate with Manchester University postgraduate life sciences students for more than five years, and evidence both for and against homeopathy was given by university researcher Austin Elliott, convincing me that it is almost certainly a placebo effect. For the occasional online polemic look for his blog, *Dr Aust's Spleen*.[78]

The UK's first and only Professor of Complementary Medicine, Eduard Ernst, who joined Exeter University in 1993, spent many years putting alternative and complementary therapies such as reflexology, acupuncture and spiritual healing through rigorous scientific tests, coming to similar conclusions that they do not work, before his early retirement in 2011 when funds for his unit dried up after a public row with Prince Charles, heir to the UK throne. Writing in *The Biologist* magazine in 2012, Ernst said that homeopathy is biologically implausible, in contrast with the laws of physics, chemistry and pharmacology, and could lead to real problems such as low vaccination rates because of homeopaths' advice not to immunise.[79]

In 2008, Ernst and the mathematician and science writer Simon Singh published *Trick or Treatment? Alternative Medicine on Trial,* which looks at 40 different alternative medical treatments.[80] During the publicity for the book launch, Singh was sued for libel by the British Chiropractic Association after dismissing their practices as bogus treatments in an article for the *Guardian* newspaper, headed 'Beware the spinal trap'. He faced personal ruin in two years of legal battle, which he eventually won in April 2010 when the UK Court of Appeal ruled that as a professional writer he could use the defence of fair comment, and the case was promptly withdrawn.

Singh's case has focused calls for a reform of the libel laws and, on 9 May 2012, the *UK Press Gazette* reported that libel reform was welcomed by the campaign group Sense About Science after proposals for reform were included in the Queen's speech, which outlines legislation for the next parliamentary session. Libel reform should also give relief and protect doctors who raise concerns about unwanted drug side effects.[81]

A 17-year-old schoolboy blogger from Cardiff, Rhys Morgan, who suffered from Crohn's disease, has also become an unlikely internet hero after similarly refusing to be intimidated by legal threats from wealthy organisations pushing miracle cures.[82]

Sense About Science and other sceptics question whether the NHS should be offering homeopathy and other such unverified procedures to patients; some doctors seem to believe that it is useful to get rid of persistent patients who have nothing intrinsically wrong with them, and anyway, homeopathy can do them no actual harm.

In protest at Boots and other UK pharmacies knowingly selling homeopathic remedies, medical students and the 10^{23} Campaign, named after Avogadro's number, organised mass overdoses on 30 January 2010. Activists purchased homeopathic remedies and then dramatically took massive overdoses, way beyond the recommended amounts, before falling lifelessly to the pavement outside pharmacies in demonstration that the remedies are in fact completely inert and harmless. The 2011 overdose event organised by Merseyside Sceptics Society was called 'Homeopathy – there's nothing in it'.

The Merseyside Sceptics Society followed this success with a Hallowe'en challenge to Sky TV celebrity psychic Sally Morgan in Liverpool on 31 October 2011, with a bid to win her the million-dollar prize offered by the James Randi Educational Foundation for anyone who can prove that their psychic gift is real. Morgan offers psychic readings on premium rate telephone lines, writes books and starred in three TV series, but has been accused of exploiting vulnerable and grieving people.[83]

For more on alternative and complementary therapies see the *Alternative Medicine: Fact from Fiction* lecture video available on YouTube,[84] featuring the author and academic Dylan Evans. He looks at a wide range of the alternative therapies practised outside medical schools including homeopathy, reiki and chiropracty, and finds that three of them, osteopathy, acupuncture and herbal medicine, may actually have significance as interventions. The key to the apparent success of the others may simply be the elements of shamanism that they incorporate: time, ritual and touch.

Placebos: a placebo is a fake, pretend or otherwise simulated medical treatment, medicine or procedure, usually used scientifically to test whether some other new treatment is actually effective. It can show when reported improvements are simply because people who believe that they are receiving medicines, even if they are not, will often get better, suggesting that belief and the brain play a critical role in our health.

The placebo effect is so powerful that modern medicines have to be very effective indeed to show up as statistically better than placebos. Placebos are used as controls in medical trials. Placebos can be completely inert, or sugar pills, which are coloured and designed to look exactly like the medicine being compared.

In the most statistically powerful version, a double blind trial, not even the researchers administering the treatments, or the patients receiving them, know whether the pill contains active ingredients or the placebo. This is in case unconscious body language cues accidentally give information to the patients. The results and which people received which version are only revealed at the very end when computer-generated randomisation patterns are uncovered.

Some research has been done on placebos themselves to investigate how powerful the effects are, and according to Austin Elliott of Manchester University, two pills are more effective than one; yellow or red coloured pills are more effective than white ones; invasive procedures that involve touching, such as injecting a weak saline solution, are more effective than pills; and repeated procedures, such as coming back the following week for another injection, are more effective than one-off interventions.

For the technically curious, and if you want my best guess, which you probably haven't asked for, the extraordinary power of placebos (or the apparent success of homeopathy, if you prefer) may be down to a neurotransmitter signalling cascade that activates the reward centres of the brain by providing endorphins and dopamine, our own natural painkillers. Or you could just eat some chocolate. For lots more on placebo effects see Dylan Evans' excellent book *Placebo: Mind over Matter in Modern Medicine*.[85]

In 2012, homeopathy was dropped at degree level at Bristol University, Derby University closed its complementary medicine department, and the University of Westminster closed most of its 14 BSc degrees in seven different complementary disciplines, retaining only acupuncture and herbal medicine.[86]

Twenty years of UK health scares

From the late 1980s, a sequence of health issues that were poorly communicated and poorly understood developed into health scares. They followed rapidly one after the other, even overlapping at times.

One of the most politically sensitive UK health scares was triggered by a junior Health Minister, Edwina Currie, in December 1988. During a BBC television interview, she claimed that 'most of the egg production in this country is now, sadly, affected with salmonella', a known bacterial cause of food poisoning. Sales fell by 60 per cent as millions of people stopped eating eggs, and many stopped eating chicken too, causing huge financial damage to the poultry industry as 400 million unwanted chickens were slaughtered. Currie, who initially refused to retract her statement, eventually had to resign. At the time her portfolio of responsibilities included my employers, UK Transplant Service. She was the minister we reported to, and for whom I organised photo opportunities and publicity events.

By 1994, a flesh-eating superbug was apparently ripping through hospitals and communities – a scare that turned out to be nothing more than the normal incidences of drug-resistant necrotising fasciitis that our hospitals see every year. Once the media spotlight was turned on them, these isolated cases of a little known but terrifying infection appeared to be a new epidemic sweeping the country.

In 1995, medical research seemed to show that women taking the contraceptive pill to avoid pregnancy were more at risk of developing blood clots in their leg veins than other women. According to Dr Christine Roke of the New Zealand Family Planning Association, women not on the pill and not pregnant have a 1:30,000 chance of a blood clot in a leg vein. Pregnant women have a 30:30,000 chance of a blood clot. Women taking contraceptive pills containing oestrogen have a 3:30,000 or a 6:30,000 chance of a blood clot depending upon the type of pill. The higher the oestrogen dose, the higher the risk, so second generation pills had a lower dose. Third generation pills were expected to be even safer, but the published studies in 1995 seemed to show otherwise, with the scientific research showing that women on the newer, low dose pills were developing more clots. The inexplicable results have now been explained as due to differences in the groups of women taking the pills, and differences in the way they were taken, with higher-risk women more often being prescribed the newer pills. The health scare caused by the original science publication caused many women to come off the pill, leading to a rise in unwanted pregnancy, and a rise in complications from blood clots among the now pregnant women.

This was followed by the first cases of new variant Creutzfeldt-Jakob disease appearing in humans in 1996 after it became apparent that new types of bovine spongiform encephalopathy had spread into cattle from scrapie-infected sheep that had been ground up and added as extra protein-rich meal to cattle. The intensively bred cattle needed supplements as they couldn't otherwise cope with the demand of giving 20 litres rather than six litres of milk a day, which let the animals meet the economic returns required by supermarkets.

It appeared that in a cycle, sick and dying cattle had in turn been fed back to sheep in sheep nuts, giving our modern, larger sheep the extra protein they need to feed the twin and triple lambs growing inside them during the winter months as a consequence of breeders developing sheep that can become pregnant at any time of the year. Government relaxation of animal feed rules to lower cooking temperatures and to include wider sources of protein, such as dead animals unfit for human consumption, may have eventually led to this new variant CJD outbreak.

With supermarkets almost completely replacing traditional high street shops and demanding ever more reliable supplies of standard-sized meat cuts, farmers bred bigger and more productive animals to meet their demands. Supermarkets also wanted cheap, standardised, lower fat milk and butter, so feed suppliers turned to ever more marginal feed ingredients (such as dead sick animals) to keep costs down. Farmers simply bought the cheapest (safely government regulated) feed available.

This vicious circle also drove the move towards industrialisation of the scale of animal movements – with a typical purchase of several pens of sheep from different suppliers sold in the north of England markets being mixed in large holding pens, before being transported overnight in huge livestock lorries and spread over dozens of farms in the south and west the next day. These finishing farms were owned or leased in the south by the biggest industrial-scale farmers so that they could meet their supermarket contracts for a constant supply of standard-sized joints. Meat had become a traded commodity, not the outcome of several generations of careful nurturing of best primestock by family farms.

The UK and its industrialised food system was ripe for an epidemic disaster. BSE and CJD were followed in 2000 by foot and mouth disease, spread overnight into dozens of farms after a major livestock sale and over-night distribution of animals that had been penned together, incubating the disease. Another crisis, blamed by some on the government's relaxation of animal feed and public health guidelines. Rural areas virtually shut down for nine months and thousands of prime healthy animals were destroyed.

The subsequent explosion of red tape, tagging, record keeping and reg-ulations for farmers was the last nail in the coffin, changed farming in the UK for ever and drove thousands of smaller farms out of livestock and dairy production. Meanwhile the industrial scale and commodity broking agribu-sinesses received millions of pounds in compensation from public funds and were back in business the next day. From the small farmers' perspective, the other winners were industrial scale hauliers from unaffected urban areas who picked up lucrative contracts to clear the mounds of slaughtered animals. And the huge firms of city-based accountants and business consultants, who were offered what should have been the farmers' rural economy regenera-tion payments as consultancy fees, to advise on modernising and diversifying rural enterprises. With the impersonal and industrial scale working of the major supply chains exposed, the public lost much of its confidence in British food.

Then MMR and the imagined link between autism and measles vaccines hit the news. In 1998, a London doctor, Andrew Wakefield, published a research paper in the medical journal *The Lancet* that suggested a causal link between the triple measles, mumps and rubella vaccine, and autism in young patients who had been inoculated. The media scare and furore following this saw vaccination rates fall dramatically all over the UK, and the eventual disgrace of Andrew Wakefield after being found guilty of professional misconduct and being struck off the medical register by the General Medical Council in 2010. On 6 January 2011, a *British Medical Journal* article by editor-in-chief Fiona Godlee, Jane Smith and Harvey Marcovitch declared that 'clear evidence of falsification of data should now close the door on this damaging vaccine scare', while in an accompanying editorial journalist Brian Deer explained how the case against MMR was fixed.[87]

References

1. Animals (Scientific Procedures) Act 1986, www.legislation.gov.uk/ukpga/1986/14/contents.
2. Boyd Group, www.boyd-group.demon.co.uk.
3. James Gleick, *Chaos – Making A New Science*, Cardinal Books, 1988.
4. Donatella H. Meadows (ed. Diana Wright), *Thinking in Systems*, Earthscan, 2009.
5. BBC Trust review of impartiality and accuracy of the BBC's coverage of science, June 2011.
6. *Guardian*, 21 July 2011.
7. Press release, Department of Health Media Centre, 20 December 2011.
8. NHS core principles, NHS Choices website, www.nhs.uk/NHSEngland/thenhs/about/Pages/nhscoreprinciples.aspx.
9. *Guardian*, 2 June 2012.
10. *Guardian*, 13 March 2012.
11. Martha Nussbaum, *The New Religious Intolerance: Overcoming the Politics of Fear in an Anxious Age*, Harvard Press, 2012.
12. *Daily Telegraph*, 16 March 2012.
13. BBC News, 19 July 2010.
14. Steven Levitt & Stephen Dubner, *Superfreakonomics*, Allen Lane (Penguin), 2009.
15. David Nutt, *Drugs Without the Hot Air*, UIT Cambridge, 2012.
16. *Guardian*, 31 May and 11 June 2012.
17. Magic mushrooms' effects illuminated in brain imaging studies, press release, Imperial College, London, 23 January 2012; PNAS, 23 January 2012 and *British Journal of Psychiatry*, 26 January 2012.
18. *Guardian*, 23 May 2012.
19. *Guardian*, 12 June 2012.
20. *The Men Who Made Us Fat*, BBC2, 14 June 2012.
21. *BMJ* press release, 14 May 2012.
22. *Guardian*, 22 December 2011.
23. 'Obesity – working with communities', NICE guidance, 2012.
24. *Sunday Telegraph*, 5 February 2012.
25. *Guardian*, corrections column, 5 March 2012.
26. NICE consults on updated recommendations for treating fertility, press release, NICE, 22 May 2012.
27. Donna Dickenson, *Bioethics: All That Matters*, Hodder, 2012.
28. *Guardian*, 7 April 2012.

29. *Guardian*, 28 May 2012.
30. *Guardian*, letters, 31 May 2012.
31. *Guardian*, 26 May 2012.
32. *Daily Telegraph*, 10 April 2012.
33. *Guardian*, 29 December 2012.
34. *Guardian*, 10 April 2012. For the dangers of hospital against home births see Levitt & Dubner, *Superfreakonomics*, page 133.
35. *Guardian*, 20 & 21 December 2011.
36. *Daily Telegraph*, 4 July 2012.
37. *Transforming Social Care*, Centre for Social Justice, May 2012.
38. *Guardian*, 7 May 2012.
39. *Guardian*, 7 May 2012.
40. *Guardian*, 12 June 2012.
41. *Guardian*, 7 May 2012.
42. *Guardian*, 23 January 2012, 11 December 2011, 27 October 2011, *Guardian*, letters, 16 November 2011, 12 November 2011.
43. *Guardian*, 26 November 2011.
44. *Guardian*, 28 February 2012.
45. *Guardian*, 16 March 2012.
46. *Daily Telegraph*, 16 March 2012.
47. Dylan Evans, *Risk Intelligence: How to Live with Uncertainty*, Free Press, 2012.
48. *Guardian*, 17 January 2012.
49. Allyson M. Pollock, *NHS plc: the Privatisation of Our Healthcare*, Verso, 2004.
50. *Daily Telegraph*, 12 April 2012.
51. *The Times*, 4 November 2011.
52. Ben Goldacre, *Bad Science*, Fourth Estate, 2008, and the missing chapter at www.badscience.net/2009/04/matthias-rath-steal-this-chapter.
53. *Guardian*, 16 December 2011.
54. *Daily Telegraph*, letters, 11 April 2012.
55. *The Times*, 4 November 2011.
56. *Daily Telegraph*, 11 April 2012.
57. *Guardian*, 17 May 2012.
58. *Guardian*, 7 & 10 February 2012.
59. *Guardian*, 10 February 2012.
60. *Daily Telegraph*, 19 March 2012.
61. *Guardian*, 6 April 2012.
62. Rebecca Skloot, *The Immortal Life of Henrietta Lacks*, Crown Books, 2010.
63. BBC News, 20 May 2010,=www.bbc.co.uk/news/10132762.
64. *Guardian*, 4 February 2012.
65. See, *inter alia*, the long-running *Guardian* debates centred around George Monbiot's opinion article on 30 August 2011, and Ian Sample writing in the *Guardian*, 16 July 2012.
66. BBC News, 12 May 2006.
67. Tim Spector, *Identically Different: Why You Can Change Your Genes*, Weidenfeld & Nicolson, 2012.
68. Junk DNA and the Encode project, at www.nature.com/encode/#/threads.
69. *Guardian*, 1 March 2012.
70. *Guardian*, 27 February 2012.
71. *Guardian*, 7 November 2011.
72. 'Novel techniques for the prevention of mitochondrial disorders: an ethical review', Nuffield Council on Bioethics, 12 June 2012.
73. *Guardian*, 12 June 2012.
74. *Daily Telegraph*, 10 April 2012.
75. *Sunday Telegraph*, 15 July 2012.

76. Sir John Sulston, chair, *People and the Planet*, Royal Society Science Policy Centre Report, 26 April 2012.
77. *GP* magazine, 18 July 2012.
78. *Dr Aust's Spleen*. Be warned. http://draust.wordpress.com.
79. *Daily Telegraph*, 19 March 2012.
80. Simon Singh & Eduard Ernst, *Trick or Treatment? Alternative Medicine on Trial*, Bantam Press, 2008.
81. *UK Press Gazette*, 9 May 2012.
82. *Guardian*, 15 November 2011.
83. *Guardian*, 28 October 2011.
84. Dylan Evans, *Alternative Medicine: Fact from Fiction*, at www.youtube.com/watch?v=a1hIfH1AxoU.
85. Dylan Evans, *Placebo: Mind over Matter in Modern Medicine*, HarperCollins, 2003.
86. *Daily Telegraph*, 3 January 2012.
87. *British Medical Journal*, 2011; 342: c7452.

Part V
A bit of history

12 Health and medical PR
An alternative and potted modern history

This book argues strongly that using pictures, especially pictures with people in them, and telling a story are two of the main keys to good communications. I believe that visual impact has played an important part in the emergence of medical and health public relations as a distinct discipline. So in this chapter I would like to trace some of the contributory influences and landmarks, of both real pictures and conjured up mental images, which I think can still offer us valuable lessons today.

This is not intended to be a thorough overview of the emergence of the public relations industry itself, or a historical timeline tracing the history of medicine. The history of public relations has been adequately covered in other, more conventional, academic textbooks. (see any of Prof Anne Gregory's excellent works). And for the fascinating history of medicine I would recommend almost anything by Prof Tilli Tansey of Queen Mary, University of London.

Instead let us look at some isolated examples and incidents and trace their influence from the quirkier practices of the past to the way we frame public relations activities today. Some still lurk in our collective unconscious, shaping our opinions and purchasing decisions, and revisiting them might help us as modern public relations executives better understand our publics, their prejudices and some of their stranger pseudoscientific notions.

Florence and the PR machine

Mary Seacole (1805–1881) was voted in 2004 the greatest ever black Briton. After being told that no more nurses were needed by the War Office, she took herself to the Crimean War in 1855 to help wounded soldiers, following in the footsteps of the Lady with the Lamp, Florence Nightingale. She first visited Florence's hospital in Scutari, and then put herself in personal danger by going forward to the front line on the Balaklava battlefield to tend wounded soldiers, giving them food and drink, and cleaning and bandaging their wounds.

Florence Nightingale (1820–1910) was much better at her own PR than Mary Seacole, in spite of Mary's later book about her exploits, so for many years history has given Florence all the credit. However, even if Mary Seacole does really deserve much better recognition for nursing under fire, Florence Nightingale had a more significant impact on public health and public understanding of science.

Florence realised that she would get just one chance to make her case for better nursing of wounded soldiers to Queen Victoria (1819–1901, taking the throne in 1837), her government and the British parliament. Florence's findings were later published in their own pamphlet.[1] Florence was originally allowed just a few pages as an appendix to a Royal Commission report in 1857 on the disastrously high army losses in the Crimea. And so she invented a new way of expressing statistics, an idea so radical that it could be argued today that it was the public relations coup that founded the British National Health Service.

Florence's stroke of genius was to visually present the soldiers' death rate data as a rose diagram or coxcomb (predating the word graph by more than 30 years), which divided a circle into 12 equal monthly segments. It then superimposes as pie chart blocks the death rates from wounds in red; death from other causes in black; and most damningly, deaths from preventable diseases and infections such as dysentery and cholera (which we would today call hospital-acquired infections) in blue. This blue segment hugely outweighed all the other causes of death by July 1854, proving that the infectious aftermath, not the war itself, was the biggest killer. See Diagram of the Causes of Mortality in the Army in the East; the image is now copyright expired and in the public domain and can be seen in the Wellcome Trust collection.[2]

This graphic was a forerunner of today's pie charts, and in his BBC television series in 2010, *The Beauty of Diagrams*, the brilliant communicator and mathematician Marcus du Sautoy, Oxford Professor for the Public Understanding of Science, says that Florence Nightingale's data graphic was hugely influential. It raised the idea that infectious diseases were a serious cause of death everywhere, not just in the Crimea, and that, crucially, they could be combated with better hygiene. But rather than the Lady with the Lamp, Wikipedia credits William Playfair with books he published in 1786 (graphs) and 1801 (pie charts) as the inventor of graphic presentations of data, so perhaps Florence was simply the first to present medical data like this.

Like many people, I always believed that through her own efforts (and those of the largely unsung Mary Seacole) in improving hygiene, Florence had reduced the death rates from the unsanitary hospital conditions. But other authorities now say that she never claimed this herself, attributing her small success to improving the soldiers' nutrition, and that the death rates did not start to fall until six months later when a task force flushed out the hospital's sewers and the whole ward area was properly ventilated.

Florence certainly returned from the Crimea with some sort of disease herself, which made her an invalid for the next 53 years. Natasha McEnroe, the director of the Florence Nightingale Museum, responding to letters in the *Guardian* in March 2012 which suggested that Florence had become a laudanum addict, said that there is no evidence for this and that Florence had probably contracted brucellosis, the third most common fever in the Crimea after typhoid and typhus.

We now have a much better understanding of bacteria, microbes and the diseases they can cause. The medical profession resisted the idea that microscopic organisms, invisible to the naked eye, could cause so much trouble for hundreds of years. Antonie van Leeuwenhoek (1632–1723) improved his microscopes sufficiently to see single cells, discovering bacteria in 1676, calling his findings animalcules, or tiny organisms swimming about; he sent his drawings to the Royal Society in London. But it was 1680 before his findings were finally accepted by them. In her turn, nearly 200 years later, Florence Nightingale sowed the seeds of modern nursing by showing that diseases could be prevented, but even she did not fully link cause and effect.

In 1860, Florence Nightingale founded the first professional nursing training course at St Thomas' Hospital, now part of King's College London, and her influence and work can be directly traced through to today's NHS. I leave it to you as students of health and medical public relations to decide whether the truth matters more than the myth, if the eventual outcome was that attitudes and practices were changed and lives saved.[3]

Broad Street pump

Around the same time, in 1854, a terrible outbreak of cholera hit an area of Soho in London, which was not yet connected to the new London sewer system. Near Broad Street, 127 people died in just three days, rising to 500 people within a fortnight, and people were fleeing the area. At the time many physicians still thought that diseases were transmitted by breathing bad air or miasma, but Dr John Snow (1813–1858) rejected this theory, and from talking to the people in Soho he discovered that nearly all the affected families used the public water pump in Broad Street.

Legend had it that he smashed the handle of the water pump, stopping the cholera outbreak in its tracks. We now think that it was removed by the Guardians of St James Parish, after Snow's evidence convinced them that water from this particular pump was to blame for the deaths. Snow used a map with spots marking the outbreaks to visually show that the deaths were clustered around the pump, or in homes that used water from it instead of from nearer pumps. This was the first time that a disease was identified from the pattern of infection, laying the foundation of today's epidemiology studies, and was a major landmark in public health.

The Broad Street pump was delivering water from a well that had been dug only three feet from an old cesspit. Many houses still had cesspits under their cellars, and these often overflowed with human excrement. So the authorities collected and dumped the waste into the Thames, contaminating the water that many poor people still used for drinking and washing. Snow showed that other cholera outbreaks were in areas where the water authorities were piping drinking water from a polluted section of the Thames.

In an attempt to combat cholera, typhus and the generally unsanitary conditions, the 1875 UK Public Health Act required all newly built houses to be connected to running water and an internal drainage system.[4]

Tobacco smoking

Perhaps the most influential example of modern epidemiology was the work of Sir Richard Doll (1912–2005) who demonstrated the link between smoking and lung cancer. In 1954 he was working at the UK Medical Research Council, and at the time 80 per cent of British adults smoked (50 years later it had dropped to 26 per cent). The researchers were trying to find out why so many people were dying of lung cancer in post-war Britain, and according to a BBC report marking the 50th anniversary, Richard Doll thought that the deaths were most likely caused by tarring the roads, since they already knew that tar contained carcinogens. Smoking had also been suggested, but animal experiments did not confirm the link.

The researchers interviewed 700 lung cancer patients to try to find possible causes or links to tar, and it quickly became obvious that smoking really was to blame, causing Doll himself to quit cigarettes two-thirds of the way through the study. The findings were published in 1951, but it wasn't until a second paper was published in 1954, following 40,000 doctors and conclusively confirming the link, that people took notice.

Doll's findings were so important that in 1962 the UK's Royal College of Physicians decided for the first time ever to directly promote medical findings to the public by publishing a report on the link between smoking and health. At this time doctors could still be disciplined by the medical establishment, and even struck off, for seeking to publicise themselves, for instance by freely talking to journalists. This attitude and prejudice has coloured the entire relationship between the medical professions and the media, and still persists today to a slight extent.

Millions of lives have since been saved, and since 1962 another 6 million have been lost to smoking according to the Royal College of Physicians' 50th anniversary press release in March 2012, in spite of long-drawn-out rearguard public relations campaigns by the tobacco industry.[5] These have attempted to downplay the scientific findings, avoid financial responsibility and compensation, or tried to position smoking as an issue of personal taste and responsibility.

In 1975, the US state of Minnesota enacted the Minnesota Clean Air Act, making it the first place to restrict smoking in public places and requiring restaurants to have 'no smoking' areas. In 2004, the Republic of Ireland banned smoking in all workplaces, followed by Scotland in 2006. In 2005, tobacco advertising and sponsorship was banned across the European Union, particularly hitting Formula One motor racing sponsorship and some indoor sports such as snooker. The Formula One ban was originally delayed in the UK after billionaire Bernie Ecclestone, the sport's chief executive, donated £1m to Tony Blair's Labour Government in 1997.

Politicians have found it difficult to turn down the enormous cash cow offered by taxes on tobacco products, leading to unhealthily cosy relationships with the industry. Britain's first female Prime Minister, the Conservative Margaret Thatcher, left office and took up a three-year role with Philip Morris, the world's largest cigarette manufacturers, which makes seven of the world's top 15 international brands (according to their own news releases).

In England, Wales and Northern Ireland, laws were passed in 2007 banning smoking in workplaces and enclosed public spaces, and the age for buying cigarettes was raised from 16 years to 18 years. In France in 2011, the first beach became smoke-free. Hospitals are finding it increasingly difficult to justify providing special smoking areas, for example in 2012 North Devon District Hospital in England banned smoking by staff or patients on all hospital property including the car parks.[6] According to NHS data released in May 2012 by the Health and Social Care Information Centre one in eight women who give birth in England are still smokers, risking serious harm to their unborn babies.[7]

Today the Royal College of Physicians is still lobbying to get cigarettes sold in plain packs rather than attractively branded packaging as young people are particularly susceptible to branding associations. A UK government consultation on plain packs was opened on 16 April 2012 by the Health Secretary, with the campaigning charity Action on Smoking and Health welcoming the move, and Imperial Tobacco saying that it was disproportionate and preposterous.[8]

This consultation has prompted the type of militant response usually only seen from animal rights activists and the anti-abortion faith groups, with academics, charities such as Cancer Research UK, and health campaigners ASH being threatened with violence and personal abuse by bloggers supporting the pro-smoking lobby Freedom2Choose, according to *Guardian* newspaper reports[9] in June 2012. Bath University has increased its security and set up a new website TobaccoTactics.org to monitor the smoking industry and its supporters' activities.

In August 2012, Australia's highest court endorsed plain packaging laws for cigarettes, against challenges from British American Tobacco, Philip Morris, Imperial Tobacco Group and Japan Tobacco, which claimed that the new rules were illegal as they extinguished trademark and brand values, part of the companies' intellectual property rights. Australian campaigners are now asking for an extension to the law, banning cigarette sales to anyone born since the year 2000.[10]

Brands and branding

Our modern consumer society could not develop until there were recognisable things to buy, and sufficient leisure time and spare cash for people to spend on holidays and household goods. Before the Industrial Revolution, hand-crafted things were too expensive for most people, but mass production in factories meant that the rising middle classes, and even some poorer people, could now afford household goods and luxuries such as blankets, sheets and mass-produced cooking pots.

Most everyday things in Victorian times were still made at home from basic ingredients or raw materials, sometimes now by following increasingly popular printed receipts or recipes. These gave ideas for sewing clothes or cooking meals, but also for making household cleaners based on salt and vinegar, ink from crushed oak galls, or medicines, salves and other treatments.

The role of health public relations harks back to the earliest days of branding and advertising, when their own patent medicines started to be produced by street corner pharmacies. These would also supply other health and hygiene products such as new household cleaners, and in rural areas the patent medicines were sold by travelling snake oil salesmen. They all made extravagant claims for the efficacy and cure-all properties of their nostrums. These increasingly dubious claims in turn prompted some of the first consumer legislation for public protection.

Today, much of the World Wide Web's innovation, charging strategies and successful conversion of public curiosity into profit, is being driven by the pornography industry (and more recently by online gambling and video game playing). Two centuries ago, the new health and medical markets provided similar drivers, leading early developments in the field of advertising and marketing.

As director of the Research for Health Charities Group in the 1990s, I often got the chance to visit the museum and archive belonging to the world's largest medical charity, the Wellcome Trust, in London. The Wellcome Collection has extensive examples of early medical and health paraphernalia including advertising leaflets, bottles and medical devices which provide an invaluable record of early pseudoscientific claims (see www.wellcomecollection.org).

Soap and hygiene

Sunlight Soap was the world's first branded soap, wrapped in standard-sized bars and sold since 1884. Its manufacturers, Lever Brothers, now part of Unilever, are usually credited with inventing the concept of branding. Their innovation of wrapping soap bars in what was basically a brightly coloured advertising leaflet enabled consumers to identify a distinct, consistent and widely available product, which in its turn spawned today's advertising and marketing industries.

Early Sunlight Soap advertisements used what are clearly the forerunners of today's public relations messages, or possibly spin, such as the 1915 patriotic posters showing soldiers firing from the trenches surrounded by wooden cases of the soap, captioned 'The *CLEANEST* fighter in the world – the British Tommy'.

Advertisements for Ivory Soap from the same period show homoerotic pictures of sailors communally bathing in wooden tubs on deck, an early example of using sexual images to sell in advertising. In America around 1911, the generally acknowledged first clear example of sex being used to sell was created by a woman copywriter for Woodbury's Facial Soap, with the strapline 'The skin you love to touch', and the pictures showing a romantic couple embracing.

This early emphasis in advertising innovation by soap companies was continued into the brands' early relationship with the broadcast media, with the advent of commercial sponsorship of radio and then television programmes. This led to the name we still have today, 'soap operas' or 'soaps' for a particular genre of emotional and relationship-based drama programmes usually involving a series of continuing episodes.

Patent medicines

The British Empire grew out of the United Kingdom's overseas territories and other trading posts around the world from the 1750s onwards. With Britain's growing colonies, this Empire eventually covered one-fifth of the world's population, and brought with it exposure to a whole series of health threats and diseases for the British citizens who governed it, and who had no inherited or naturally acquired immunity to these new challenges.

This created a ready market for the new patent medicines among fearful but ignorant travellers and expatriates, who had no real understanding of the causes or course of diseases, and no effective treatments or painkillers, apart from alcohol and opium.

The new medicines, known as specifics, cures, nostrums, and later as quack remedies or snake oil, were often sold in distinctively shaped bottles and jars and shipped out to India, America and the other colonies, where British families eagerly consumed them in preference to the dubious and uncivilised local treatments available from the native healers.

In a curious modern reversal, many of those traditional natural and native remedies are now just as eagerly consumed by citizens in rich countries of the developed world who distrust what they see as the artificially and factory-produced drugs available in the US, UK and Europe from big pharma, and which have been safety tested on animals.

As branding forerunners, these early patent medicines often used unusually shaped bottles and jars, sometimes embossed with the product or maker's names to guarantee authenticity. According to antique bottle collector Mitch Brown, perhaps the most distinctive and highly collectable today are the violin-shaped pressed-glass bottles with embossed lettering and dates invented by Robert Turlington in 1754. He was trying to stop the counterfeiting of his Turlington's Balsam of Life, a hugely popular specific containing 27 ingredients, which he had been making by royal patent and exporting since 1744.[11]

Many of the patent medicines contained alcohol, even ones intended for children, and several contained opium (or laudanum, which is a tincture or alcoholic extract of opium) to soothe and numb pain. Some were simply wine or spirits diluted with water and coloured and flavoured with vegetable dyes, but some were based on toxic solutions of acids or contained traces of more positively harmful ingredients.

Within 100 years there were more than 1,000 registered proprietary medicines being produced and marketed in Britain. In the US, the market and supply lines for British patent medicines had collapsed with independence, but American patent medicine producers quickly filled the gap with concoctions claiming to contain rare and exotic ingredients to cure all ills.

Among these, Clark Stanley's Snake Oil Liniment, purportedly made from rattlesnake fat, became one of the most well known. It was claimed to cure rheumatism, neuralgia, sciatica, lumbago, sore throats, frostbite and toothache. It even contained some active pain-killing ingredients – such as camphor and red peppers – along with the turpentine and beef fat, according to Joe Schwartz, director of McGill University Office for Science and Society, writing for the Montreal *Gazette* in February 2008.[12]

From 1875 the UK Sale of Food and Drugs Act, mainly concerned with food adulteration and safety, formed the basis of most British food law until 1955. In

1906, the US passed the Pure Food and Drug Act, which limited some of the claims that medical companies could make, and manufacturers started removing many of the most dangerous ingredients. In 1909, as the medical establishment tried to stamp out quacks, the *British Medical Journal* tested and analysed the efficacy of patent medicines, printing 'Secret Remedies, What They Cost and What They Contain', which is still reprinted today.[13]

Drugs and medicines

Meanwhile many genuine plant-based medicines were also being refined and tested, and finally aspirin, the world's first synthetic drug, was commercially developed as a painkiller by Felix Hoffmann, a chemist working for the German manufacturer Bayer, in 1899. It has recently been reinvented as a wonder drug to treat cancer and heart disease. Bayer was forced to give up the patent for it in 1919 under the Treaty of Versailles.[14]

The modern medical era is reckoned to date from 1928 when Scottish biologist Sir Alexander Fleming (1881–1955) discovered the first successful antibiotic treatment, penicillin, extracted from a mould or fungus, for which he won the Nobel Prize in 1945.

Drugs and medicines today have a strict legal definition. The European Union Directive 65/65/EEC defines drugs as any substances designed to prevent or treat diseases in humans or animals, distinguishing them from borderline products intended for personal hygiene, cosmetic, functional foods and foodstuffs, though sometimes the distinctions and efficacy claims are blurred.[15]

A huge range of policies and regulations affect the production, safety, labelling, advertising, marketing, distribution and sales of drugs today, distinguishing between prescription drugs that cannot be sold across the counter without a physician's prescription and patent medicines that can be sold freely. Many of these are covered in the European Union by Directive 2001/83/EC, among others.

But, popularly, the term drugs, as contrasted with medicines, is also used to describe a range of mood and mind-altering recreational, narcotic and intoxicant substances. According to the drug policy foundation Transform, in the UK, drugs legislation started with the Poisons Act in 1858, which expanded the Arsenic Act of 1851 and regulated the sale of poisons in an attempt to control crime – and specifically murder – rather than pharmaceutical science.

In 1860, the Second Opium War ended and the British opium trade was legalised after centuries of smuggling Indian opium into China. In 1868, the US Pharmacy Act and, in 1869, the UK Pharmacy Act regulated the sale of arsenic, prussic acid, cyanide and opium. In 1920, the UK Dangerous Drugs Act extended the 1916 Defence of the Realm Act, which treated drug-taking as a criminal matter of national security. Today many critics of the pharmaceutical industry routinely refer to medicines as drugs, whereas industry supporters prefer the terms pharmaceuticals or medicines.

In 1948, the Labour Government Minister for Health Aneurin Bevan (1897–1960) officially started the UK's National Health Service, launching a dream that good healthcare should be available to all, regardless of wealth.[16] According to the official NHS Choices website, this meant that for the first time hospitals, doctors, nurses, pharmacists, opticians and dentists were brought together under one umbrella organisation and healthcare was free for all at the point of delivery. The central principles were clear: the health service will be available to all and financed entirely from taxation, which meant that people pay into it according to their means.

Medical practitioners in the UK have to be registered with the General Medical Council and are now governed by the 1983 Medical Act. The GMC's role is to protect, promote and maintain the health and safety of the public by ensuring proper standards in the practice of medicine. The Act gives the GMC four main functions:

- keeping up-to-date registers of qualified doctors;
- fostering good medical practice;
- promoting high standards of medical education and training;
- dealing firmly and fairly with doctors whose fitness to practise is in doubt.

In spite of these scientific advances and the formalisation of conventional medicine, the British public still spends millions of pounds every year on patent medicines and other forms of complementary therapies. This prompts periodic outcries from medical establishment figures who do not think that homeopathy and other alternative medical treatments should be available and funded through the National Health Service, as in their view any successes are largely due to the placebo effect (see Chapter 11, 'Complementary and alternative medicine, placebos', p.153).

But it raises the question for public relations practitioners (and taxpayers), does it matter if sick people get better because they have been properly treated by a qualified medical practitioner, or if they simply get better because their disease was largely imaginary and they just believed that they were going to get better? Does it similarly matter if a religious adherent believes that prayer can help cure illness and, if so, should the NHS also fund hospital chaplains, imams or rabbis? If so, what about witches, mediums and crystal-gazers?

Fresh air, exercise and electricity

Ozone is an atmospheric gas formed from three oxygen atoms, a harmful and highly reactive pollutant at ground level. But it also protects us from damaging ultraviolet light from the Sun when it is in the upper atmosphere or ozone layer. It accounts for the distinctive and easily detectable smell of lightning storms, as ozone can be formed at ground level when strong electric charges or ultraviolet rays react with air containing hydrocarbons or smog. It is named from the Greek for smell, because of its distinctive odour, slightly similar to chlorine, which in turn forms one of the main salts found in seawater.

In the Victorian age, people believed that ozone was good for you rather than harmful. Today we know it causes heart attacks, asthma and respiratory illness.

However, ozone can also be made by your white blood cells, which use it to attack invading microbes. But the Victorians particularly liked it, as they did most things electric. They also thought that the fresh smell of the seaside was caused by ozone, which started the craze for seaside holidays and bracing walks along beaches, promenades and coastal paths. Today we think that they had simply mistaken the smell of rotting seaweed for the smell of ozone.

The concept of fresh seaside air being good for you was later encapsulated in the iconic promotional poster in the Victoria & Albert museum collection, 'Skegness is SO bracing', designed by John Hassall in 1908, which shows a rotund fisherman skipping along the beach. This poster image of the jolly fisherman was originally designed as an advertisement for the Great Northern Railway to promote train travel, and continued to be used by the London & North Eastern Railway from 1925, becoming so famous and recognisable that it is still promoting the chilly seaside town of Skegness today.

Note that in PR terms, train travel is an abstract concept, so it is difficult to get customers to visualise it unless an actual destination or concrete outcome such as going to the seaside is suggested. Thus we have two incorrect myths, healthy ozone and the smell of the sea, and the power of a strong visual image in the jolly fisherman (with a sprinkling of nostalgia for a bygone age), still being used today to promote a thoroughly healthy activity, taking brisk exercise and relaxation away from work on your holidays. Do the misconceptions matter?

More electricity, mesmerism, spiritualism and pseudoscience

Electricity has been used in medicine from quack treatments in the 1700s through to modern therapies.[17] Franz Anton Mesmer (1734–1815), a German physician, developed the theory of animal magnetism, which was based on the belief that the astrological movements of the planets, moon and stars in the sky exerted a tidal magnetic effect on special fluids in our bodies and therefore on our health.

Mesmer claimed that he could cure diseases by channelling this magnetic influence, sometimes touching his patients for hours on end with a metal rod, or later with his hands alone. He was elected to the Bavarian Academy of Sciences in 1775, curing many patients before moving to Paris in 1778 where he practised until 1785, all the time attempting to get Royal Academy of Sciences recognition of his treatments. His mesmerism teachings were taken up and practised by Harmony Societies, a network of supporters' groups that raised a total of 20,000 francs for Mesmer. Their members later modified his treatments themselves, leading to long-running arguments with him.

Mesmer's techniques, today called hypnotism, were adapted by the religious groups called Spiritualists in the 1840s for their séances. They claimed that mesmerism-induced trances allowed living people or mediums to communicate with spirits in the afterlife or spirit world, and therefore receive moral guidance from the inhabitants of the afterlife and, ultimately, from God. Mesmerism subsequently became associated with faith healing and clairvoyancy.

Meanwhile Luigi Galvani (1737–1798), a physician and lecturer in anatomy at the University of Bologna, Italy, found by accident in 1771 that a frog's severed legs twitched when its nerves were touched with a metal knife while preparing to cook it. Or his wife did, but he's usually credited with the discovery. And so he found out that animals themselves contained electricity, providing a scientific basis for medical electrical treatments.

Galvani concluded that there were three different types of electricity: natural electricity that produces lightning; artificial electricity produced by friction, which we know today as static; and animal electricity (echoing Mesmer's term animal magnetism). Galvani's experiments also showed that electric currents were produced when two different types of metal touched each other.

Similarly to Mesmer's practices, quack treatments using galvanism quickly became popular. The treatments were based on belts made of copper rings and zinc plates, and also bracelets, rings and headbands, which people thought could be activated by sweat. The remnants of these folk beliefs still persist today, with some people wearing copper bracelets to ward off rheumatism and other ailments.

In 1801, using Galvani's discovery that two metals together produce an electric current, Alessandro Volta (1745–1827), professor of physics at the University of Pavia in Italy, invented the first functioning electric battery, called the voltaic pile, made of alternating stacked discs of zinc and copper separated by pieces of cardboard soaked in brine. He disagreed with Galvani, claiming that the muscle contractions caused by a metal knife touching nerves were in fact due to the excess or defect of electricity in different parts of the animal's body, similar to the effect of the two different metals in his voltaic pile.

After a long and fierce debate between Galvani and Volta, medical papers, experiments and treatments based on galvanism began to appear, spurred by the observation that the muscle contractions worked in both dead and living animals, so fuelling speculation that drowned or asphyxiated people could be revived.

Using voltaic piles, electric currents were passed through gold leaf connected to the battery and placed on the patient's skin. This was used to treat paralysis, cramp, tetanus and tumours, with short breaks needed between each set of contractions. Passing a current through the head could treat headaches or mental illness.

In 1831, Michael Faraday (1791–1867) discovered electromagnetic induction, leading to the development of magneto-electro machines that could deliver a steady but interrupted supply of electricity, now called an alternating current, giving us devices that could be used effectively in medicine.

Catching the zeitgeist, and reflecting public and academic fascination with electricity and the re-animation experiments of Galvani and Volta, Mary Shelley (1797–1851), wife of the poet Percy Bysshe Shelley and daughter of feminist philosopher Mary Wollstonecraft, published her gothic horror novel *Frankenstein* in 1818.[18] The book describes a deranged scientist's successful attempt to create a living being from the stolen and reassembled parts of human corpses, sparked back to life by electricity. Thanks, Mary.

Bodysnatching

In the UK, the Murder Act of 1752 said that only the bodies of executed murderers could be legally dissected for medical studies. But the rise of formal scientific training in universities meant that the demand for bodies was far greater than the possible supply of murdered corpses. Anatomy teaching was so hampered at the time by the lack of fresh cadavers that grave robbers, bodysnatchers or resurrection men stepped in to supply bodies. Grave robbing became so common that family members would watch over a relative's body until burial, and often then watch over the grave at night for some time afterwards. In some places guard watchtowers were built in cemeteries.

The need for fresh corpses was still not met, prompting criminal suppliers to take even greater risks. In 12 months between 1827 and 1828, two Irishmen, William Burke and William Hare, murdered 17 people in Edinburgh, Scotland, and supplied the corpses to Dr Robert Knox, a surgeon, for anatomy studies with Edinburgh Medical College students. The pair were eventually arrested but the evidence against them was largely circumstantial, so Hare was offered immunity if he testified against Burke, who was consequently hanged in January 1829.

The public were outraged at the crimes and a Parliamentary Select Committee recommended changing the law to make more bodies available so that anatomy studies were possible. The Royal College of Surgeons opposed the change in 1829, and the original bill was withdrawn. In 1832, a new version of the Anatomy Act finally made dissection of donated bodies legal for doctors, anatomists and medical students, and required anatomy teachers to be licensed, causing the illegal market in cadavers to collapse.

A massive scandal in 1999 at Alder Hey Hospital in Liverpool, England, uncovered evidence that pathologists had been routinely retaining dead children's hearts and other organs for teaching and scientific research. Under the law this was a legal but possibly unethical practice, since relatives' specific consent was not obtained, unlike the usual practice for transplant organs. This widespread practice by pathologists for their heart research was first revealed and publicly criticised at Bristol Royal Infirmary in 1996. The public outcry caused by these scandals led directly to the law being revised, and the scientific use of bodies for research or organ transplantation is now covered by the Human Tissue Act of 2004 and regulated by the Human Tissue Authority.[19]

Dead and undead

Apart from the possibility of having your dead body stolen and cut up by medical students, one of the biggest concerns for the seriously ill Victorian was the possibility of physicians giving up on you before you were really dead. This fear has been overtaken today by concern that terminally ill patients will not be allowed to die in peace by their doctors without frightful and invasive interventions. Or helped to die, or euthanised, if physically unable to kill themselves, when the suffering becomes too much.

The Victorian answer, prompted by the fear of being buried alive during epidemics of cholera or simply if knocked unconscious, was to create coffins equipped with signalling devices that could be used by people to raise the alarm if they revived. The fear of premature burial was given widespread publicity at the time and gripped the public imagination, reflected by and further fuelled by the works of American author Edgar Allan Poe (1809–1849), who is credited with inventing the detective story.

In Poe's short mystery story, *The Fall of the House of Usher*, published in 1839, the main character Roderick Usher suffers from anxiety and hypochondria. He has a sick twin sister Madeline who falls into deathlike states or cataleptic trances. During one of these, Roderick assumes that she has died and puts her in the family tomb under the house for two weeks before her final burial. During a massive storm Madeline dramatically reappears in the house, grabs her brother and both fall dead.

Poe returned to this theme in several of his other works, most notably *The Premature Burial*, published in 1844, in which the main character constructs an elaborate tomb equipped with signalling devices to raise the alarm in case he is buried alive.

The Victorians were great inventors, so many types of these coffins were designed, usually incorporating flags to be raised, bells operated by wires that would ring above ground, ladders to reach the surface, escape hatches, glass panels and a few even had speaking tubes and feeding funnels, although many didn't provide any way of breathing fresh air. Some graveyards employed watchmen to listen out for the sound of bells and whistles if buried people were signalling for help.

In the 1980s, arguments played out in the media about organ transplants centred on whether doctors could know that the donor of a heart or kidneys was really dead when certified as brain dead, if they were still being maintained (or kept alive) on an artificial ventilator (then commonly known as life support machines). Eventually the establishment, and most medical and religious authorities, accepted the legal, ethical and actual definition of death as being when the brain has ceased to function meaningfully, as measured by the tests to determine brain stem death.

Quite aside from the ethics of transplantation, people were starting to get concerned about heroic medical interventions in accident and emergency and intensive care units which seemed to prevent the patient's dignified death. The right to life articulated by the Victorians had become a concern about the right to die. This concern spread to a general ethical feeling that, since suicide had been decriminalised in the UK, then perhaps terminally ill patients whose prognosis was of increasing pain, mental incapacitation through dementia, or steadily increasing loss of bodily functions and dignity, should be allowed to die, or be assisted to die, at a time of their own choosing.

Various legal appeals tried to establish whether relatives could ask doctors to withdraw positive interventions such as intravenously feeding patients in persistent vegetative states. Or if the relatives would be prosecuted for assisting terminally ill patients to die, or whether they would be prosecuted for travelling with terminally ill patients who wished to end their lives in the Swiss clinics provided by Dignitas and other welfare organisations. Eventually in 2009, the UK government issued new guidance that clarified the enforcement of the 1961 Suicide Act, after a legal case brought by Debbie Purdy questioning the circumstances when relatives who help someone will be prosecuted, and when it is not in the public interest to do so.

In March 2012, a new UK landmark in the right-to-die debate was reached by a 58-year-old paralysed man called Tony Nicklinson, who suffered a massive stroke in 2005 which left him completely unable to move below the neck or speak apart from blinking an eye, and therefore unable to carry out any bodily functions for himself. He sought the legal right for a doctor to end his 'indignity'. He won the right for a full hearing from a high court in the UK to establish whether he had the right to choose when he would like to die. This case was significant since his incapacity meant that he would be unable to administer any poisons or drugs himself even if supplied with them, which had formed the basis of argument in previous assisted suicide cases, but would require the action of a doctor to kill him, at a time of his own choosing.

In August 2012 the UK High Court's Lord Justice Toulson ruled that, while such cases were deeply moving, the questions they raised were too significant to be decided by them. He said that it was not for the court to decide whether the law about assisted dying should be changed and, if so, what safeguards should be put in place, saying that these matters were for parliament to decide for society as a whole, not for a court in ruling on an individual case.[20]

Five years previously, when I chaired a public debate 'The Right to Die: The Choice to Live' on this issue in September 2007 at the Science Museum's Dana Centre in London, in the end vote the overwhelming majority of the audience wanted the law changed to allow physician-assisted dying. Although I agreed with the general principle of self-determination, it did leave me concerned that if allowed, we would be shifting the burden of moral responsibility from the individuals who wanted to end their own life, and their relatives, to the doctors who would then be expected to administer the poison. Is this reasonable?

The Nicklinson debate received widespread media coverage as it pushed the boundary of medical ethics, and revived public concerns about euthanasia and eugenics, in addition to all the religious faith-based objections. During BBC broadcast news coverage of the case, Tony Nicklinson was described as suffering from 'locked-in' syndrome, which more usually refers to people who are completely unable to communicate with their carers, but still definitely alive, and possibly conscious, according to their brain activity. When Tony Nicklinson sadly died, a week after losing his court case, on 22 August 2012, the BBC Radio 4 Six O'Clock News again described him as locked-in.[21]

A very few successful attempts have been made recently in providing completely locked-in patients with brain scanners, or brain-machine interfaces, allowing their brain activity to be measured and then translated into letters and words on a computer screen so that they can laboriously write messages for their carers using thought alone. For these patients, until now, no one has even known whether they were conscious or could hear, so any decisions about ending their lives would have to be taken by surrogates such as doctors, carers or family. But in Tony Nicklinson's case, he could communicate his wishes, although only via a computer reading his eyeblinks.

So, from a public relations perspective, should the doctors and ethics pundits who were invited to discuss Nicklinson's immensely important case in those national news broadcasts have taken up precious airtime by making the distinction between completely locked-in and unable to communicate at all, and someone in Nicklinson's position? Or was a greater good served by allowing the wider definition to pass (as it did in every broadcast I heard) and concentrating on the deeper ethical issue of the right to euthanasia on demand? I am grateful to Fabio Turone of the European Union of Science Journalists Associations for pointing out to me that Tony Nicklinson's position still met the wider definition of locked-in as defined in the *Journal of Neurology*.[22]

As an endnote to this right-to-die debate, at exactly the same time that Tony Nicklinson's supporters were campaigning for his right to a dignified death, doctors were facing a legal challenge from the family of a 55-year-old Muslim man from Manchester, England, who were opposing an application to the court of protection in London to avoid having to resuscitate him or put him on a ventilator if his condition became life-threatening.[23] The family claimed that their religion required everything possible to be done to keep him alive, in spite of his apparent persistent vegetative state (see Chapter 11, 'NHS issues: ageism').

UK National Health Service

If Florence Nightingale was one of the unwitting founders of the National Health Service, as we saw at the start of this chapter, then Beatrice Webb (1858–1943) was its midwife. A radical social reformer, she co-founded the London School of Economics and the *New Statesman* magazine, and from 1905 to 1909 was a member of the Royal Commission on the Poor Laws and Relief of Distress, which reported to the UK government in two forms – the Majority Report and the Minority Report.

Webb's Poor Law Minority Report of 1909 proposed a radically different system, which would 'secure a national minimum of civilised life, open to all alike, of both sexes and classes, by which we meant sufficient nourishment and training when young, a living wage when able bodied, treatment when sick, and modest but secure livelihood when disabled or aged'.

According to NHS Choices, the National Health Service's website (see www. nhs.uk), the NHS was created so that good healthcare should be available to all, regardless of wealth. It was launched by the Labour Government Minister of Health Aneurin Bevan in July 1948 and based on three core principles:

- that it meet the needs of everyone;
- that it be free at the point of delivery;
- that it be based on clinical need, not ability to pay.

Your job as a public relations practitioner, should you choose to accept it, either in the UK, somewhere in Europe, in the US, or elsewhere in the world, is to try to uphold a similar set of principles for communication. People have a right to know stuff, especially when the information affects something as fundamental as their health.

In the UK, currently undergoing a major health service reorganisation that many view as the commercialisation and privatisation of a previously state-provided function, standards have not significantly changed in the last year. Nor have waiting lists or waiting times. Nor have success rates for treatments, or staffing levels. What has suddenly changed is the public's perception.

Public satisfaction with the NHS in the UK has just suffered the biggest one-year fall since surveys began in 1983, from 70 per cent in 2010 to 58 per cent in 2011, according to the annual British Social Attitudes survey, now carried out by the King's Fund health and social care thinktank, after government funding was withdrawn last year.[24]

This drop cannot be because of a non-existent steep decline in services. It is a fall in reputation caused by public perception. The King's Fund thinks this may be because of negative media stories dominating the agenda, or possibly as a surrogate vote expressing dissatisfaction with the present government and its handling of the health service. Which brings us neatly back to where we started in this book's Introduction.

According to Glen Whitman,[25] the Two Things about public relations are:

1. Perception is reality.
2. Perception is rarely reality.

References

1. Florence Nightingale, Notes on Matters Affecting the Health, Efficiency, and Hospital Administration of the British Army: Founded Chiefly on the Experiences of the Late War, *Presented by Request to the Secretary of State for War*, Harrison and Sons (privately printed for Miss Nightingale), 1858.
2. Wellcome Trust, Wellcome Library reference: GC M:WA100 1858N68n.
3. For more on Florence Nightingale see the National Archives at www.nationalarchives.gov.uk/education/lesson40.htm.
4. For more on John Snow and the Broad Street Pump see the Wellcome Trust website at www.wellcomecollection.org/Cholera.
5. 'One hundred million years of life will be lost by those smoking now', Royal College of Physicians, press release, 6 March 2012.
6. *North Devon Journal*, 31 March 2012.
7. *Guardian*, 25 May 2012.
8. *Guardian*, 14 April 2012.
9. *Guardian*, 2 June 2012.
10. *Sydney Morning Herald*, 22 August 2012.
11. For Turlington's Balsam bottles see www.antiquebottles.com/turlington.
12. *The Gazette*, Montreal, 23 February 2008.
13. 'Secret Remedies, What They Cost and What They Contain', *British Medical Journal*, BMJ 2009; 338:b1624.

14. Aspirin patent see the *New York Times* website, http://inventors.about.com/library/inventors/blaspirin.htm.
15. Taiwo Oriola, Cardiff University Law School, Research Paper 4.
16. NHS Healthcare for all, see www.nhs.uk/NHSEngland/thenhs/nhshistory/Pages/NHShistory1948.aspx.
17. Electricity in medicine, see the Institution of Engineering and Technology website, www.theiet.org/resources/library/archives/exhibition/medical/mesmerism.cfm.
18. Mary Shelley, Maurice Hindle, *Frankenstein*, Penguin Classics, 2003.
19. Human Tissue Authority, see www.hta.gov.uk.
20. *Guardian*, 17 August 2012, and further analysis during the following week.
21. BBC Radio 4, *Six O'Clock News*, 22 August 2012.
22. G. Bauer, F. Gerstenbrand & E. Rumpl, 'Varieties of the Locked-in Syndrome', *Journal of Neurology*, 221 (1979): 77–91.
23. *Guardian*, 24 August 2012.
24. Public satisfaction with the NHS and its services, King's Fund, 6 June 2012.
25. Glen Whitman, the Two Things game at www.csun.edu/~dgw61315/thetwothings.html.

Index